Canon T70

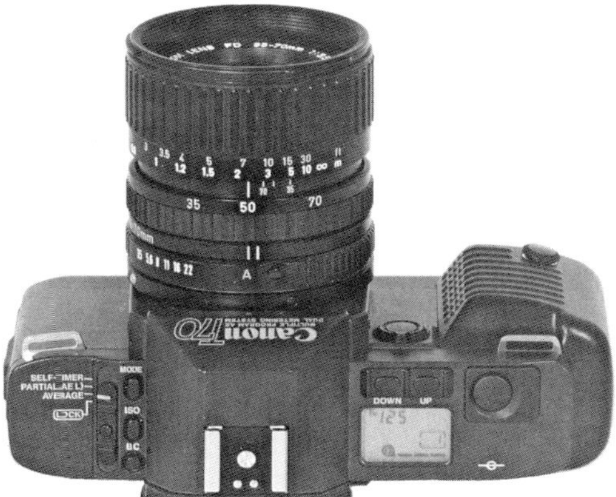

Günter Richter

HOVE ~ FOUNTAIN BOOKS

CANON T70

First English Edition December 1986
English Translation from the original German
by Liselotte Sperl
Edited by George Wakefield
Series Editor Dennis Laney
Typeset by Direct Image Photosetting, Hove
Printed in Great Britain by
Purnell Book Production Ltd.

ISBN 0-86343-059-7

Published by
HOVE FOUNTAIN BOOKS

45 The Broadway
Tolworth
Surrey KT6 7DW

34 Church Road
Hove
Sussex BN3 2JG

U.K. Trade Distribution by
Fountain Press Ltd
45 The Broadway
Tolworth
Surrey
KT6 7DW

U.S.A. Distributor
Seven Hills Books
49 Central Avenue, Suite 300
Cincinnati
Ohio 45202

CONTENTS

Preface

Electronics and automated manufacturing techniques have given us increasingly sophisticated cameras in recent years. Each manufacturer claims that his models are easy to use and that he has solved all the problems for the photographer. If we believed all these claims we would expect that all of these cameras could turn a blind person into a Michelangelo.

It is true that the technical refinement of modern cameras has been continuously increased. And to the same extent their operation has been simplified so that even a complete novice is able to produce technically perfect photographs. The emphasis lies on the word "technical", because a correctly exposed and sharp photograph does not imply that it is also a good picture. There is a paradox in this simplicity which is due to technology and which is not restricted only to the camera construction. It is found everywhere and in everything that surrounds us. Enormous technical progress, particularly in electronics, has made it possible to pack a variety of facilities into a small chip so that now we find this simplicity of use is no longer so simple; the bewildering choice of options confuses us.

The Canon T70 is a good example. If you wish to get a general idea of what this camera can do and what it displays, warns about, bleeps or even manages to accomplish of its own accord, then you will give up in confusion. But if you take the camera into your hand and try out all the functions, one by one, then it all becomes quite clear. However, to be able to do so presupposes a certain knowledge of photographic principles and of photographic techniques. This I have set out to describe in this book.

The T70 is an exceptionally good SLR camera. You would not do it justice if you restricted yourself solely to using it in Program mode. We shall first look at the T70 and its facilities from the viewpoint of its practical application, without wasting too much time in technical detail. The first consideration will always be ease of understanding.

However, before we get stuck into the practical side I should like to define a few basic concepts. If you are not familiar with terms such as aperture and shutter speed, and what effect these have on the final picture, then you will not be able to develop as a photographer. It is essential to be fully aware of these functions because only then will you be able to use the different exposure programs offered by your T70 to full advantage.

After introducing the camera I shall show a few examples which, I hope, will inspire you to take your own photographs and which should help you to avoid some common and quite avoidable mistakes. Finally I shall discuss the optical accessories offered by Canon and by other manufacturers for the T70. Reading this book may even help you to combine the enjoyable hobby of photography with some other activity in which you may be interested.

The New Style Camera

When Canon introduced the AE-1 in 1976, it caused a furore. Today, electronics dominate camera design and a whole new generation of photographic tools have had to follow these new standards. The A-1, which followed about two years later, continued this development by offering better integrated, and thereby more effective, electronics. Digital electronics that operate the systems by means of codes rather than voltages, which may be subject to fluctuations, have arrived in camera technology.

These days Canon scarcely mention that the T70 has an even more effective electronics system than the A-1, the star of yesteryear. The normal photographer will not know what do do with technical details such as flow diagrams and breakdown of integrated circuits, but the additional features offered by the T70 will be of interest to him. Canon have continued to develop the concept and performance that had been introduced with the AE-1 and A-1. The following important aspects are useful in practical application:

1. Provision of a transport motor will now automatically transport the film. Winders are dead! This feature has been adopted as a modern standard; it not only renders the rapid transport lever superfluous by providing an integrated motor, with very little increase in the size of the camera, but also brings about some useful little features such as automatic film insertion and winding of the film to the first frame. The film is also rewound by motor. However, it is difficult to convince the Japanese that this can in no way be described as "automatic", at least in the form it is offered on the T70 and in some compact cameras such as the AF35M II. If it is necessary to depress a button before anything happens then it is not automatic. Now that the very remarkable compact Canon MC does actually offer automatic rewinding for the first time it may be possible to persuade them to use the term correctly.
2. The T70 offers the ideal shutter speed priority mode with a

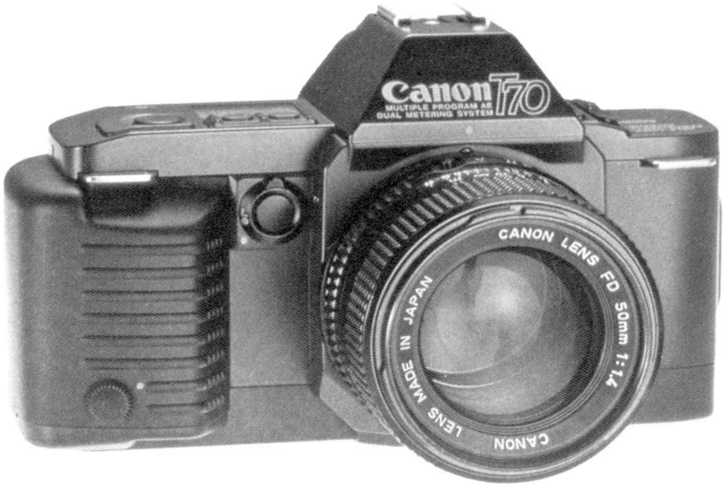

The Canon T70, the camera which would like to be identified with a computer.

unique feature that is new to Canon: it will automatically switch to aperture priority mode if, for the preset time, the greatest or smallest aperture opening would not be able to produce a correct exposure.

3. Canon have found the optimal solution to the problem of exposure correction under difficult subject situations, such as high contrast, backlit shots, etc. It is possible to change from the normal centre-weighted integral metering to selective metering of 11% of the viewing field. To use this metering technique to full advantage it is possible to store the metered value in this operational mode by lightly depressing the release button. This makes it possible to meter the important detail in the frame quickly and correctly and make full use of the automatic feature as well.
4. Apart from the shutter speed priority mode, which may be switched off, there are three other program modes. The actual worth of these programs is a matter of personal taste. The T70 offers the choice of working aperture priority mode to offer you photographic convenience when you are using special lenses or close-up accessories without data

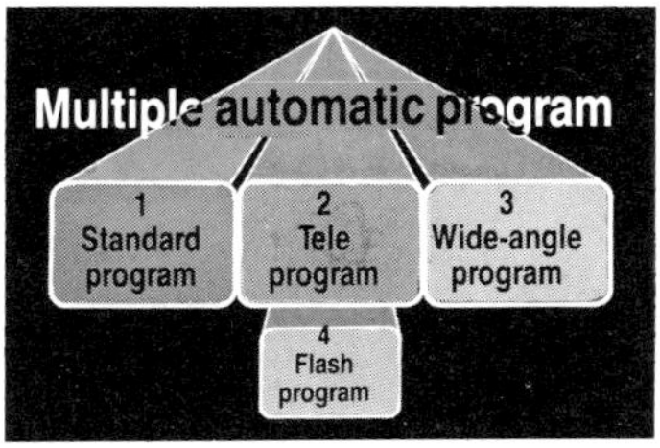

A program mode with three choices: standard, wide-angle and telephoto, finally justifies the arguments made in advertisements in favour of the usefulness of a program mode.

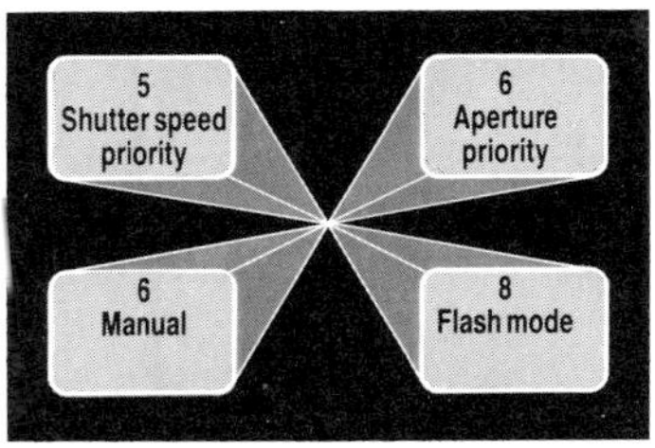

Counting also the manual exposure setting, the Canon T70 offers eight different shooting modes.

transfer to control the aperture. The open aperture priority mode as a separate program is dead; may it rest in peace.

5. All settings on the T70 may be achieved by activating a few buttons. There are no setting rings or knobs.
6. A large LCD display on top of the camera gives you more information and detail than any conventional camera. The display is always limited to the data required at any time and is therefore functional and clear. The display in the viewfinder is illuminated and logically divided into two sections, showing the important and variable data. The aperture is digital. It couldn't be better.
7. The T70 offers the ideal solution for flash photography in flash program mode, provided you are also using the Speedite 277T. Even competitors offering internal metering with flash (TTL-flash mode) cannot offer such simple and reliable handling as provided by Canon with the infrared-setting flash. This method is indisputedly the superior alternative in flash photography.
8. The data back with additional control features provides the

The liquid crystal display (LCD) is a treasure trove of information, but at any one time the display shows only the information which is logical and useful.

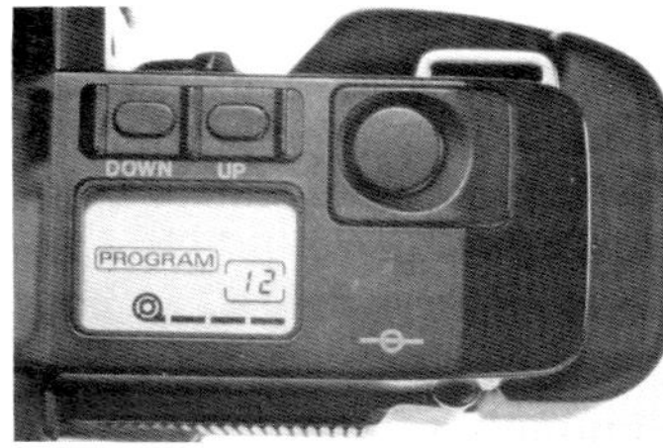

greatest flexibility for long exposures, interval shots, and so on.

9. The T70's highly developed and efficient electronics provide information and visible and audible alarms and thus you are assured of the greatest possible functional reliability and convenience

The great bonus is that all this doesn't cost the earth. On the contrary, it is offered at a most reasonable price, almost sensational, considering the complete set of features and the wide variety of functions. The reason for this lies in Canon's policy of consistent development of their ideas and production methods, which started with the AE-1. The great production runs introduced with the AE-1 were considered unique at the time; the same production policies are applied and even enhanced for the T70. This makes it possible for Canon to improve the price/output ratio for modern high-performance cameras and the T70 is yet another Canon camera setting the standards for the market.

Reflex is Best

The Canon T70 is a camera which can do almost everything. This versatility is due not just to its highly sophisticated technical specifications, but primarily to its basic form as an SLR camera. I shall now describe in general terms what this means.

The single lens of your camera is not a restriction, but a virtue. It means that if you are looking through your viewfinder you are looking directly at the selected subject. This offers many advantages.

1. You can be sure you are seeing exactly that which will be captured on film. Cut-off heads, which you may have come across when using a compact camera with viewfinder, are a thing of the past. The framing is correct, regardless of how close you are to the subject. This means that you are able to take extreme close-ups with SLR cameras, which might be completely impossible with other viewfinder systems.
2. Only the view directly through the lens makes it possible to compose a picture properly and precisely. Only if the viewfinder image and the image projected onto the film are identical is it possible to ascertain whether elements of the picture composition such as separation of lines and alignment of details are correct.
3. The viewfinder image shows you the exact position of the section of the view with maximum sharpness. In other words, focusing to the greatest precision is made possible with the least effort. This is particularly important when focusing with very long lenses or extremely close-up where precise focusing is essential.
4. The reflex viewfinder presents you with the image at exactly the same size and perspective, which corresponds to the characteristics of the lens used at the time, regardless of the focal length used. The optical impression produced by a super wide-angle, for example, is completely different from the characteristics of a telephoto lens. This preview of the final picture saves you having to estimate what the image will be like from the impression the human eye can produce; this would be exceedingly difficult for the extreme focal lengths. The reflex viewfinder is essential for careful image creation particularly for extreme focal lengths

The secret of the view through the lens is the hinged mirror, which is positioned at 45° behind the lens and directs the

The T70 at a Glance

1. Remote control terminal
2. Shutter release
3. Shift button (up)
4. Liquid crystal display (LCD) panel
5. Shift button (down)
6. Exposure preview button
7. Shutter speed lock lever
8. Accessory shoe with flash contacts
9. Battery check button
10. Mode selector lock button
11. Film speed setting button
12. AE mode selector
13. Back cover latch with lock button
14. Battery chamber cover
15. Rewind button
16. Rewind button unlocking lever
17. Tripod socket

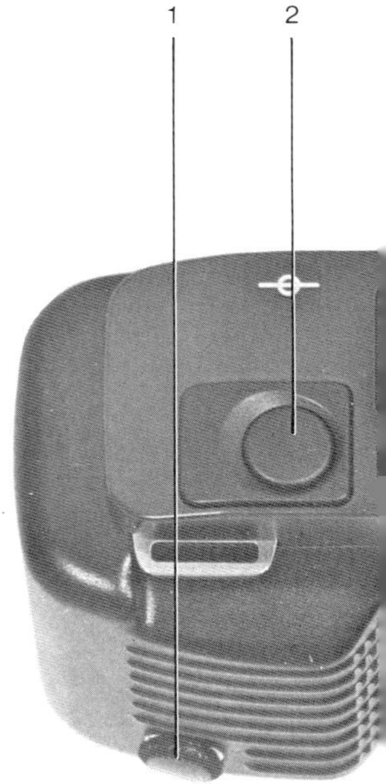

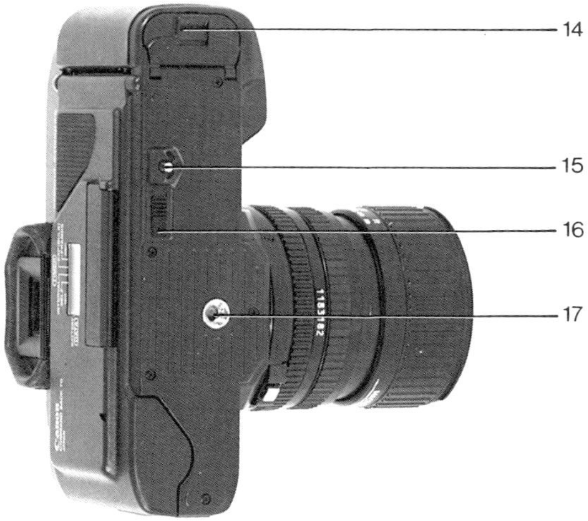

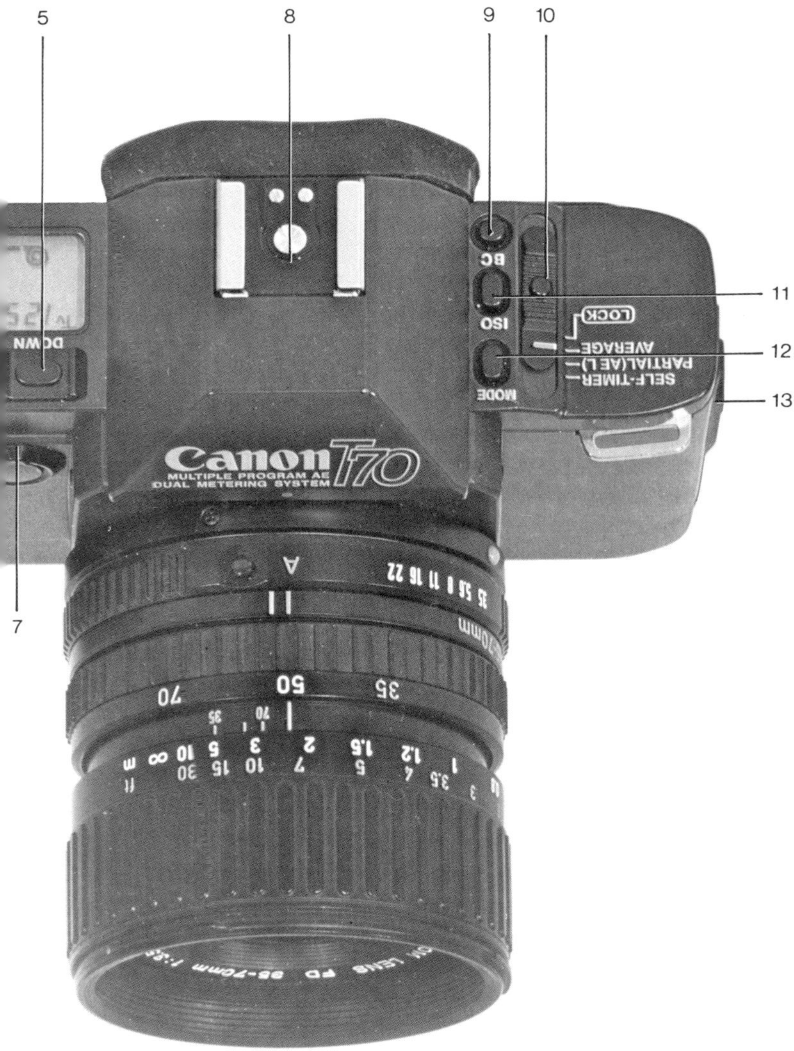
5
8
9
10
11
12
13
7
Canon T70
MULTIPLE PROGRAM AE
DUAL METERING SYSTEM

incoming rays vertically upwards. At the same distance at which the film is behind the mirror is a ground glass screen to receive a sharp image in this plane. A pentaprism is arranged above the focusing screen which redirects the rays to the eyepiece at the rear of the camera. Without the pentaprism the image viewed through the eyepiece would be inverted and viewable only from the top. The prism turns the image back so that it may be viewed correctly, even if the camera is turned to take an upright picture. The image on the film is laterally reversed and stands on its head; but this is of no consequence as it is reversed when the slide is projected, or the negative printed on paper. The photographer is thus always able to view the subject exactly as seen by the naked eye and from eye-level.

During exposure the hinged mirror would be in the way, so when the release button is depressed, shortly before the

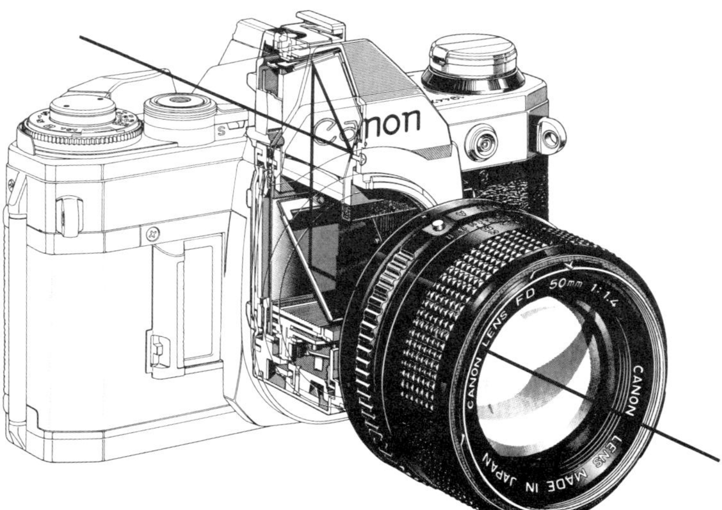

The inside of a single lens reflex camera. The example here is a 35mm reflex camera with mini computer, the Canon AE-1.

shutter sequence is activated, the mirror folds away in front of the lower surface of the focusing screen. This ensures at the same time that no undesired stray light enters with the rays from the subject. Now the light can enter straight through the open shutter and expose the film. As soon as the shutter has closed again, the mirror will fold down and your T70 is ready to act once again as an excellent viewfinder.

The EMAS Shutter

Another abbreviation to add to your vocabulary. EMAS: This is Canon's term for the Electro Magnetic Attraction Shutter which is used for the first time in this form in the T70. To be exact it ought to be called "EMAS II", because the T50 also possesses an EMAS shutter, but Canon improved on the principle for the T70.

First let us consider what a shutter is and what it does. If you remember the description of the reflex viewfinder you will recall that there is always light in the reflex housing and in the viewfinder. The shutter which controls the duration of light that is allowed to get to the film therefore has to be situated behind the mirror in order not to obstruct the viewfinder. This means that the "dark room" is just the small space at the rear of the camera housing.

All modern SLR cameras have the so-called slit or focal plane shutter. This consists of two shutter blinds, of which the first one opens at the start of the exposure and the second one closes the opening again at the end of the exposure time. The EMAS shutter of the T70 consists of two metal blades which traverse the focal plane in a vertical direction, i.e. the shorter distance across the frame. The shorter distance which the shutter blinds have to traverse makes it possible to achieve a shorter synchronisation time for electronic flash. The slit shutter presents one problem which is expressed by its name: the whole frame is completely exposed to the light only for a very short time. For very short shutter speeds it is necessary

The T70's focal plane shutter consists of metal blinds which travel vertically.

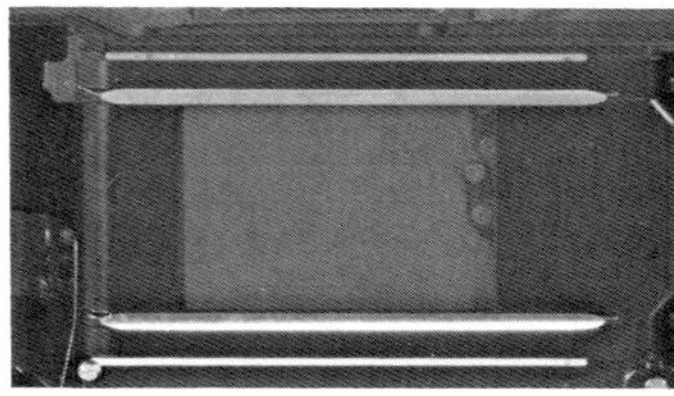

that the second blind follows the first before the first has reached the other side. This means that for short times a slit of varying widths moves across the frame, exposing the film in strips. If you take an exposure with an electronic flash which has an illumination time of between $^1/_{1000}$ second to $^1/_{50000}$ second, using a shutter speed where the frame is exposed in strips, then the flash would illuminate only the strip that was exposed at the instant of the even shorter flash illumination time, the rest of the frame remaining unexposed.

For the Canon T70 the shortest time possible to synchronise an electronic flash is $^1/_{90}$ second, this is called the X-synchonisation time. The actual flash synchronisation time is taken to be $^1/_{85}$ second. Short flash illumination times are particularly important for fill-in flash in daylight. But this may be achieved only if the traversing times are short. The shutter blinds of the T70 achieve a time of 7.5 milliseconds. This time cannot be greatly improved on as the blinds have to be accelerated and decelerated without causing harmful vibrations which would result in the pictures being blurred.

The T70 adjusts the shutter speeds continuously from $^1/_{1000}$ second to two full seconds in the appropriate shooting modes. In shutter speed priority mode or in manual mode you may also use the usual fixed shutter speeds within the same time range. The current consumption of the EMAS shutter is particularly low, but the purely electronic shutter setting "B" for long shutter speeds requires a lot of current. And although the T70 offers a variety of functions, including the integral motor, it will work with two 1.5 V AA size batteries.

What Effect has the Shutter on the Picture?

The main function of the shutter in your T70 is to regulate the amount of light that will expose the film, and to ensure that when the subject and prevailing lighting conditions have been assessed, the film with its fixed speed will produce a useful image. Apart from this the shutter speed will affect the manner in which the subject with all its details is represented in the picture. This is obvious if you think about it. Let us assume we take a moving subject at a speed of, say, $^1/_{1000}$ second, then the subject will have little or no chance to show its movement within this short space of time, it will therefore be shown in sharp focus; the movement will be frozen. If the same subject is taken at a speed of $^1/_{30}$ second, then the movement will be clearly shown in the image, as it probably moved quite some distance in this relatively long time. The result: the contours become blurred, the image is no longer sharp. But this is only one component of the movement. The second is to be found with the photographer. After all, we are only human, and more jittery than we think. If we hold our camera and depress the release, the support we provide is far from firm and steady. Any movement, however slight, will be transferred to the camera and the final image, but this time the whole picture will be blurred. If we shake the camera, as this is generally called, then the image will generally be useless. Camera shake ruins the best composition. The only remedy in this case is to attach the camera to a tripod. Any subject movement will still be shown by a blurring of the contours, which can be desirable and most effective, but the non-moving details in the image will be sharp.

Camera shake is the one source of many a bad picture for the amateur photographer. To start with, many hold their cameras badly. The index finger hovers over the release button, ready to pounce like a hawk and so push the camera violently. This method is bound to produce bad pictures. Make sure, therefore, to adopt good habits; always hold the camera so that the pressure on the release button is produced by the finger joint, and not by the whole arm, the rest of the body should be absolutely still. Only then will you be able to produce sharp images. A fast shutter speed alone is no guarantee of sharp images. If your pulse is racing to catch that special fleeting moment, jerking the camera, even at $^1/_{500}$ second, will blur the image for sure.

There is one golden rule that you should always keep in mind. It is so simple that you won't be able to forget it. Taking the reciprocal of the focal length of the lens in mm and expressing this value as a fraction in seconds will give you the lower limit for hand-held shots. In other words, this means that using a standard 50mm lens and as a general guideline to fix shutter speeds, then the longest shutter speed for hand-held shots is $^1/_{60}$ second. For a 135mm telephoto lens you will need $^1/_{125}$ second and for a 200 mm telephoto you will have a reasonable chance of producing a sharp image at $^1/_{250}$ second.

The Eyes of your T70

The lens orders the light rays and composes an image of your subject, first in the viewfinder, and later during exposure, on the film. Before we go into more detail, we need to define certain terms which are important in understanding the effects of various functions. One term that has been mentioned several times already is "focal length". If you hold a lens so that the sunlight passing through produces a small bright and hot spot on your skin, then the distance between the lens and the plane on which the spot is produced is the focal length of the lens. The lens will reproduce subjects at infinity sharply at this point. If you hold the lens in front of a wall, opposite a window, then it will produce a laterally reversed, upside-down image of the window, and the scene outside. The image can be focused, i.e. made sharp, by adjusting the distance between lens and wall. Again you have found the focal length of the lens.

Let's stay with the single lens for demonstration purposes. If

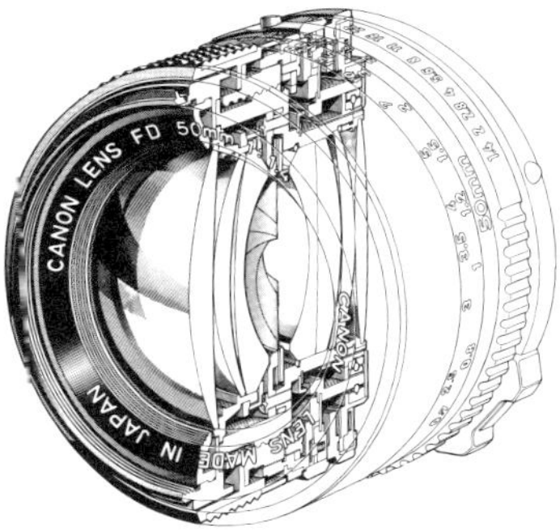

Modern lens systems for reflex cameras are very complex. The Canon FD lenses are particularly sophisticated to provide for genuine shutter speed priority.

we look at a strongly-curved lens, we note that it has a short focal length, the rays converge at a relatively short distance behind the lens. The image produced shows the details rather small, but it comprises a large section of the scene. If you repeat this experiment with a less strongly curved lens you will find that its focal length is rather longer; and a subject is represented at a larger scale. Those principles of refraction apply also to multiple lens systems, which is what we actually use in our picture-taking equipment.

The focal length of a lens is its most important characteristic. This is stated in millimetres and engraved on the lens. For small format cameras, i.e. 24x36mm, of which the Canon T70 is one, a 50mm lens is considered the standard lens. Focal lengths of 35mm and shorter are considered wide-angle lenses and from 100mm upwards we talk of telephoto lenses.

A set of interchangeable lenses available for the T70 turns your camera into an instrument for almost unlimited photographic expression. For this reason we shall discuss at some length the concept of focal length and how the scale of representation within the given format opens up a wide range of different technical and creative possibilities. I touched on this subject earlier when mentioning movement blur. It is logical that the effect of camera-shake is four-times as large for a 200mm telephoto, compared with the standard focal length of

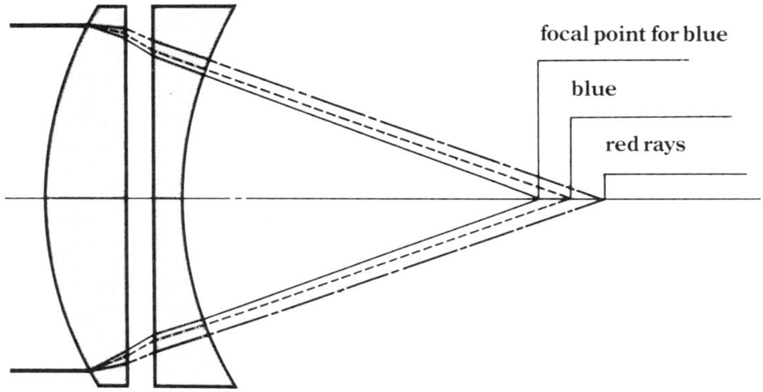

The focal length of a lens element or lens system is different for different wavelengths. The blue rays, for example, intersect before the red rays. It is the optical designer's duty to correct these so-called colour aberrations which are due to the dispersion of light in glass. This is achieved by the use of different types of glass, radii of curvature, and air gaps.

50mm. After all, the telephoto manages to depict everything four times as large in your given format. The effect is that of a telescope. If you have ever used such an instrument you will have noticed how easily the image will shake. It will be still only if you hold the telescope absolutely steady. Consequently, when taking a picture with a long lens you need very fast shutter speeds to counteract the exaggerated movement of the lens.

The Misunderstood Lens Speed

You may think that this means that some lenses work faster than others. Technology and the language of technology moves in wonderous ways. Some loosely-used terms were adopted over the years to mean particular things. The term "speed" of a particular lens means the largest opening of that lens and tells you how much light is allowed into the system of lens elements. It is obvious that the bigger the "hole", the more light may enter the lens. You are therefore still able to take pictures with a fast lens, even if the available light is limited.

Lens speed is expressed by a ratio, e.g. 1:2.8. This value is obtained by dividing the focal length of the lens by the effective diameter of the opening and is engraved on the lens. This ratio is usually written as f/2.8.

In technical photographic circles the lens speed is usually called the "relative aperture", or "aperture ratio" which is a better descriptive term. In principle one might think that great lens speed is a very desirable feature. But the joy is not entirely unalloyed. The faster the lens, the greater the lens diameter to allow more light into the system, the heavier, bulkier and less handy is the lens itself. That is not all. The bigger the lens relative aperture, the more difficult it is for the lens designer to correct the unavoidable reproduction errors, which are characteristic of any optical system. This means that a lens with high performance and relatively high speed will be an expensive affair. Therefore you should always keep in mind, when deciding on a lens, that lens speed alone is not the only criterion of its performance. A fast lens is not necessarily a better lens, it simply extends the photographic day.

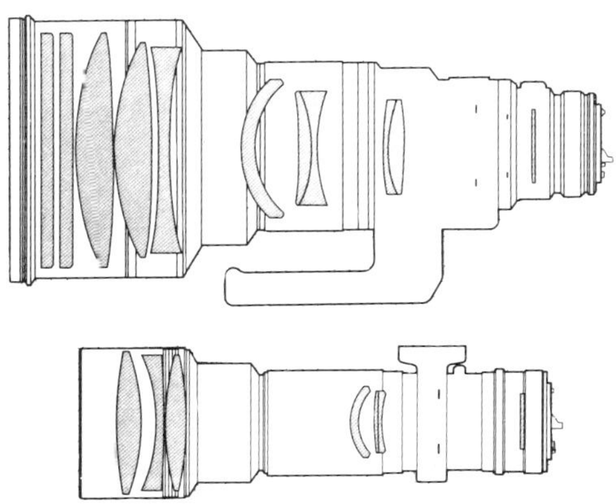

A comparison of these scale drawings of the FD f/2.8 400 mm L (top) and the FD f/4.5 400mm demonstrates the optical complexity necessary to produce the greater lens speed.

Light Value – Aperture

If we compare the lens of a camera with our eyes, we find several similarities. Not only does it project the image onto the film in the way the lens of the eye projects an image onto the retina, it also possesses an aperture, just like the human eye, which is adjusted to allow the correct amount of light to enter. The iris of our eye fulfils this function, it contracts to an increasingly smaller aperture the brighter the light, and our eye is thus able to adjust to a wide range of light intensities. The lens of a camera is also equipped with such an adjustable aperture, called the iris diaphragm, which functions according to the same principle. Exceedingly thin overlapping metal blades allow continuous contraction of the diameter of the light rays entering the lens and the aperture is thus the second control element of exposure, the other being the shutter speed, as discussed above. These two control functions provide us with a wide range of settings for the exposure.

If we wish to obtain reproducible exposure values for different lenses then it will be necessary to agree on a standard. The relative aperture, which we discussed for lens speed, will be useful here and, as it is based on the relationship between lens focal length and aperture diameter, it is generally applicable. Consequently, an f/2.8 telephoto lens will produce the same exposure as a standard f/2.8 lens. Only the diameter of the aperture will be much bigger in the telephoto lens than in the standard lens.

The relative aperture serves as the so-called aperture value, generally referred to just simply as the "aperture". An international sequence of aperture values divides the overall range of effective openings which are useful for photographic use. These are known as f/numbers and the sequence runs thus:

f/1 - f/1.4 - f/2 - f/2.8 - f/4 - f/5.6 - f/8 - f/11 - f/16 - f/22 - f/32

The smaller f/numbers correspond to the larger apertures.

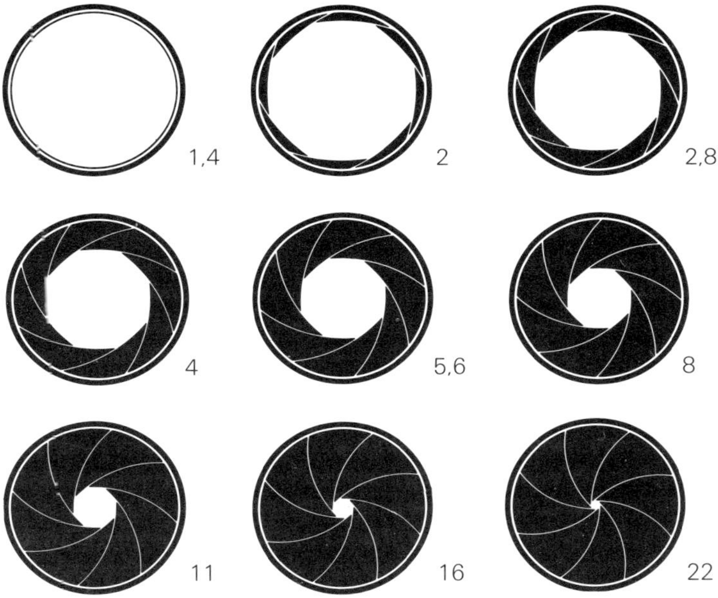

Aperture values and the corresponding diaphragm openings demonstrated in this example of a f/1.4 50 mm lens.

This may be confusing to start with. But the reason soon becomes apparent when you get used to the idea that the aperture is the focal length divided by aperture diameter.

Just as with shutter speed, each aperture stop corresponds to a doubling or halving of exposure. At aperture setting of f/4 twice as much light is allowed to reach the film as for aperture f/5.6. On the other hand aperture f/2.8 allows only half the amount of light to enter compared with aperture f/2.

What Effect has the Aperture on your Pictures?

As with the shutter, the function of the aperture is not limited to exposure regulation. The effective aperture diameter determines the size of the beam of rays entering the camera. A narrow beam, the result of a small aperture, results in quite a different representation of the image compared to a wide beam. We now have to consider the phenomenon of "depth of field", a term which is of extreme importance in the language of photography because it is one of the most crucial factors in picture creation.

Strictly speaking, a lens is capable of representing in sharp focus only the information from one plane. It follows that all our pictures would then be unsharp to a great extent. However, we know from practical experience that this is not so. The reason lies in the resolving power of the human eye. If the subject is considered as being represented by tiny dots, these dots are smallest in the plane of focus and get larger behind and in front of this plane, turning into increasingly larger discs. Our eye is able to discern this difference only after a certain point before and beyond the plane of focus and we therefore perceive the picture as being in sharp focus within the range between these points. This is what is meant by the depth of field.

The extent of the depth of field depends on two factors: on the aperture diameter of the lens and on the distance setting. A narrower light beam, resulting from the light passing through a smaller aperture produces the unsharpness discs at a relatively larger distance in front of and behind the focusing plane, than a wider light beam from a larger aperture. We should remember one important rule:

small aperture = large depth of field

The aperture diameter is the key to a further effect which is generally considered separately, although it is a consequence of the above rule. Taking several pictures at different aperture settings from one position, they will each have a different depth of field, always depending on the focal length of the lens. Taking an aperture setting of f/4, a telephoto lens (a system with long focal length) will produce a much shallower depth of field than a wide-angle lens. This is quite logical; the light has to travel a greater distance within the lens to get to the film plane, than in the wide-angle lens. Consequently, the opening diameter of the telephoto lens has to be much larger if, for the same aperture value, the same amount of light has to arrive at the film plane. In turn, large aperture openings mean broad beams of light and therefore larger unsharpness discs.

In this connection I would like to refer back to the subject of lens speed. We know that large apertures, i.e. fast lenses, imply a reduction in depth of field. In other words, although a very fast lens is capable of producing a useful picture, even under very poor lighting conditions, the sharpness within that picture will be reduced to a very narrow depth of field. And this is the point that is always disregarded when considering the speed of a lens. You have to be clear in your mind that you will be limited to this "one-dimensional" photography, if you wish to utilize these large apertures. This means that such lens settings are quite unsuitable for many subjects. With this in mind you will not make the mistake of considering lens speed as the universal solution to all your problems. In many

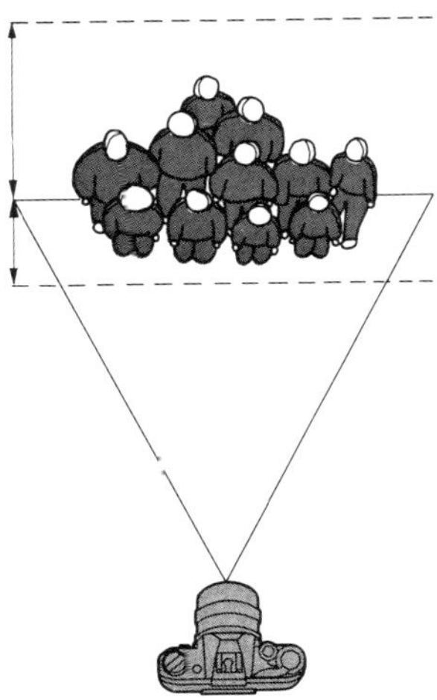

The depth of field is less in front of the plane of focus than behind.

situations you would be better advised to use fast films and a smaller aperture; this will produce a sufficient sharpness range and cover your subject adequately under prevailing lighting conditions.

Now we have to consider this other factor which determines depth of field: the distance setting. The shorter the distance at which you focus the subject, the smaller will be the depth of field. And there is no way round it. There is only a narrow margin for close-ups and it is technically impossible to depict three-dimensional objects in their entirety in sharp focus. Not even a small aperture will be able to counteract this effect entirely. In the extreme close-up range the depth of field will shrink to just a few millimetres.

It follows therefore that the aperture and the shutter speed are both important means to picture creation. Generally speaking it will be necessary to find some sort of compromise as these two factors are mutually opposed. If you are after as large a depth of field as possible and choose therefore the smallest possible aperture, you will find that the required exposure time increases accordingly. Somewhere along the line you will come up against a limit. The longer the time, the greater the danger of camera shake, and what is the point of great depth of field if the whole picture is quite blurred. If, on the other hand, you wish to capture fast movement, then you need a fast shutter speed. Let's say that $^1/_{1000}$ second seems suitable. Then it will be necessary to open up the aperture to allow through sufficient light to expose the film adequately. This means you are reducing the depth of field; what you gain on the swings, you lose on the roundabouts. The decision; sharpness of contours against depth of field will therefore represent a compromise determined by certain practical circumstances: photographic intent, subject movement, lighting conditions, focal length and subject distance.

Once you have experimented with all these factors in mind you will develop sufficient flair to handle your camera's controls just as if you were driving a car. You will be able to select the most suitable combination without difficulty.

The Lens Mount

After the introduction of interchangeable lenses it was necessary to think about a suitable coupling between the camera body and the optics. Some manufacturers stayed for a rather long time with the screw fitting. This produced a very secure connection, but it was rather inconvenient for a fast change. Canon decided very early in its manufacturing history on the bayonet mount, and this has been generally accepted as the most suitable type of fitting. It it not surprising, however, that each manufacturer likes to do his own thing and so we find that these bayonet fittings are all just that bit different. However, this presents no problem for you as the proud owner of a Canon because Canon offer the widest possible choice of excellent lenses.

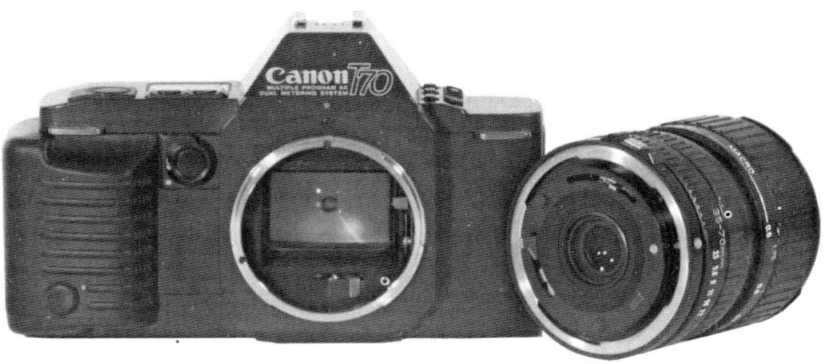

The large, practically wear-proof Canon bayonet allows more than 50 high performance lenses to be used with the T70.

It has always been one of Canon's principles that the contact surfaces of the bayonet, which are critical for accurate data transfer, are not exposed to any friction. Canon's lens "trade mark" used to be the chromed clamping collar which ensured secure contact to the camera. The lens itself was not subject to any twisting movement and therefore to no friction. Since then the Canon FD lenses have undergone some slimming-down, optically as well as mechanically. They now have to be turned, both for inserting and removing, but they have not lost the advantage of friction-free coupling. The contact surfaces between lens and camera body are still in very firm contact. It may seem to you that these surfaces are moved against each other when the lens is inserted, but this is not so. In fact only the outer ring of the FD-bayonet is turned, the inner part with all the coupling elements does not move in the slightest from the position in which it was inserted into the camera. Canon engineers have moved the earlier clamping ring into the interior of the lens and transferred its duties to the mounting ring. The advantage lies in a much more compact overall construction.

Let us take this opportunity to examine the coupling elements on the rear of the FD lens to help us understand the functions of the individual levers and contacts.

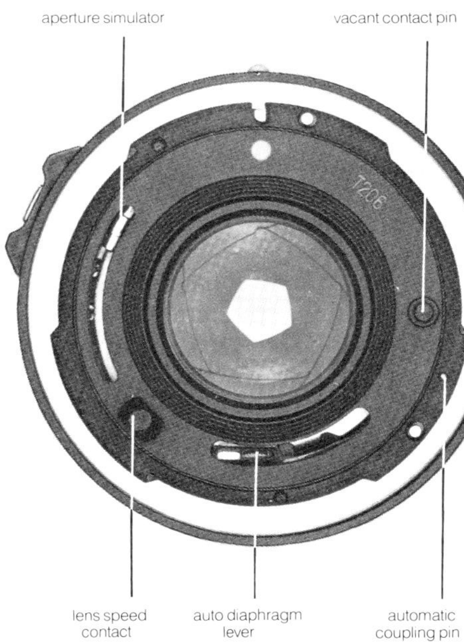

The coupling elements of a Canon FD lens.

The spring-back diaphragm lever is activated by the pressure on the release button via a counterpart in the camera body, closing the iris diaphragm to the selected value. If this lever is fixed at its right stop by the plastic adapter, which is available as an optional extra, then the auto diaphragm function is inactive and the aperture ring will directly activate the iris diaphragm. This is necessary whenever an accessory is used which is not directly coupled. If you are using an older FD lens with the chrome ring then it is possible to engage the auto diaphragm lever directly at the right stop. Some older style lenses have no catch but a separate locking lever instead. Do not forget to release the auto diaphragm lever before attaching a directly coupled lens, otherwise the camera may be damaged.

The aperture-simulator reports the selected position of the aperture pre-selection ring to the camera's metering system in order for it to be able to calculate the difference between the light metered at the greatest possible lens opening and the value that would be obtained with actual working aperture.

The Automatic Control Pin is usually embedded in the contact surface. It is extended only after the aperture ring is brought into the Automatic position by simultaneously depressing the locking button. This is the reason why it is impossible to attach FD lenses in Automatic position to accessories if they were not designed for operation with shutter speed priority or program modes. Such equipment is not equipped with a socket into which the control pin can fit. The control pin's function is to transfer the signals in program and shutter speed priority modes.

The Lens Speed Contact informs the camera's metering system about the speed of the lens used at the time. This means you need not worry about any lens speed setting on the camera. This contact has the further task of taking some other corrective measures necessary for open aperture metering.

The Vacant Contact Pin may be found in all Canon FD lenses that Canon ever built. Some lenses even have two. We have to make do with the explanation that this is meant for later developments, as I was unable to obtain a better explantion from Canon.

Inserting the Batteries

Before we go any further we ought to get the camera into a position where we can actually see how it will react to changing the settings and what we can see through the viewfinder. The most important thing to do is insert the batteries, because it won't work without electricity. Some traditionalists may disapprove, but if we are making use of modern electronics of which Canon is one of the leaders, then we have to have batteries. After all, nobody these days would think to look askance at a car just because it doesn't run on oats!

The Canon T70 is quite frugal in its power consumption. It requires just two 1.5V AA size batteries. These are available all over the world; even the medicine man in the jungle uses them in his portable radio! As an added little benefit, this type is also the cheapest. When selecting the batteries you have three choices:

1. **Alkaline Batteries.** No doubt, these are the first choice as they are high performance batteries which should last at normal temperatures for about 60 24-exposure films. In temperatures below -10°C their useful life reduces to about seven films and at -20°C they will manage only three! In Europe you should always ask for alkaline batteries. In some far-off countries it may be possible that these are not available, and then you will have to do with ordinary carbon-zinc batteries.

2. **Carbon-Zinc batteries.** In principle these even cheaper 1.5 V carbon-zinc batteries are just as suitable as the alkaline batteries, but they don't last as long. At normal temperatures they will expose about 20, 24-exposure films. However, their voltage drops considerably at low

temperatures and they will expose only one film at temperatures of around -10°C. In temperatures below this they will not perform at all.

3. **Nickel-Cadmium Batteries.** Nickel cadmium batteries of the same size have a lower voltage of only 1.3V. They are rechargeable and as such suitable for very active photographers. The lower voltage affects the number of films that may be exposed with a set of fully charged batteries. At normal temperatures they will expose about 30 films of 24 exposures. At the lower temperature ranges these batteries perform better than carbon-zinc and even alkaline batteries. They manage about 15 films at temperatures of -10°C, and at -20°C even seven films. For this reason they would be the ideal power source for Arctic explorers, or even just enthusiastic winter scene photographers!

Always check the batteries when you're buying. There are some makes on the market that do not fit into the T70, their contacts are too large and project too far forward. When checking the batteries the nickel cadmium types offer a smaller margin because of their lower voltage. It may be that only two "test bars" will be shown, even when fully charged, This would be equivalent to three bars with normal batteries.

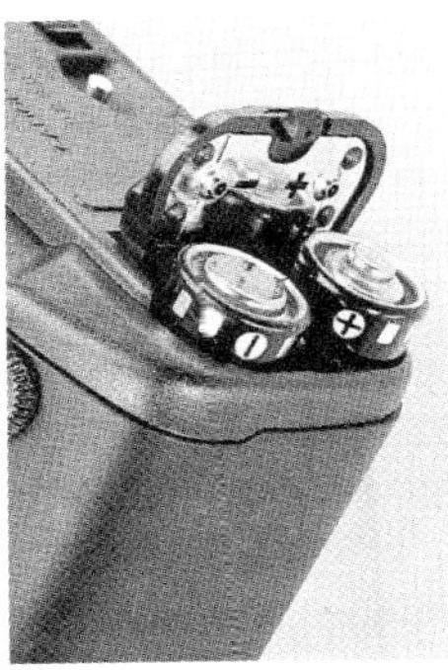

Changing batteries may be done at any time, even with a film loaded. The battery compartment is easily accessible.

As mentioned previously, you will need two batteries. Don't touch the contacts as this might encourage corrosion and lead to poor contact later on. It is always a good idea to wipe the contacts with a dry cloth before inserting them in the camera.

The battery compartment is located at the bottom of the handgrip and can be easily opened by hand. The polarity of the batteries is indicated in the compartment. The battery nearer to the front of the camera has to be inserted with the positive contact pointing downwards, the battery at the rear, the other way round. Always make sure that the polarity of the batteries is correct; the camera cannot work otherwise. Close the battery compartment by pushing the cover down.

To check the state of charge of the batteries simply switch the camera on. This is done by pushing the main switch forward to one of the battery positions and depressing the battery check button marked "BC". The LCD display at the top should display three horizontal bars to indicate that the

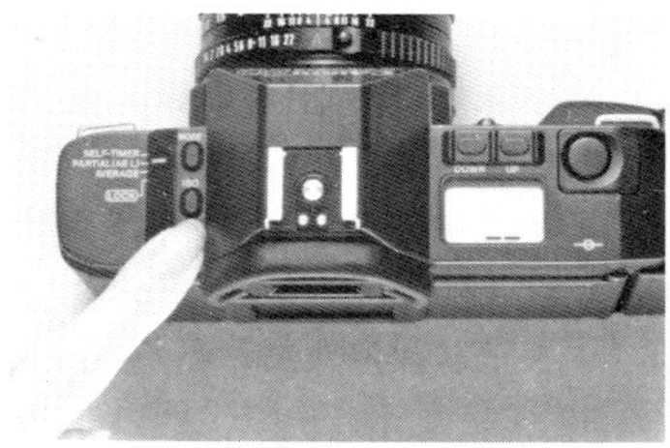

One, two or three horizontal bars indicate the battery condition for battery check.

batteries are fully charged. If the display shows only two bars, then the batteries are still useful for some more shots, but they are on their way out. If the voltage level is insufficient, then only one bar will blink, or there is no display at all. If there is no display it is worth checking whether the batteries had been correctly inserted.

If the camera is not to be used for some time, then it is wise to remove the batteries. Exhausted, or partially exhausted batteries tend to leak and this could damage the camera. Always store still useful batteries in a cool, dry place.

Batteries which are not performing satisfactorily at very low temperatures need not be thrown away, they should recover at normal temperature. When taking pictures in very low temperatures always keep the camera protected against the worst of the cold conditions as long as possible and keep two spare batteries in an inside pocket to keep them warm. If the set in the camera fails, you can exchange them for those kept warm in your pocket and give the others a chance to warm up. Changing them round in this way will probably keep you going even in the coldest situation.

Fitting the Lens

A modern SLR camera is generally sold as an entity in itself, without a lens. The SLR offers almost endless combinations with the wide variety of lenses available for each make and model. You have the choice at the point of purchase to choose the equipment that will be your ideal combination. Gone are the times when every camera was sold together with a lens, regardless of whether the customer wanted the one offered or not. You should therefore carefully consider all the available alternatives and make a well-informed decision. You could start with one of the macro lenses with normal focal length, such as the Canon FD 50mm f/3.5 Macro. This lens offers, at a small cost in lens speed, a much wider range of applications than the standard lens. Or you may choose a zoom lens, ranging from wide-angle to standard focal length, perhaps the Canon FD 28-55mm f/3.5-4.5, or the FD 35-70mm f/3.5-4.5, or even the FD 35-105mm f/3.5, which cover a greater range around the standard focal length. If you chose one of these lenses later on, then the standard lens will have been superfluous.

The camera body is protected by a cover. This has to be on the camera if no lens is attached. This is an absolute must, as the interior has to be protected against dust and foreign bodies as well as against physical contact. The mirror box is very delicate and essential to your camera's good performance;

remember that the image on the focusing mirror is projected by it and its alignment is therefore critical. Never touch any part of the camera's interior as any fingermarks on the mirror could damage its surface. The same applies to the rear element of the lens; always protect this by putting on the back cap whenever the lens is not in use. To remove the cap turn it to meet the left stop, which is when the red arrow at the back points to the red domed button. Never set the lens down with the back exposed, as this could damage the contact elements. It does not matter if you set the lens down on its front, even without lens cap. The only exception is the Canon 7.5mm f/5.6 fisheye, because the front element in this lens protrudes from the front of the mount.

To fit the lens to the camera, hold it in your hand so that the red domed button points upwards, align it with the red point beneath the legend "Canon" at the camera lens housing, lower it into the camera body and secure it with a short turn clockwise. It is important that the chromed release button on the lens is not depressed, otherwise it will not be able to engage into the right position.

When changing a lens put the lens cap on first. Hold the lens so that the right index finger rests on the release button. Depress the release button, and turn the lens to the left until the red button points upwards and remove the lens. Don't forget to immediately put on the rear cap. You align the arrow on the outside of the cap with the red dot at the rear of the lens or the red domed button. The cap will align easily in this position with the bayonet fitting, and can be secured by turning. If you are not inserting a lens in the camera, protect it with the body cap. This is also marked with a red dot, which is aligned and the cover turned to secure.

The Viewfinder

Looking through the viewinder you will see the bright focusing screen, unencumbered by any display. Any necessary data that

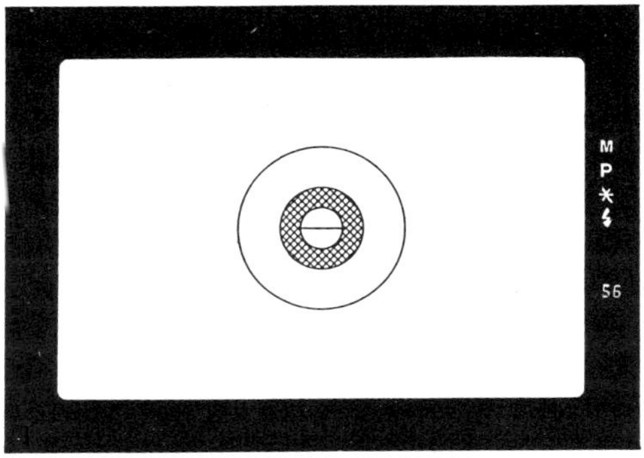

The larger circle at the centre of the viewfinder of the T70 indicates the metering area for selective metering. Only the relevant shooting mode symbol (M, P, *, ϟ) flash will be illuminated at the side of the viewfinder.

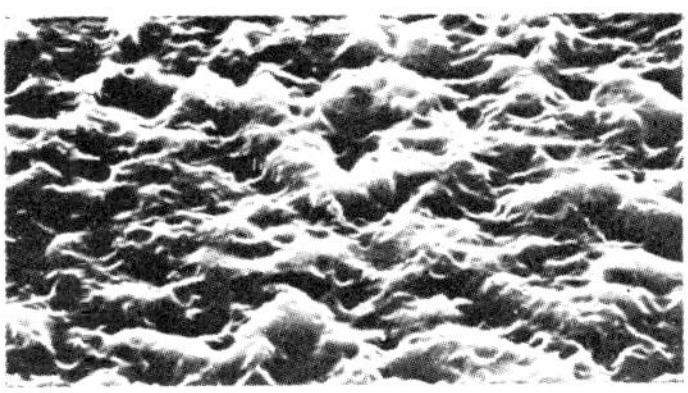

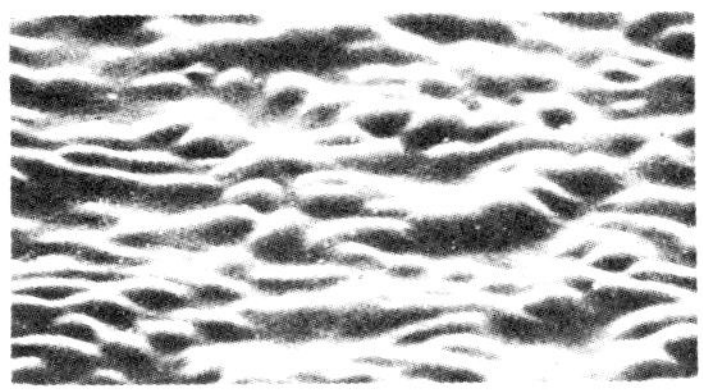

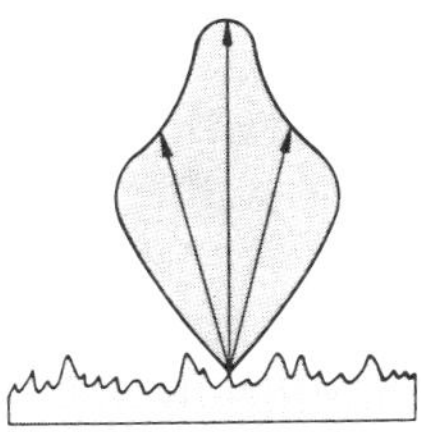

Sand-blasted focusing screen

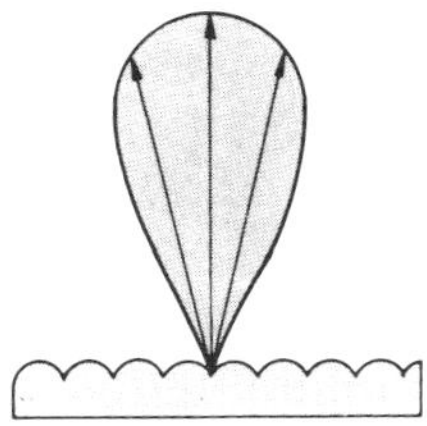

Laser-matt focusing screen

The surface of a conventional focusing screen is sand-blasted. This produces a rather uneven and rough surface (top left). The diagram beneath demonstrates how the intensity of lateral rays is considerably reduced. Canon produce their focusing screens now by a laser method. The result is a much more even surface (top right), giving a much better illumination of the viewfinder image. To date Canon is the only manufacturer using this method.

you may have to keep sight of, such as exposure values and warnings, are all displayed in illuminated figures. At the edge of the viewfinder frame therefore you will sometimes see a red "M" flashing; this will occur if the aperture ring has been turned from position "A", which will be necessary whenever you want to shoot with "automatic" switched off. If the green "P" is illuminated it means you are shooting in program mode. An illuminated red asterisk means selective metering and a flash symbol means that the equipment is ready to shoot with an appropriate Canon flashgun. The aperture values are digitally displayed in half-stops and this information will appear in all exposure programs.

In order not to confuse the view too much, only the pertinent information is displayed at any one time. The brightness of the the LEDs varies and is shown in one of four intensities according to the brightness in the viewfinder. You are thus not dazzled by the display in dim conditions, but are able to read the display clearly, even in bright sunshine.

The viewfinder display does not darken until a focal length of 400mm. For focal lengths in excess of this the edge will start to lose intensity, but this has no effect on the final picture. The focusing screen is a Canon E-type which has been produced by modern laser technology and is particularly bright and clear. You will be able to focus on any part of this screen. The presence of a split image indicator and a microprism ring makes this the most universally suitable focusing device ever invented.

The Special Split-Image Indicator

Split-image indicators are well known in SLR photography as focusing aids. These are formed from two horizontal glass wedges at the centre of the ground glass screen. They are arranged opposite to each other such that they split the central circular disc. The image lines here are out of alignment with each other as long as the lens is not set to the required

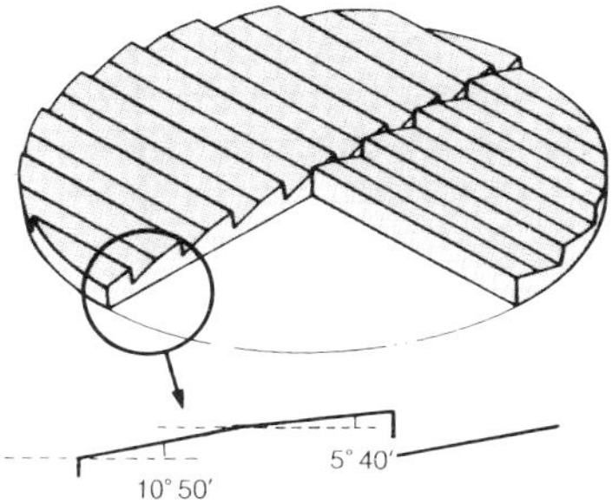

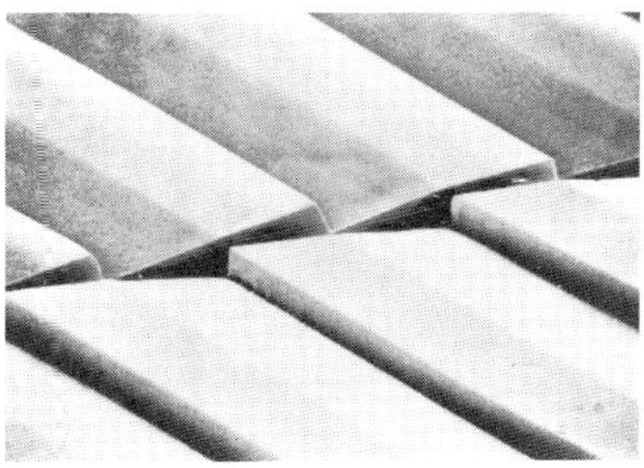

Canon's new split-image rangefinder is composed of a large number of wedges with differently angled sides. This construction counteracts darkening at small apertures.

distance. As soon as the subject is focused by the lens, they coincide and show the picture with all lines properly aligned. This aid is appreciated in particular by those who wear glasses, as they are very useful for objects containing straight lines and where the alignment of lines is easily discerned.

But it is just this feature that presents a severe restriction for subjects which are quite irregular in shape and have no distinct lines. There is another serious defect, characteristic of all split image indicators. As soon as the aperture of the lens drops below about f/4 they black-out on one side. In that event they are useless as focusing aids and, to make matters worse, this dark area in the centre of the viewfinder is rather distracting. The critical lens aperture value is attained by many modern zoom lenses where the maximum aperture often drops to f/4.5 at the long focal length. The same applies when using tele converters, or accessories for close-up photography.

Canon can claim that they are the first manufacturers to

successfully solve this problem. The so-called "new split image indicator" no longer darkens for even small effective apertures and therefore remains useful even under these difficult circumstances. This is an important point to remember, as the non-interchangeable focusing screen would present a source of constant annoyance, in particular when using one of the zoom lenses in the ranges f/3.5-4.5, that Canon likes to recommend.

Fast lenses offer a smaller depth of field and therefore more precise focusing with a focusing screen. However, the split image indicator is adjusted for a fixed aperture of f/4 and as such does not benefit by this fact.

The selection of the line structure for focusing with the split image indicator is most important. It is quite easy to try and align two lines which may belong to two different distances and you may have focused quite precisely using a wrong alignment.

Microprism Screen

The second focusing aid in the centre of the focusing screen is the microprism ring, arranged around the split image indicator at the centre of the viewfinder. These microscopically small prisms literally break up the image into a shimmering picture. Only sharply focused subject details will produce a clear non-scintillating image. These two focusing aids complement each other ideally. The microprism ring allows focusing on fine non-geometrical details, whilst the split image indicator is ideal for straight lines. The merging into a clear image in the microprism ring is an unmistakable sign of sharp focusing on finely detailed subjects. The unmistakable clarity of the effect makes it unnecessary to slowly home-in on the subject, as is necessary with the matt focusing screen, and is therefore much faster.

As with everything else, the microprism ring also has its limitations. In principle the same limitations apply as with traditional split image indicators (i.e. not the new Canon versions, as are fitted to the T70). The microprism ring becomes useless as a focusing aid for apertures of about f/5.6 and smaller, as individual prisms start to darken. A sort of structure results which still allows the image to be seen, but the actual job of focusing can no longer be usefully performed. Generally you will not be working with an effective aperture of f/5.6 or smaller when you are using one of the FD lenses. However, it may be the case when using one of the special lenses or a telephoto lens, that the lens speed drops to or below this value. This eventuality should not be disregarded; just think of a teleconverter which doubles the focal length of the lens used while at the same time reducing the lens speed by the equivalent of two stops. A lens of f/4 is thus converted to a new system with a maximum aperture of f/8.

Or let's think of the situation when we are engaged in macro photography. As soon as the lens is extended by intermediate rings or by bellows, less light is allowed to arrive at the film plane. In other words, the values engraved on the lens are no longer true, having lost one or two aperture stops. The effective lens speed available at fully-open aperture, which is essential in obtaining the necessary conditions to use focusing aids such as the microprism ring and split image indicator, no longer apply. Under these circumstances you will have to go back to using our good old friend, the focusing screen, and you will have to focus on any suitable part within the viewfinder frame.

Viewfinder Accessories

As we are already dealing with this subject, we might as well cover accessories and their usefulness. There are all sorts of things that may be attached to the eyepiece to make life easier and focusing more precise. In every case it is necessary to remove the eye cup by simply sliding it out.

Eyesight correction lenses. These are available in ten strengths, from +3 to -4 dioptres and help people with long or short sight. Some sight defects such as astigmatism cannot be corrected by such lenses. When choosing an eye correction lens you can use your spectacle prescription as a guide, but it is always better to try it out to ensure that it is suitable.

Magnifying Lens S. This may be pushed onto the eyepiece with its square adapter and is particularly useful for macro photography and reproductions, and also for slide duplicating. The magnifier is adjustable to your eye within the range of +4 to -4 dioptres and magnifies the centre of the viewfinder image at a magnification ratio of 1:2.5. It is, of course, no longer possible to use any of the other focusing aids; you therefore focus on the focusing screen. The magnifier may be folded away in order that you can check the entire viewfinder image after focusing.

Angle Finder. This is fixed in a similar manner to the other viewfinder accessories. The device bends the rays so that you view the image at a 90 ° angle and this makes it possible to hold the camera upright, while at the same time focusing on an object near to the ground. It is also very useful in macro photography and for reproductions, for example on a copying stand. Angle Finder A2 is the simpler of the Canon models. The object viewed through the angle finder is upright, but reversed left to right. Angle Finder B is also equipped with a reversing prism, so that the object is viewed in its correct orientation.

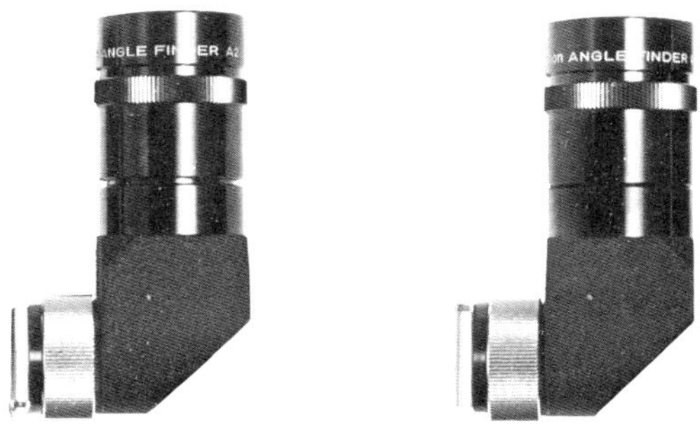

The Canon angle-finders A2 (left) and B (right).

The viewer of the angle finder is adjustable. By a simple movement you can turn it to view the subject from the side or from the top. The eyepiece of both these models has dioptre adjustment in the range of +2 to -4 dioptres. To set the dioptre adjustment the lens is turned until the outer circle in the viewfinder centre, this is the line designating the metering field for selective metering, appears in sharp focus. Here again, only long- or short-sightedness can be corrected, other eye defects can only be adjusted by wearing suitable glasses.

The Liquid Crystal Display (LCD)

One of the most important new developments that Canon offers with the T70 is the type and manner in which the information is displayed. Up to now one had to set switches and read counters. The T70 organizes it all from one central display window. The versatility of this new display and setting system is unsurpassed by any other make. So computer technology has finally conquered camera construction technology. Most of us are familiar with LCD displays in the pocket calculator and other modern gadgets around the house. The T70 may claim to belong to the new generation of cameras, both in its construction and its operation.

I shall not discuss at this point all the possible displays, as it might be confusing. In any case, the display never shows all the functions at once and to show you here a presentation of all the possible displays would definitely not clarify matters; it would rather give the impression of being complicated and quite impossible to grasp. I shall therefore reserve these examples for more realistic demonstrations and shall confine myself to describing how the LCD display is able to inform.

To start with, there is the selected exposure program, starting with the program mode with its three different forms comprising shutter speed priority, working aperture priority mode and shooting with program mode switched off. The shutter speed is displayed in whole numbers. It is not necessary to see the shutter speed in the viewfinder and it was therefore omitted. Depressing a button will display the film speed in ISO numbers.

The rest of the possible displays are entirely new and unique. The T70 can show you in the LCD whether a film has been loaded and it keeps track of film transport, both during shooting and when the film is rewound by the built-in motor. The frame counter is also part of the display, a definite improvement for ease of reading. The battery state may be checked by a touch of a button, and if you are using the self-timer, the remaining time is counted down on the display. In position 'B' it is possible to time the exposure by a very precise stop watch function. In short, this must be the most universal display on any camera to date.

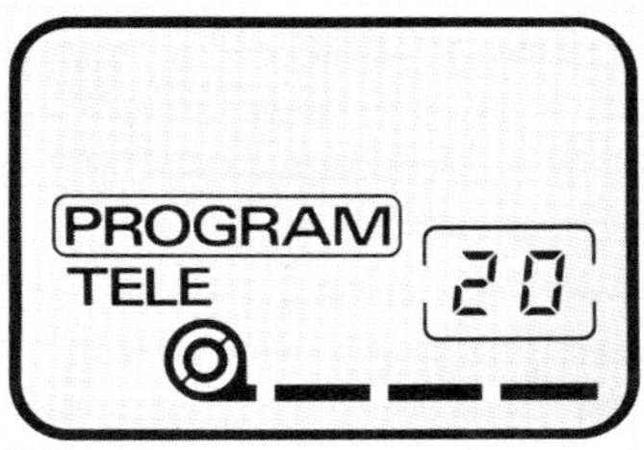

The functional clarity of the T70 LCD display is highly advanced and superior to that of any other camera. In addition it supplies some information that we have had to do without so far.

It is quite obvious that the display will only function if the main switch has been turned to one of the three shooting mode positions. Only the symbols for film loaded and ready to shoot, film transport and frame counter are visible even if the camera is switched off.

Should you insist on taking your T70 with you into the sauna, which I am not really recommending, then you would be in for a surprise. The entire display will turn black as soon as it is exposed to temperatures in excess of 60°C. This is due to physical reasons and does not mean that it will stay like this. As soon as the camera is brought back into normal temperatures and allowed to adjust, it will again show you its usual face. Similarly, in extremely low temperatures the display will respond more slowly. This too should not give cause for concern; as soon as you get yourself and your camera out of the inclement conditions, everything will return to normal.

There is one point though where the LCD display has limitations: it does not last for ever. After about five years the display will fade until it reaches a point where it cannot be read at all. At this stage you will have to go to your Canon dealer and ask for a new display to be installed, at a cost, of course.

The Buffer Battery

A modern electronic display such as the LCD depends on electricity. The camera's memory too depends on a constant source of electricity to remember the settings and values. Consequently the camera would also forget the set film speed and even the counter position if both AA batteries were exhausted or were being exchanged. To avoid this Canon have built in a buffer battery which stays in the camera. This buffer battery has a life expectancy about equal to that of the LCD and should be replaced together with the display. It is a 3V lithium battery, type CR1220, switched in parallel with the main voltage supply. It will activate as soon as the voltage of the two AA batteries drops below the minimum required level.

If the display "ISO 100" flashes after new batteries have been inserted and the camera is switched on, then this signifies that the buffer battery has come to the end of its useful life. You would have to re-set the film speed, but the frame counter display would be lost. In principle the camera is fully functional even without the buffer battery, provided it has the AA size batteries. But this event should hardly occur as the internal battery's useful life is much longer than that of the LCD and in the event of the LCD being at the end of its life, both would be replaced.

The Selective Metering System

The T70 not only has highly sophisticated electronics inside it, it also has a highly sensitive and accurate exposure meter which can be switched to work in one of two functional modes. The T70 can therefore offer you everything from rigid overall metering to very selective and considered metering of individual subject details. The superior metering facility, together with its flexibility, puts this camera in a class of its own as it will meet even the most demanding requirements that a professional photographer may expect from his instrument. The T70's internal metering system depends entirely on the viewfinder image. An aspherical prism lens arranged behind the pentaprism directs the viewfinder rays upwards and focuses them on the metering cell. This method ensures absolute exactness, because the metering cell "sees" exactly that section which is seen through the lens with the focal length used at the particular time.

You may have noticed that nothing seems to be happening in the lens itself when you turn the aperture setting ring, and with good reason. As we are using the camera at this point mainly as a viewfinder, we are not bothered that there is rather a lot of light available for viewing though the viewfinder. The lens has been constructed to allow the aperture to be fully open to provide a bright image in the viewfinder. If the aperture were to be stopped down, the amount of light allowed into the viewfinder would be greatly reduced. Not only this, the smaller aperture would result in greater depth of field and make precise focusing even more difficult. Of course, the aperture is required as a light value during the actual exposure and the value selected at the aperture ring or by the automatic program mode is at this stage only simulated by the camera's electronics. Immediately after the release button has been depressed, the auto-diaphragm will close the aperture to the selected value. The aperture opens fully as soon as the exposure has been made and your T70 is again ready to act as the perfect viewfinder.

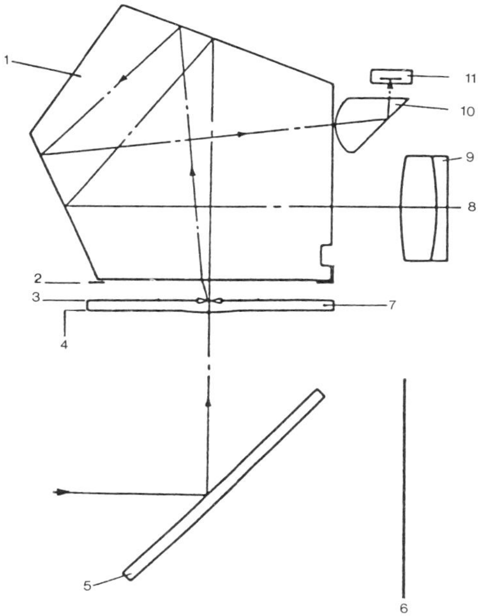

Viewfinder and internal metering system of the Canon T70

1 pentaprism
2 finder mask
3 focusing surface
4 Fresnel surface
5 fold-away mirror
6 film plane
7 focusing screen
8 exit pupil (16mm)
9 viewfinder eyepiece
10 prism lens
11 metering cell

Naturally there is a difference in metered value between metering with open aperture and with working aperture. This difference has to be taken into account by the camera's electronics. Whenever you are looking through the viewfinder the camera displays the calculated exposure values, at open aperture, of course. To do this the aperture simulator on the lens, which we discussed before when describing the coupling elements, reports to the metering system what aperture has been pre-selected on the aperture ring. If the camera is in automatic shooting mode, then it is already informed of all the necessary parameters. Based on this information the camera will calculate the difference between the metered value at open aperture and the value expected at working aperture. The displayed values are therefore always in agreement with the values when the exposure is actually made.

You may have noticed a peculiarity when looking through the

viewfinder and comparing this view with the final image. In the viewfinder your subject is often seen sharply defined against a blurred background and you are then very surprised to find that in the final print the whole image is sharp, including the background. The clear distinction between subject and background has been lost and may ruin the composition you intended to show. The reason for this phenomenon is easy to understand; the image in the viewfinder was seen at fully open aperture, resulting in a shallow depth of field. But when the exposure was actually made, the aperture was stopped down, perhaps to f/8, which would result in a considerably greater depth of field. You should therefore always keep this difference firmly in mind and calculate the depth of field for various working apertures which are always displayed in the viewfinder to assist you. With some experience it will be almost second nature to you that a wide open aperture results in a shallow depth of field and a small aperture in the greatest possible depth of field.

A Measure for all Things

The calibrated value is the ultimate measure for the light meter of the T70. After all, it has to compare the metered brightness in the viewfinder with some known standard in order to draw a meaningful conclusion as to how bright this brightness really is. Photographic designers have agreed to use an average grey tone with 18% reflectivity as standard.

Let's follow this train of thought for a while as it will help to explain a wider aspect that cannot be better explained elsewhere. If you have ever taken pictures of a snow-covered landscape or brightly-lit white sand, or similar light-flooded bright scenes you may have found that your camera, which has always proved most reliable, produced rather underexposed pictures; people and shadows were much too dark, the gleaming white surfaces rather grey. How come? This is not due to a camera malfunction. No, on the contrary, the light meter compared what it "saw" with the calibrated 18% average grey and came to the conclusion that this amount of light needed only a very short exposure, if the film was not to be over-exposed, and this is how the underexposure came about.

Or let's take the opposite situation. You point your camera at a person clad in black, standing in front of a dark background. Again, the metering system compares the reflected light with the calibrated reflectivity and concludes that a lot of exposure is necessary. Result: the person's face is too pale, the black dress grey. The metering system performed its duty perfectly and exposed the supposed grey area correctly.

These extreme cases serve to demonstrate that even a modern metering system is unable to think ahead. In unusual situations, such as shots against the light, subjects with extreme contrasts and extremely dark or white surfaces, depend on your interference. You could, of course, just shoot away in program mode, regardless of any special circumstances, and accept any failures without worrying too much, but you wouldn't do your T70 justice; it is capable of serving you much better than simply just as a snapshot camera.

Centre-Weighted Integral Metering

If you push the T70's main switch to the first position bearing the legend AVERAGE, then the metering cell will meter the

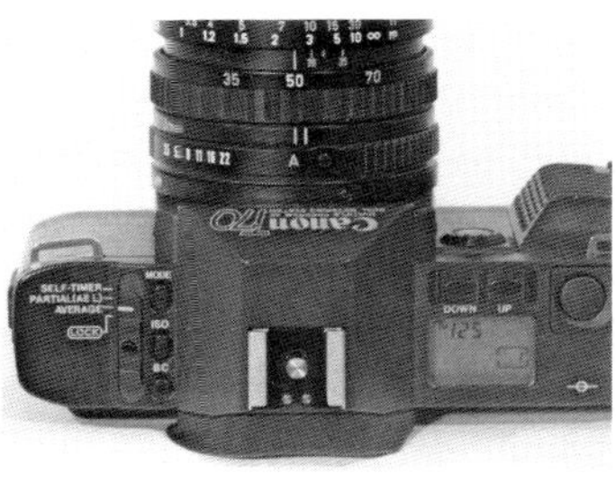

The main switch at the top left of the camera serves at the same time as the switch for centre-weighted integral or selective metering

light from the entire viewfinder frame, but the light from the centre section will be given more importance than the outer section. To be precise, the metering sensitivity drops sharply towards the edges. The upper part of the frame, taking a picture in horizontal format, contributes very little. This is to counteract the relatively great brightness of the sky, which is usually in this section of the frame. The diagram of the metering characteristics show clearly the distribution of metering zones across the frame. This type of metering characteristic has proved very successful over the years, particularly in automatic exposure programs. However, in situations with great contrast or unusual reflectivity this method is not suitable.

The T70's main switch is designed such that the centre-weighted integral metering is the general metering method, i.e. AVERAGE is the selection when switching on the camera. This is in line with the general design of the camera. The user of a program mode camera, having no technical experience in this field, and who is interested mainly in shooting automatically, will be able to switch on and start. In principle

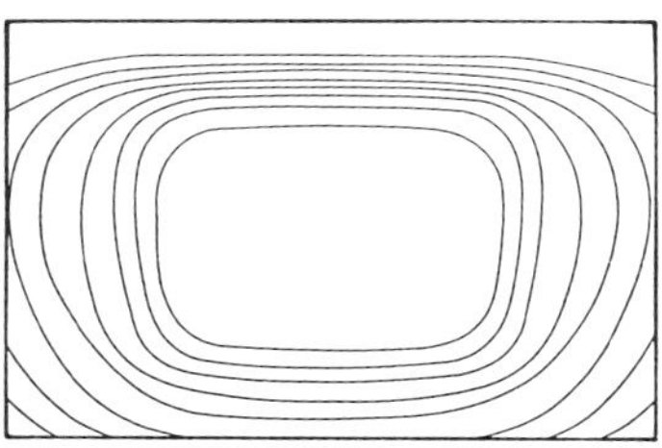

Arrangement of measuring zones for centre-weighted integral metering

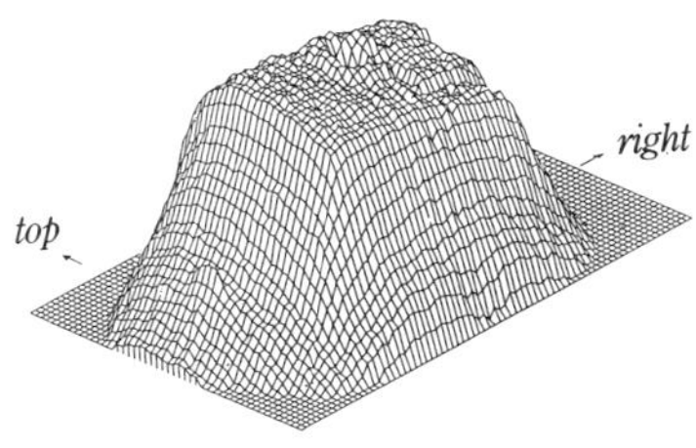

Three-dimensional computer representation of metering response for integral metering

one can say that integral metering produces the best results, as long as there are no particularly bright light sources in the picture and the reflectivity characteristics of the subject do not deviate greatly from the norm and there are no unusual illumination situations. The integral metering method is not suitable for the following circumstances:

If you wanted to photograph a sunlit snowscape, the result would be underexposed, similarly with a bright beach bathed in sunlight, here too the picture would be underexposed. If the subject is against a prominent large white wall or other very bright background, then it would be underexposed. Another example is the stage actor in a bright stage spotlight. Here the actor would be overexposed. If a highly-reflecting surface, such as water, is in the centre of the metering field, it would trick the metering system into thinking that the subject was a lot brighter than it was and lead to underexposure. In views through an arched gateway or through a window, the dark, large frame would cause the bright sky to be overexposed. As the film would find it difficult to handle such high contrasts it is advisable to keep such framing relatively small, then the light meter can expose mainly for the bright main subject and the balance will be restored.

Integral metering is independent of the shooting mode the camera is using at any particular time. In other words, you may use it in all automatic modes, as well as with manual exposure. Only the operation of the main switch is, in my opinion anyway, rather impractical. It is not possible just simply to switch into integral metering as would be best in practice. The main switch, which is a slide, has to be moved carefully to its first position. This requires concentration and a gentle touch, it cannot be done quickly. The slightest excess pressure and the switch moves on to the selective metering position.

Selective Metering

A very slight touch, pushing the switch further beyond

AVERAGE will select PARTIAL (AE L), the position for selective metering. I would like to mention at this point that the T70's main switch is definitely designed for the left thumb. If your ring and middle fingers press against the camera's bottom plate, you could operate this switch quite comfortably, if only there were not so many positions! Don't use any other finger, as this would definitely be most impractical, using the left thumb it is even possible to operate the switch with leather gloves.

In selective metering the photocell will measure only the light from approximately the centre circle in the viewfinder field, about 11% of the overall area. This makes the T70 an extremely fine precision tool in the hands of an experienced photographer. It is important, though, that the photographer takes a very active part. If the selective metering is performed correctly I can guarantee that you will not be disappointed in any of your pictures. The difficulty lies in finding the most representative point in the composition. Using this metering technique you should master even the most difficult situations such as shots against the light, etc. Simply point the metering field at a section which does not contain any excessively bright

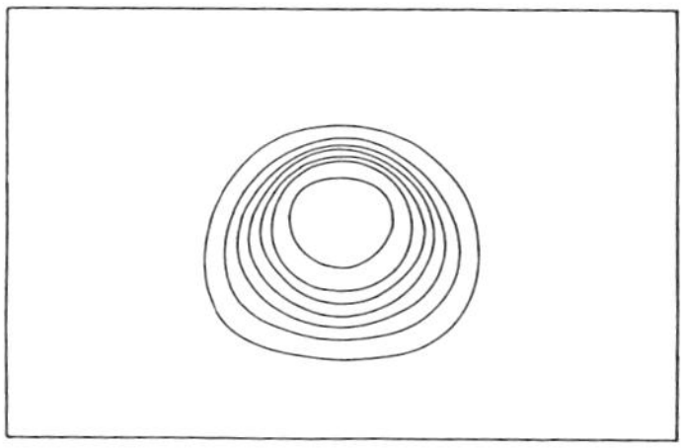

Arrangement of measuring zones for selective metering

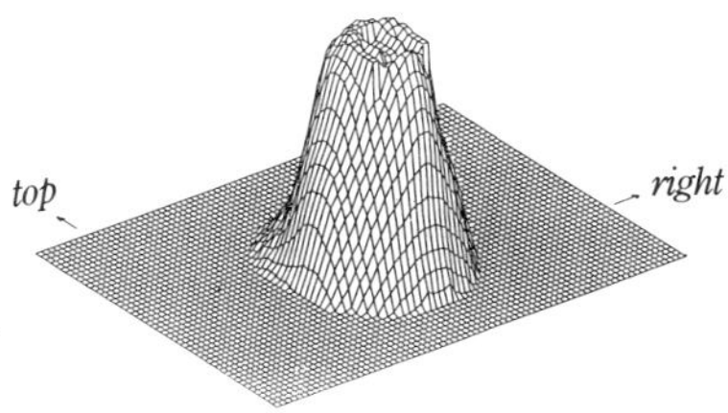

Three-dimensional computer representation of metering response for selective metering

or highly reflecting areas. You also need to consider that slide film reacts slightly differently from print film. Colour print film should be exposed for the shadow parts, i.e. it is better to choose the darker sections in the composition. Slide film should be exposed for the brighter parts as it reacts to strong general illumination with rather washed-out colours and bleached lights. It is advisable to use the brighter, but not the brightest, sections in the subject for selective metering with slide film.

I would like to warn you against one thing though, don't overdo this compensation of exposure for the most important sections of the composition, as many photographers seem to do. We see such photographs as examples in brochures and manuals. A person standing against a bright sky will be too dark if no compensation factors are applied. At the same time, the comparative sample with selective metering tends to look quite awful at times, as it is usually much too bright and does not convey the mood of the situation. In my opinion such shots are for the wastepaper basket. Always try to retain at least a hint of the original mood by allowing the selective metering to include a little of the excessively lit areas. We should not forget that the human eye too tends to see everything a bit darker in such a situation. This is the reason why these comparative pictures often look so awfully bright and unnatural and do not show the situation as we tend to see it.

Selective metering is generally only practicable together with memory lock, at least in automatic shooting mode, and this we shall discuss in the next chapter. If selective metering has been chosen, a red star symbol will illuminate at the right edge of the viewfinder frame on pressing the release button slightly.

As amazing as the possibilities are that selective metering offers, the novice is advised not to plunge straight in, but to try integral metering first. The selection of the relatively small area used for metering in selective mode requires some experience and badly applied selective metering will produce worse results than properly applied integral metering. In the hands of an experienced photographer the T70 used in selective metering mode becomes an excellent instrument that will be able to cope with the most difficult situations. After all, this is the first Canon camera equipped with a metering system than can be changed by switch to suit the situation. Switchable systems are no absolute novelty, but they are not the rule either.

Exposure Test

The release button on the T70 has two functions. A slight pressure switches the metering system on, activating the viewfinder display. The LCD display changes according to the exposure program and shutter speed appropriate at the time, provided, of course, you have moved the main switch from the LOCK position. The actual exposure is triggered only after a firmer pressure, easily discerned by the pressure point.

It is possible at any time to check the data for the selected program or for the preselected settings by simply depressing the release button slightly. The aperture value will illuminate in the viewfinder in half stops, the shutter speed is shown in the LCD display. There are also alarms for incorrect exposures and an alarm warning against camera shake for slow shutter speeds.

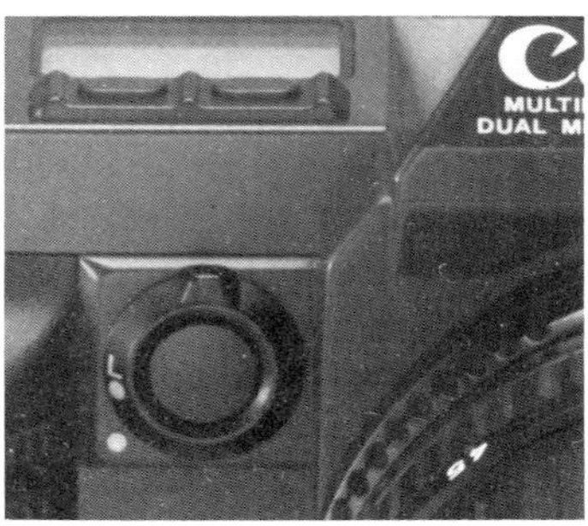

The metering system can be switched on by depressing the release button or by switching on the exposure test key; this leaves the right index finger free to operate the function keys in shutter speed priority

It is also possible to check the exposure values by slightly depressing the exposure test key at the front right of the camera. This key is designed to be activated by the right middle finger which is positioned in this location for normal camera support. It is therefore possible to look through the viewfinder while at the same time activating the exposure test key and, with the right index finger, one of the two UP or DOWN keys, in order to decide, either in shutter speed priority mode or in manual mode, which shutter speed will result in a more suitable aperture value.

Memory Lock

The release button has an extra function in the selective metering mode; at the first stop it not only switches on the metering system, it also remembers the exposure value until you either release the pressure and thereby switch off the metering system, or depress the button completely to expose. This manner of operation is very practical and used for the first time in a Canon camera; some previous models were somewhat impractical because it was necessary to operate several switches.

The point of the memory lock is as follows. If you set the exposure for a certain section of the subject by slightly pressing the release button and at the same time keep this value automatically in memory, you have the fastest and most accurate method of correction at your fingertips. Instead of having to work out complicated correction factors, you simply choose the required section to correctly represent the entire frame, i.e. you may exclude particularly bright or dark areas which would have misled the integral metering. To what extent the exposure is thereby corrected depends on you; the slightest movement from side to side, or up and down, will result in different values. But the advantage of fast automatic metering and setting remains fully at your disposal. As soon as you release the pressure on the release button and the metering system switches off, you can depress it again slightly, point to a different detail, a different section, and you can store the new values. In other words, you are not stuck with one setting, but have complete flexibility at all times.

Just as in selective metering, the memory lock can be used in any exposure program, although it seems pointless to use this facility in program mode. Then there is shutter speed priority mode, and in this shooting mode selective metering with memory lock is the ideal combination. If you are not a total beginner in SLR photography and are looking only for some assistance from program mode, you can be totally in charge in any conceivable situation using shutter speed priority mode with selective metering and stored settings.

The T70 in Practice

We now know quite a lot about focal length and lens speed, shutter and aperture. We also got to know the camera itself. Now we ready to start in earnest.

Loading the Film

Loading the film into the Canon T70 has changed the concept of film loading altogether. I never counted myself amongst those critics who found it altogether too difficult to load a film into a 35mm camera, but now even they have to stop their moaning. Canon has simplified this procedure so that even a child of five could manage it. Canon opened up the field of photography to a new generation!

First you set the main switch to one of the shooting modes, except to self-timer of course. We need electricity to load the film, this is not surprising, as soon as technology takes over it needs current to make it work. The back can be opened by sliding the left thumb over the (upper) locking lever and pushing the lever down. If you have just bought the camera then the film pressure plate may still have a plastic foil to protect it. This should be removed as it is no longer needed.

The open back panel exposes one of the most delicate parts, the shutter. Under no circumstances touch it as a forceful thumb could cause irreparable damage. The film pressure plate and the guide rails should not be touched either.

Insert the film cassette in the chamber on the left, so that the end of the film points to the right. It is easiest to put the cassette in, top first, sliding it on the rewind fork and then lowering the bottom into the chamber. The film end is then pulled across to lie flat over the film window, to reach as far as the orange marking at the bottom next to the takeup reel. If the film end has been pulled out too far, take the cassette out and turn it back by hand. If the film reaches the orange marking, the lower perforations will engage in the sprockets.

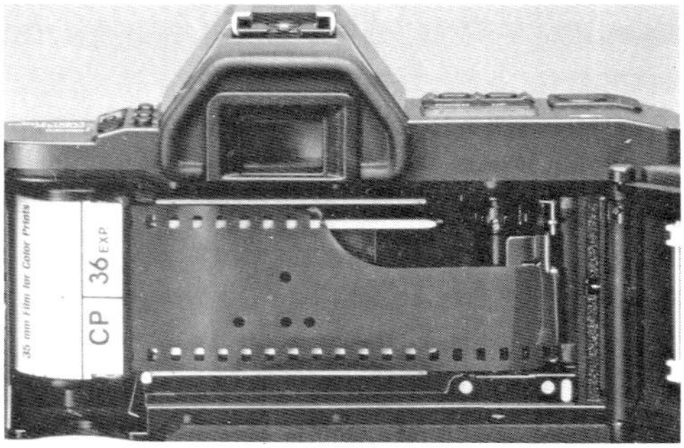

Insert the film cassette and close the camera back, the camera will do the rest.

As soon as the cassette is in the camera, the LCD display will show the cassette symbol and a box with the frame number, even if the camera is not switched on. This display is always visible. As soon as the camera back is closed after the above described procedure, your T70 will spring into action, automatically, without depressing the release button or any other action by you. It will transport the film to the first frame and trigger the necessary two blind shots. If the film is correctly loaded, three horizontal bars will appear in the LCD, seemingly extending out of the film cartridge and moving from left to right. If these bars are not displayed, then the back has to be opened again and the film newly loaded. These bars are always visible as soon as the camera is ready to shoot (they are normally vertical), even if the main switch is on LOCK.

During film transport up to the first frame, the film speed is displayed, either as the basic 100 ISO, or for any other previously set value. The film speed display disappears and remains discreetly stored in memory, but can be recalled any time by slightly depressing a key.

As soon as the film is advanced to the first frame the number "1" appears in a small box at the bottom right of the display. This modern form of frame counter goes up to No 39, and when the film is rewound it counts backwards. The LCD display is much easier to read than conventional frame counters. The frame number remains even if the camera is switched off.

The selected exposure program, and, if appropriate, the set shutter speed, is also displayed together with the frame number.

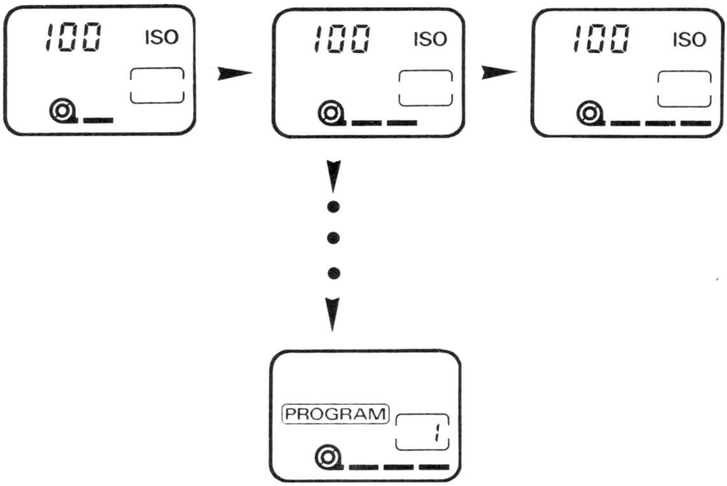

Three bars, seemingly coming out of the film cartridge symbol, indicate correct film transport during automatic film advance to the first frame

Setting the Film Speed

We have to tell the camera the speed of the film that is loaded at a particular time, only then will it be able to calculate the appropriate exposure values. The generally accepted standards for film speed used to be the DIN standard in Germany and ASA values (American Standards Association) elsewhere. The DIN and the ASA values were equivalent, only the numbers were different. Later it was decided to combine the DIN and the ASA standards to one uniform standard, the result: the ISO standard, an abbreviation for International Standards Organization. The well-intentioned fathers of standardization had the following in mind:

ASA 12	=	DIN 12	=	ISO	12/12°
ASA 16	=	DIN 13	=	ISO	16/13°
ASA 20	=	DIN 14	=	ISO	20/14°
ASA 25	=	DIN 15	=	ISO	25/15°
ASA 32	=	DIN 16	=	ISO	32/16°
ASA 40	=	DIN 17	=	ISO	40/17°
ASA 50	=	DIN 18	=	ISO	50/18°
ASA 64	=	DIN 19	=	ISO	64/19°
ASA 80	=	DIN 20	=	ISO	80/20°
ASA 10	=	DIN 21	=	ISO	100/21°
ASA 125	=	DIN 22	=	ISO	125/22°
ASA 160	=	DIN 23	=	ISO	160/23°
ASA 200	=	DIN 24	=	ISO	200/24°
ASA 250	=	DIN 25	=	ISO	250/25°
ASA 320	=	DIN 26	=	ISO	320/26°
ASA 400	=	DIN 27	=	ISO	400/27°
ASA 500	=	DIN 28	=	ISO	500/28°
ASA 640	=	DIN 29	=	ISO	640/29°
ASA 800	=	DIN 30	=	ISO	800/30°
ASA 1000	=	DIN 31	=	ISO	1000/31°
ASA 1250	=	DIN 32	=	ISO	1250/32°
ASA 1600	=	DIN 33	=	ISO	1600/33°

So far, so good. If you check the cardboard box of your film you will find the film speed stated in ISO, sometimes the ASA values are given as well. If you look at a modern camera or a flashgun, or read in some photographic literature, then you suddenly find terms such as "ASA/ISO", "ISO/ASA" or just simply "ISO" followed by two numerical values, e.g. ISO 100/21°.

The T70 avails itself of the ISO standards and you set the film speed ISO or ASA values, which are identical. You will find this value on the film cartridge, and you use the first half of the ISO pair. To set the value the camera has to be switched on. The key with the legend "ISO" is to the right of the main switch. To

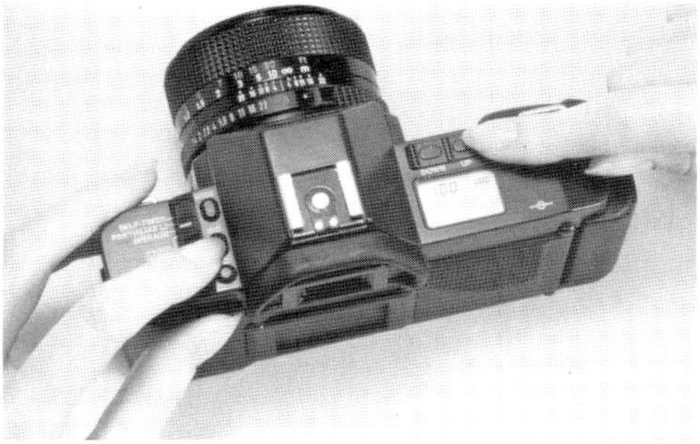

To set the film speed all you have to do is depress the ISO key and one of the UP or DOWN keys.

set the film speed keep this key depressed and at the same time depress the appropriate DOWN or UP key until the required value is displayed in the LCD display. As soon as you release the ISO key the film speed display disappears, you can forget about this setting and leave the rest to the camera's electronics.

Generally you will use the same film speed and will not have to touch this setting. Only when you change film speed do you have to take care not to forget to change this setting, otherwise you will end up with a whole roll of incorrectly exposed film.

Spoiled for Choice

Choosing the film is one of the most important decisions you have to make. First there is the basic decision whether you want to look at your photographs on paper, or as slides. You will have to decide between colour print film (assuming you wish to photograph in colour) and slide film. This sets the scene, although you may be able to get very good or at least acceptable prints from your slide film, it requires a certain amount of luck. Paper prints from slides are sometimes poor. The reason for this lies partly in the material and to a great extent on the quality of the picture. Although it is possible to produce excellent enlargements from slide film, in practice these are somewhat difficult to achieve.

But paper prints are sometimes no different. Looking at

some mass-produced paper prints, which seems the only affordable way to produce pictures these days, you may ask yourself if you took them with a sophisticated camera such as the Canon T70, or with any cheap little camera. Too dark, too light, colour wrong, anything is possible it seems other than a good print from your nice clean negative. I have to advise you therefore not to judge your T70's performance on the enlargements you get from the processing lab. They are not always perfect but can be a degradation of the original. Another bit of advice; be critical. Peculiar hues are generally the result of incorrect filtering during printing and not your fault. Pictures that are too dark are the result of underexposed negatives, or else the lab has made a mistake. If this is the case you should refuse the prints. Processing and printing labs are not universally known for their excellence: they often leave it to the customer to complain as their form of quality control. So it is up to you to accept bad quality or to do something about it. After all, they think you won't mind coming back next week for the reprints and it saves them extra effort!

You may have come to the conclusion yourself that every pleasure has its price. But if you are using slide film you have a much better chance of obtaining acceptable results, provided you used a good quality film from a reputable manufacturer. In this case you receive the mounted slides in their original form, ready to show. Looking at a slide you can assess the quality produced by your camera. A slide is able to show much more detail than any print film, as the resolution is much higher. It is true that you need a good projector and screen to reproduce the picture to good effect. But you will be rewarded with an image in glowing colours, producing an impressive reconstruction of nature with almost three-dimensional effect. No colour print can compete with that. And on top of that it is even cheaper!

Size is an important criterion. A picture in the family album, size 9x13cm, can convey to the viewer what was going on at the time, but it may lack the proper impact. You will be astonished to see the same picture, enlarged to, say, 18x24cm. But most of us don't go to the expense of having many such enlargements made, even of our best pictures. A slide, on the other hand, is projected to perhaps 30 times the original linear size. This imbalance between original subject and picture size becomes particularly noticeable if the image was taken with a wide-angle lens. If you always show your pictures as 9x13cm prints you may as well forget about using wide-angle lenses shorter than 35mm. Very few views, perhaps those taken purely for the record, will be done justice in this way. This should always be kept in mind when taking photographs. However great the technical and personal expertise in taking the picture, it is to no avail if the second stage, the display of the picture to the viewer, is not in line with the original effort and scale in representing the subject in a realistic and convincing manner.

It is not only the type of film that you have to decide on, but also the sensitivity, that is the film speed. It is obvious that the amount of light needed to produce the optimal result for each type of film will be different. Shutter and aperture have the duty to allow the same amount of light to bombard the film surface, regardless of whether the picture is taken in brightest sunlight or in the dusk of the departing day.

The photochemical industry has made every effort to give us a great selection of different film speeds to suit almost every conceivable situation. Apart from slow and normal speed films we also have the choice of very fast materials which are capable of capturing pictures even in candlelight. At the present time a film speed of ISO 100/21° is considered normal. For slide photography we have to include Kodachrome 64 with ISO 64/19°. For your general photography I would recommend Kodachrome 64 for slides and Kodacolor Gold 100 for colour prints. Both these films are of excellent quality and I have used them for years always with good results. The new Gold 100 offers even better sharpness and very high quality indeed. The new Gold 200 is one stop faster than the ISO 100 film and has excellent sharpness.

If you are shooting with a very long lens which requires a fast shutter speed, or in situations with poor lighting, I would recommend Ektachrome 400 at ISO 400/27° for slide photography. Generally I expose this film $^1/_3$- stop faster (i.e. at ISO setting 500/28°) when shooting in normal daylight conditions. In my experience I find that overexposure with this film usually causes the colours to appear rather weak, but slight underexposure results in surprisingly intense colours. Meantime even faster films are becoming available, such as the Ektachrome XO at ISO 800/30°. If you like colour prints you have the choice between the Kodacolor Gold 400 or even the very fast Kodacolor VR 1000 at ISO 1000/31°. Both are exceptionally good films. The latter has excellent resolution, despite its fast speed. But modern technology is not satisfied. Kodak have announced in the meantime further improvements to their VR 1000 emulsion to make this type of film even more attractive. Even so, you should not use such a fast film for the field-woods-and-meadow shots. Apart from the higher price, in ordinary lighting conditions you will be forced into using the smallest aperture with fast shutter speeds, so that these two means of control are not available to you for creating the image the way you intended.

What is Meant by PROGRAM Mode?

This is the last stage in automatic exposure setting where the camera operator is relieved of any decision, the camera does it all, apart from focusing of course. This function is complemented in the T70 by automatic film transport to the next frame. It is therefore not an overstatement to talk of absolute operational convenience.

To accomplish this minor miracle the camera has first to ascertain the subject brightness. The setting of shutter speed and aperture is infinitely variable, according to a predetermined schedule. If the subject is very bright then it starts with a small aperture and fastest shutter speed of 1/1000 sec. With decreasing brightness the aperture is opened up and the shutter speed is reduced. In this connection it is nonsense to talk of the ideal aperture/shutter speed combination, such as is sometimes claimed in advertising literature. The camera simply selects a sensible combination to achieve perfect exposure, but for picture creation this may or may not be the ideal combination. This is only natural; if you leave the entire work to mindless electronics the most you will achieve is a technically correct result. To my mind the fun in photography lies in "self determination".

As far as the advantages and disadvantages of automatic program mode are concerned, it appeals to the amateur photographer who is unable or unwilling to cope with technical considerations (or those which are still left to us by modern technology) and is happy to rely on the machine's technically perfect but soulless decision. Having said this, I would not go so far as to dismiss program mode as the newest ultimate of modern technology, as we are given to understand by intensive advertising. You may be happy to start with program mode, but as soon as you have learnt enough about photography, developed a feel for your instrument and developed an eye for your subject, you will move on to Shutter Speed Priority Mode.

But Canon does not leave it simply with "program mode". For the first time here is a camera that offers variations on this theme. This confirms how far from ideal the available set of aperture/shutter speed pairs really is. The question is and always has been; what relationship should be chosen? Is it better to increase the aperture and shutter speed equally, or perhaps increase the aperture more sharply in favour of

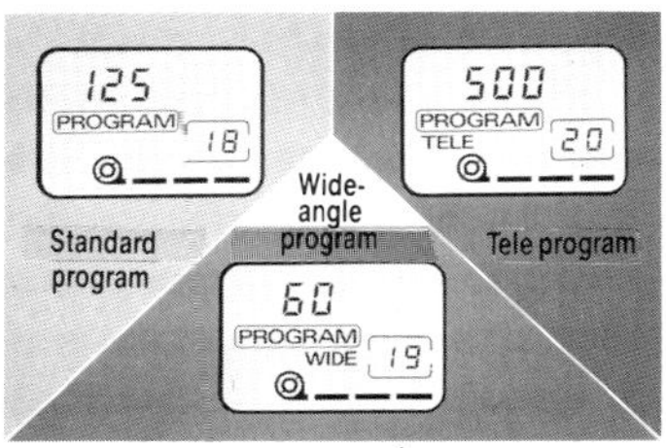

A new type of program mode; three separate program ranges allow for emphasis on either large depth of field or short shutter speeds.

shorter times? Every program mode curve has to make compromises and is therefore suitable for different applications. Canon have tried to counter the very strong argument against program modes by equipping the T70 with three programs. They have thus been able to achieve a certain control, even in automatic shooting. Modern electronics make all this possible and it seems that the future existence of program mode is assured.

The Normal Program

The T70's normal program mode is a combination of values as follows. At maximum brightness the program starts with aperture f/22. As the brightness reduces, the aperture is opened up accordingly. This process continues until aperture f/16, from which aperture value the shutter speed is also adjusted. In fact the aperture is opened up at the same rate as the shutter speed is reduced. We therefore have combinations such as aperture f/11 and shutter speed 1/500 second, and aperture f/5.6 and shutter speed 1/125 second. At aperture f/4 the program reaches the assumed limit of camera shake for standard lenses of 1/60 second. In this way, the program selects for the largest aperture of the most popular lens, the FD 50mm f/1.4, a shutter speed of 1/8 second. This is the setting limit for this lens and the program can only extend the shutter speed to the limit of the working range.

Standard program

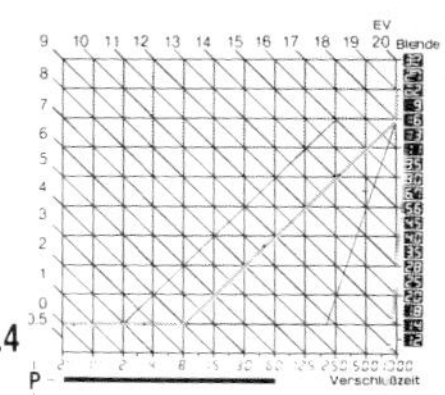

with 50mm f/1.4

The T70's standard program selects these pairs of shutter speeds and aperture values, always depending on the available subject brightness.

If you look at this sequence you will wonder why you bought a lens with a speed of f/1.4 or f/1.8, if you have to forget about 2.5 to 3 aperture stops, as these represent totally "unsteady" shutter speeds. The limit for camera shake is already attained with aperture f/4, as we have seen, all the other following program values are unacceptable, as you would not be able to hand-hold the camera for such slow shutter speeds. And there is your answer. The normal program is quite unsuitable for standard lenses. You can forget it for this lens, or you will have to make some adjustments. However, it is useful for the ever-popular standard zoom range lenses, such as the FD 28-55mm f/3.5-4.5 or the FD 35-70mm f/3.5-4.5. These lenses do not offer the very fast lens speeds and the use of this program is therefore quite realistic.

To select the normal program mode is simple. Set the main switch to AVERAGE. If the LCD display does not already show PROGRAM, depress the shooting mode selector MODE and also one of the keys UP or DOWN, until the word PROGRAM with any other additions appears in the LCD. The aperture ring on the lens is set to the small locking button next to "A" which stands for Automatic. Then you can start.

The display in the viewfinder will show a green "P" for program mode and the working aperture for the given conditions, if you depress the release button or the exposure test key. You know already that aperture f/4 is the limit in program mode if you are using a standard lens and the camera will warn you by blinking of the "P" as soon as the shutter exposure time $^1/_{60}$ second is exceeded.

If the metering system is activated, the shutter speed selected by the camera is also displayed in the LCD. It is not really necessary to check this in program mode. If the amount of light is too great even for the smallest aperture and $^1/_{1000}$ second, then the T70 will indicate this by a flashing "1000" in the LCD. The only remedy in such an event is to use a ND (neutral density) filter to reduce the amount of light and recognise that one should not use fast films in very bright conditions. Similarly, if the amount of light is insufficient then

Warnings provided by the standard program:- Danger of camera shake; Under-exposure; Over-exposure

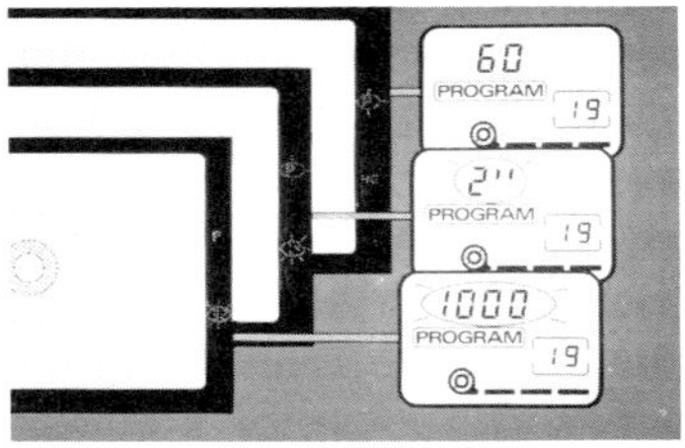

the slowest available shutter speed flashes in the LCD and the largest aperture of the lens in the viewfinder.

Theoretically it is possible to use selective metering with memory lock in program mode, but this would be a contradiction; shooting in program mode does not require any technical knowledge or decisions, selective metering requires photographic expertise and experience. The two are therefore incompatible.

The "Wide-Angle Program"

The program curve of this variant follows a much lower gradient of aperture/shutter speed ratio. The sequence is shifted by two stops in the direction of slower shutter speeds. The result is a smaller aperture for the same brightness. Smaller apertures produce greater depths of field, and this program may be considered in general outline as an attempt to reproduce the decisions normally made, or are supposed to be made, in aperture priority mode. Naturally the limit of camera shake is much sooner reached with this program. At aperture f/8 the shutter speed would be $^1/_{60}$ second. This program therefore is totally unsuited for longer focal lengths. Its main application will be with wide-angle lenses where a large depth of field is usually desirable. This program is therefore quite appropriately called "WIDE".

Based on the assumption that the shutter speed rule for camera shake permits longer times for hand-held shots,

Wide-angle program

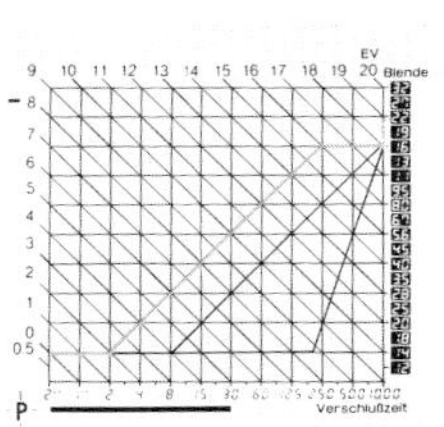

with FD 50mm f/1.4

The emphasis in the wide-angle program is on small apertures at the cost of faster shutter speeds to obtain largest-possible depth of field

Canon have provided the warning for camera shake for $^1/_{30}$ second. In other words, as soon as the program has to select a shutter speed slower than this the "P" in the viewfinder will blink, and this is the case for aperture f/5.6. All other incorrect exposure warnings are identical to that of the normal program.

Personally I cannot agree with this interpretation of the shutter speed rule for wide-angle lenses. Experience shows that the lower limit of $^1/_{60}$ second applies also to lenses with shorter focal length. The reason is not difficult to understand. The larger viewing angle accomodates a much greater wealth of detail into the frame, represented at a much smaller scale than for the standard lens. It follows that the resolution capability of film and optics have to be much higher to cope with this amount of small detail. And what happens if you take the exposure at the so-called limit of camera shake? Quite right, the resolution of film and optics may be sufficient to show the detail, but the slight blur due to camera shake begins to be superimposed on the outlines and the details lose their crispness.

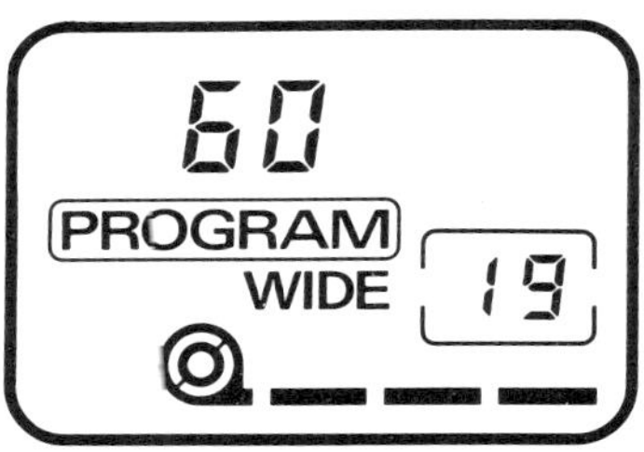

An example of the LCD display in the wide-angle program.

What does the photographer do who does not rely on the crutches of fully automatic program modes if he needs the greatest possible depth of field? Quite simple; he selects shutter speed priority, sets the longest possible hand-held shutter speed and allows the camera to do the rest. It will automatically select the smallest possible aperture for the available lighting conditions. This will result in the greatest depth of field for the given lighting conditions and no aperture priority mode will be able to do any better.

To select the wide-angle program you proceed as usual. Switch the camera on, depress the MODE key and either UP or DOWN until display shows "PROGRAM" with additional "WIDE". The lens should always be set to "A" for automatic.

The "Tele-Program"

Activating the switches in the same way as above for WIDE, you will eventually arrive at TELE. Now the program curve declines sharply down to the largest aperture opening. The necessary amount of light is permitted to enter the lens by a wide aperture which reaches its full opening already at shutter speeds between $^1/_{125}$ and $^1/_{250}$ second for lens FD 50mm f/1.4. From then on the shutter speed is continuously increased to the limit of the working range.

This program is weighted towards fast shutter speeds and is the only practical way to use long lenses. Even for aperture f/2.8 the relatively short time of $^1/_{250}$ second is still suitable, for example, for the FD 200mm f/2.8. If you are using the FD

Tele program

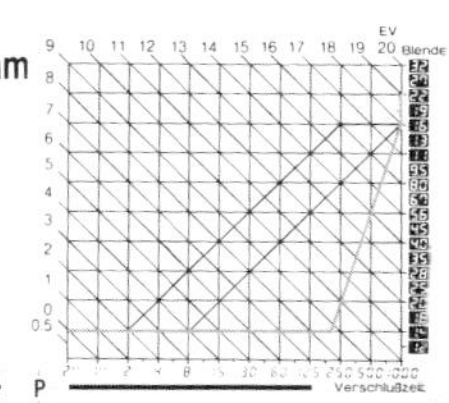

with FD
50mm f/1.4

In the telephoto program the available lens speed is taken up in preference to slower speeds before the program will select speeds slower than 1/200 sec.

300mm f/4 you obtain about $^1/_{400}$ second at full aperture and with a RF 500mm f/8 the time would be about $^1/_{600}$ second. However, you can no longer rely on the warning for camera shake, the "P" starts to blink in the viewfinder only after $^1/_{125}$ second is selected. This is much too slow for focal lengths of 135mm and longer, so you would be almost sure to get some blur even then.

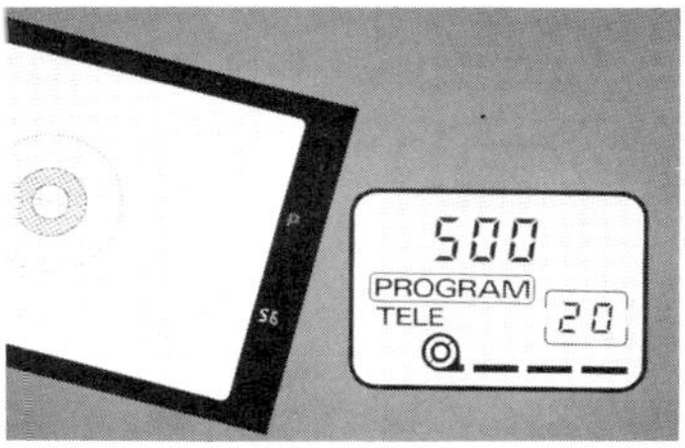

A "P" and the aperture value will be illuminated in the viewfinder in telephoto program. The LCD display gives the electronically selected shutter speed.

The name "TELE-PROGRAM" should not mislead you. In principle this program is suitable for any focal length, i.e. the standard and even the wide-angle lenses. You may use it to good effect for action photography. The preference for fast shutter speeds ensures that your main, moving, subject is sharply defined. This comes close to the principle of shutter speed priority mode without the photographer having to contribute any settings. I would recommend the tele-program even to the novice using a standard lens. He would be much better served by this program, rather than the normal program as it is able to utilise the full lens speed without exceeding the limits of camera shake, thus ensuring subject sharpness. Camera shake is a problem that many beginners have to overcome and this program is therefore particularly useful. Program mode is always represented in advertising literature as the ideal way to spontaneous action photogrphy, and I think the tele-program actually lives up to this claim.

We noted previously that the warning for camera shake comes too late for focal lengths in excess of 135mm. I can offer you an alternative, but must admit that this questions the idea of a fully automatic program mode. Switch to shutter speed priority and set the slowest shutter speed at which hand-held shots are still safe for the focal length of the lens. Let's say $^{1}/_{250}$ second. In this way you may be sure that the speed displayed in the viewfinder will not be slower without adequate warning. The shutter speed priority will extend the set time of $^{1}/_{250}$ second if it is not sufficient for the available lighting conditions, but it will issue a warning by flashing the largest available aperture value. In other words the warning will be given at the correct time.

I suppose program modes, even those in the new form of three variations such as Canon offers for the T70, are meant to save us the remaining need to think. This seems to serve the spirit of the time. Programmed for good pictures means that if you have a wide-angle lens, switch to WIDE; if you have a standard lens, switch to PROGRAM; if you have a tele, switch to TELE: and there you have it!

Shutter Speed Priority – Exposure with Brains

In my opinion the T70's most important and most useful exposure program is the shutter speed priority mode, which this camera offers in a very sophisticated form. Selective metering and memory lock make it an ideal exposure program, fulfilling the highest expectations of operational convenience, precision and versatility. Added to this is the automatic change to aperture priority if the pre-set shutter speed cannot produce a satisfactory exposure for the available aperture values. I shall discuss the latter later on.

In shutter speed priority you pre-set a shutter speed for which the camera calculates a suitable aperture for the available lighting conditions and the set film speed. You are thus able to control sharpness for every type of subject. Depending on lens focal length and movement of the subject you can select

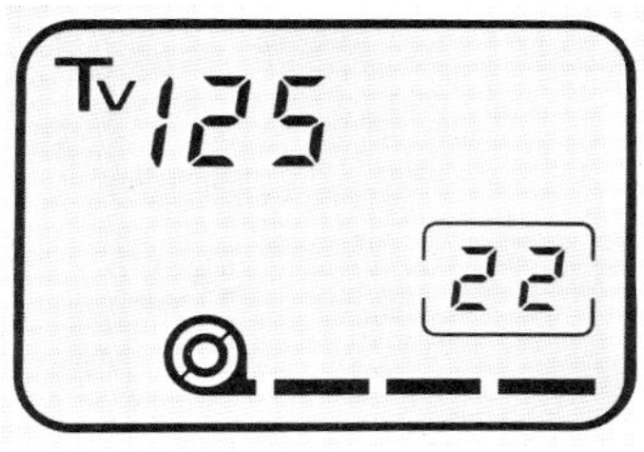

In shutter-speed priority the shutter speed is selected via the two UP or DOWN keys.

a suitable shutter speed to ensure maximum sharpness. On the other hand you could decide to show a certain amount of movement blur to convey an impression of the subject's speed. One should not forget that a movement frozen in crisp sharpness is unnatural to the eye and may sometimes be better conveyed by allowing slight blurring. The naked eye would never be able to extract one instant from the sequence of movements.

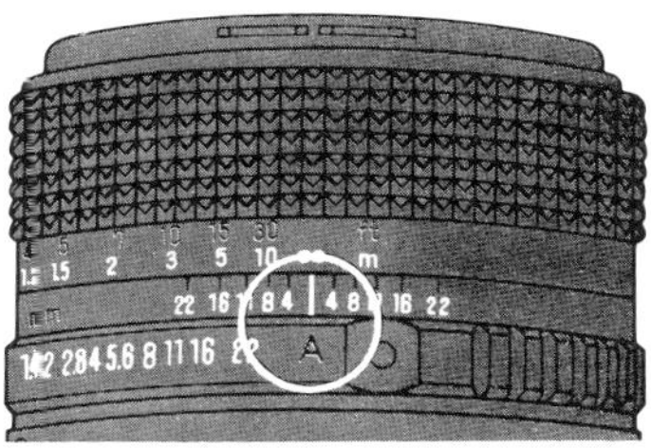

The aperture ring on the FD lens is in position "A" in program and also in shutter-speed priority modes.

Shutter speed priority mode is ideal for the majority of photographic applications, for snapshots, amongst friends and relatives, on travel, for sport, in animal photography and for hobby photography. In addition, Canon have overcome some of the limitations that earlier models suffered from. Together with selective metering and memory lock it is possible to make very fast exposure corrections for specific sections of a subject and so achieve perfect exposure. And you have automatic exposure control at your disposal without having to bow down to a rigid program mode which will allow only one interpretation of a given subject. Using shutter speed priority mode, you can avail yourself of the full creative possibilities that this excellent camera can offer.

The necessary settings are quite simple. Put the main switch to AVERAGE, or PARTIAL (AE L) if you should wish to use selective metering; set the lens as usual to "A"; depress the MODE key and one of the keys UP or DOWN until the LCD shows "Tv" and then, after the MODE key has been released, the shutter speed will be displayed. The required shutter speed is then set by depressing one of the UP/DOWN keys. If one of these keys are kept depressed, the available times will run through in sequence, which allows very fast adjustment. Tapping the keys a few times will take you through the sequence in measured steps.

Every time the release button or the exposure test key is lightly depressed the aperture calculated by the camera is displayed in the viewfinder. This is the only information that you need in shutter speed priority, as you have preselected the shutter speed in the LCD such that this is a known and, within the available aperture range, a constant value. The aperture in the display is always easy to read and is formed by a series of small luminous dots (LEDs) whose brightness varies with the brightness in the viewfinder. The display is in half-stops and as such is very accurate. In contrast to some other cameras where the display is by LCD the T70 does not need any viewfinder illumination, because the display is luminous for all data.

There is one variation to the display which I have to ask you to accept. If you are using one of the new variable speed lenses, such as for example the FD 28-55mm f/3.5-4.5 or the FD 35-70mm f/3.5-4.5, then the contact for lens aperture is calibrated for the maximum aperture, here this would be f/3.5. In other words, the viewfinder display is always told that the lens aperture value for the widest opening, whatever the effective aperture, is always f/3.5. The lens speed contact misleads the camera if the effective lens speed is only f/4.5, say, which is a full stop. This presents no problem when you are shooting in one of the automatic exposure modes, you will be misinformed, but the actual exposure level calculated by the camera will be correct. It does present a problem, however, when the automatic exposure is inactivated as you can no longer trust the display.

Canon uses digital alarms of aperture display, i.e. flashing of the aperture value in the viewfinder, to different effect. Let's first look at the incorrect exposure warning. This is indicated by a rapid flashing (at 8 Hz) of the largest available aperture value as soon as the limit of the working range is reached. This means that exposure at this setting would lead to an incorrectly exposed picture as the subject brightness is calculated to be insufficient.

As an additional function in shutter speed priority the T70 offers for the first time, automatic change-over to aperture priority. So far you have had to correct the shutter speed by hand as soon as the available lighting conditions were insufficient for the selected shutter speed. This presented a serious drawback as it necessitated a lot of manipulation if you were working in marginal conditions and wished to obtain optimal settings.

The T70 does it all automatically. If the camera detects a lens aperture limit such that it is no longer possible to gain the required amount of light by opening up the aperture, then it will automatically reduce the shutter speed. Similarly, if the lighting conditions are very bright so that the preselected time is not short enough even for the smallest aperture, then it will stop down the aperture to reduce the incident light to the required level. This means that the camera will always expose correctly, always provided, of course, that the available setting range is not exceeded.

Let's take a practical example. You have set $^1/_{250}$ second to stay within the limit of camera shake for hand-held shots with the FD 200mm f/4 lens. Using a film of ISO 64/19° or 100/21° you won't have a lot of scope for adjustment before the $^1/_{250}$ second is too fast even at fully open aperture. The T70 does not stop the shooting sequence for this reason, but indicates a warning in the viewfinder by flashing slowly (at 2 Hz) "4.0", the largest aperture. This means "beware, the selected shutter speed is insufficient, the camera has extended the time". Unfortunately, and this is a real handicap, the viewfinder display does not tell you what time has been selected. It is impossible at this point to check in the viewfinder whether it is still possible to safely expose without serious risk of camera shake. You will have to take your eye from the eyepiece and check the LCD display which shows the shutter speed in whole stops. This too is a matter of trial and error because, as soon as you try to look at the LCD display, the camera will no longer be pointing at exactly the same point, and, in particular in selective metering, you will find it almost impossible to align the camera in its former position without checking in the viewfinder. Canon deserves full praise for the automatic change-over to aperture priority when the range is limited, but the lack of viewfinder display of the effective shutter speed is a real drawback. If you carry on shooting with the aperture flashing in the viewfinder you will still obtain perfectly exposed pictures, whether they will still be acceptable, remains to be seen. This puts the whole idea of automatic change-over in question: unfortunately, Canon stopped short just as developments became really exciting.

Similarly to the warning for changeover to slower shutter speeds, the display will flash the smallest aperture value, again at a slow rate, if the exposure control switches to shorter times. In this, much rarer, case, the arguments set out above do not apply. There cannot be any objections against shorter times; nothing can go wrong. In this case the change-over is perfect.

If the largest available aperture value blinks at a rapid rate (8 Hz) in the viewfinder, then you are warned that you've reached the limit. The available light cannot be stretched even at slowest shutter speed to produce a correct exposure. In this case the said longest time blinks at 2 Hz in the LCD.

If there is danger of overexposure, then aperture value f/27 or f/32 blinks in the viewfinder, and also the fastest available shutter speed of $^1/_{1000}$ second, this applies also if you have set a slower shutter speed as the camera would have already reset the effective shutter speed and has to give in only when the effective working range is exhausted.

If you want to make sure that the set shutter speed is not accidentally moved, then you push the locking ring around the exposure test key to the right to "L", pointing the camera in the shooting direction. Now you can play as much as you like with the UP and DOWN keys, the shutter speed display in the LCD won't budge.

Manual Exposure Control

A camera's suitability for creative photography is usually judged by the criterion of whether or not the automatic control can be switched out. In the case of the T70 it suffices to select shutter speed priority, a mode in which you preselect the shutter speed, and then select the required aperture value on the lens. The display in the viewfinder will show what aperture value the camera would select for your preselected shutter speed. You could use this value as a reference point for corrections if you wished to achieve special effects. As soon as the aperture ring on the lens is moved from the automatic

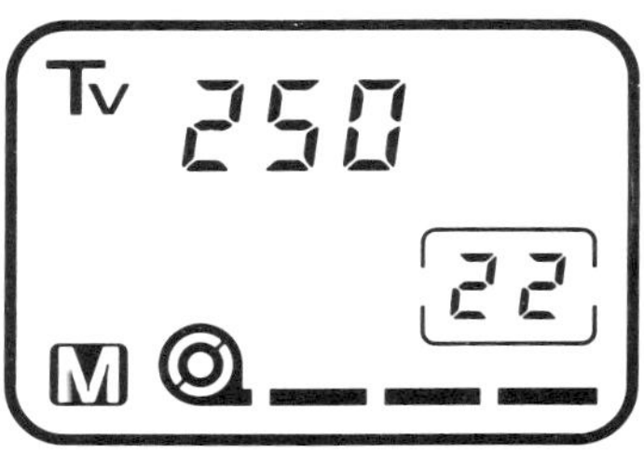

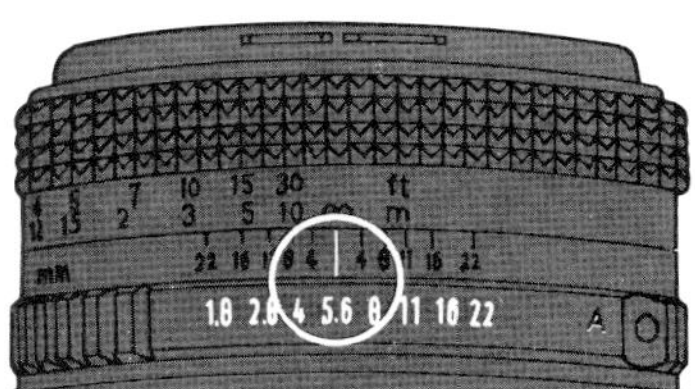

For manual selection of the exposure you start in aperture priority. Simply select the required aperture at the lens.

position, a red “M” blinks in the viewfinder to warn you that the automatic exposure is inactivated.

The incorrect exposure warnings are as usual. The smallest available aperture value flashes to indicate danger of over-exposure, in this case complemented by flashing of the shutter speed in the LCD. The largest aperture value of the lens in use flashes for overexposure and, just as for underexposure, the shutter speed in the LCD. The fact that automatic is switched-off is also indicated in the LCD by an “M”.

You will probably not need manual exposure control very often, as the T70 in principle offers everything for all conceivable corrections by selective metering and memory lock, and this is much quicker and simpler than any manual setting. However, if you like to use special effects filters, then the manual mode comes into its own. Let’s say you use one of the grey graduated filters, such as are available from Cokin, to darken the sky in colour photographs, then this would only be possible in manual setting. The automatic metering would view the image through the filter and take an average, instead of exposing for the foreground without sky which would completely ruin the effect.

I need to point out another limitation. If you are using the T70 with one of the variable focal length lenses, you should not expose in manual mode. We have already mentioned this elsewhere. The display in the viewfinder is unreliable as it always indicates the largest available focal length for the lens, regardless of the effective speed set at a particular instant. But you will need the aperture value indicated in the viewfinder as a reference point for your own, usually different, selection in order to achieve the special effect. Generally it is much easier to handle the situation with selective metering and memory lock, instead of working out complicated calculations and manipulations, which would be necessary with automatic inactivated. Unless, of course, it is absolutely necessary, as mentioned above in the case of the graduated filter.

Rewinding the Film

Having played around with the camera and tried out several possibilities you should not be surprised if the camera suddenly bleeps at you without any apparent reason. This acoustic signal indicates a compulsory stop, you have reached the end of the film! The frame number and the three bars for the film advance check flash in the LCD display.

Rewinding the film is done by simply depressing a button. The film starts moving back into the cassette as soon as the release button at the bottom of the camera, and simultaneously the release lever, are depressed. The three horizontal bars in the LCD run from right to left, indicating movement back into the cassette. As soon as the film is completely rewound the film cassette symbol begins to blink and the transport bars disappear. The camera switches off and sets itself into normal operational state by performing a dummy exposure. The cassette symbol flashes as long as the camera

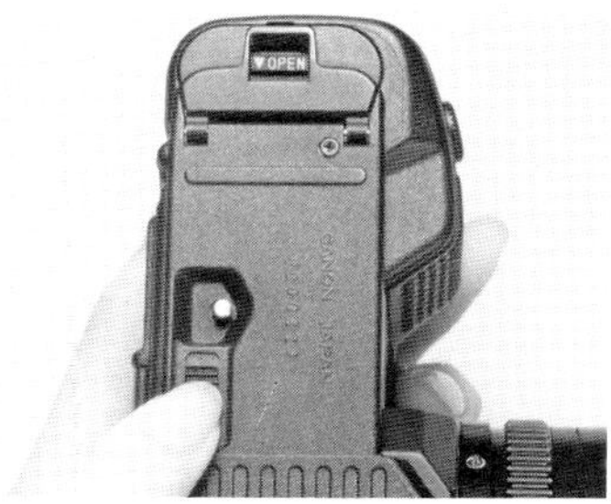

To start automatic film rewind the release switch is pushed and rewind button depressed.

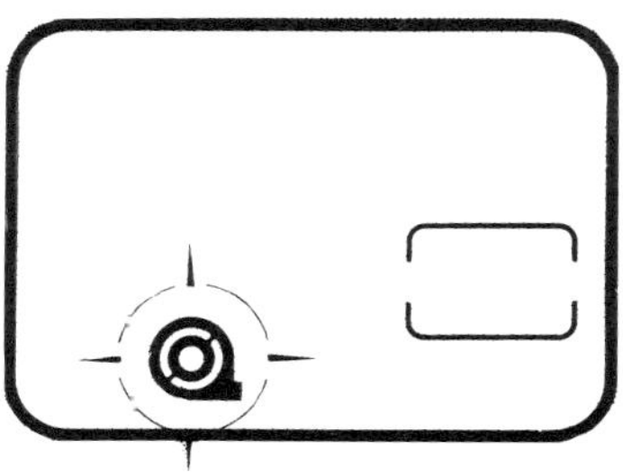

As soon as the film is completely rewound into the cassette the LCD symbol will blink.

remains switched on. If you do not remove the exposed film, i.e. the camera back is not opened, then the flashing symbol will reappear as soon as the camera is switched on again to remind you that the film needs changing.

The film is completely rewound into the cassette. It is therefore impossible to remove partially exposed films and to re-insert them later on. This has the advantage that you could not be tempted to re-insert an exposed film and thus ruin 72 frames.

Using the Self-Timer

We sometimes take pictures of our friends or relations and wish that there were a helpful genie pushing the button at the right moment so that we could also be in the picture. Or perhaps there is the occasion when you want to put yourself against an interesting background. The Canon T70, like the genie of the lamp, can fulfil your wishes. It does not present any problem to present-day technology to introduce a delay which will activate the shutter after a given time when the release button is depressed. I am talking of course about the self-timer.

You will have to contribute one little extra effort. The camera has to be positioned on a firm surface, or better still be fixed to a tripod, but this is not always available. After all, most of us buy a compact SLR camera such as the T70 because we want to use a handy device without the need for dragging bulky equipment around with us. But a table, a bench, railings, etc usually provide suitable support. You have to make sure, though, that the camera is firmly supported, after all there is quite some movement within the lens and camera during exposure which could upset its equilibrium. If balanced precariously on the edge of a precipice your T70 will have taken its parting shot!

Set up the camera and switch it on by pushing the main switch to its furthest position. In this position the camera is set to integral metering; the choice of exposure program is up to you. Focus and check the settings by depressing either the release button or the exposure test key. Now you can fully depress the release button to start the self-timer sequence. Take care not to stand in front of the camera when depressing the release button as the camera takes its final exposure measurement at this point and your presence in front of the lens would cause a wrong reading. If you do not actually look through the eyepiece at the moment of release it is necessary to cover it, otherwise stray light entering through the eyepiece may falsify the exposure. Canon recommends that the eye cup is removed and the little rubber cover placed over the

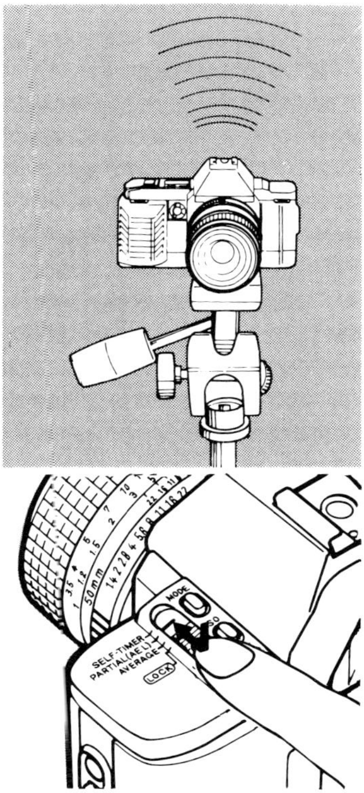

For self-timer shots the main switch is pushed forward; bleep-sounds will indicate that the sequence has started.

eyepiece. This cover is quite neatly accomodated in the anti-slip pad of the shoulder strap. To my mind this seems to be an unnecessary effort just for self-timer exposures. It will suffice if you hold your hand in front of the eyepiece at the moment of release.

The T70 will bleep during the self-timer sequence. The little box showing the frame number disappears in the LCD and the remaining time to shutter release is displayed instead. The frequency of the signal increases in the last two seconds to indicate that it is time to say “cheese”.

The delay mechanism of the T70 is a modern, electronic device and no longer the old-fashioned, mechanical retard mechanism. It is therefore quite easy to interrupt the sequence, if necessary. Therefore it is no problem to stop the self-timer after it has already counted down 5 seconds if the baby decides to have a tantrum at the wrong moment. It is sufficient to depress the “BC” battery knob or to return the main switch to another position, for the countdown to be interrupted. You can restore order to the family circle and re-start as soon as everyone has calmed down.

After the exposure with self-timer has been completed it is necessary to reset the main switch to LOCK, or any other exposure mode, otherwise it will continue to use this sequence as soon as the release button is depressed.

The self-timer is not only useful for self-portraits. It can be quite useful in situations where you need longer exposures in poorly lit situations and you need to use slow shutter speeds for hand-held shots. Under these circumstances you could look for a suitable support, a balustrade, windowsill, etc., on which you can support the camera. Even some vertical support, a wall, a tree, can serve to brace your elbow, or arm, or simply your bent knee if you can find a raised support for your foot. Having found the correct position, you hold the camera firmly and release, concentrating fully on holding the camera as still as possible. With a bit of practice and some luck you will be able to produce some good shots which would otherwise have been impossible.

Then there is the added security of being able to release with the self-timer from a tripod if you don't have the cable release handy. However, you can use the self-timer sequence only for camera-controlled shutter speeds. For technical reasons, in position "B" (bulb) (following the longest available camera-controlled time of 2 sec), the use of the self-timer is not possible. The special application of the self-timer on the T70 has a further significance because the camera is not equipped with a direct contact for a cable release. This has to be connected via the special adapter T3 which is placed between the remote release socket and a cable release.

Long Exposures

Even after reaching the upper limit of the T70's working range there is no need to call it a day. The only thing that has reached its limit is the exposure metering and automatic setting. You can still continue to take pictures. Set the camera to "Tv", as for shutter speed priority, depress the DOWN switch until the LCD display arrives at the end of the available shutter speeds, marked "bulb". This position corresponds to the "B" position and is derived from the days when the shutter was activated by a rubber ball, or bulb. If the release is depressed in this position then the shutter will remain open until you take your finger off the release button. In other words, the duration of exposure is determined by you and, theoretically at least, is unlimited. The shutter of the T70 is electronically activated, even in this mode, but the current consumption is extremely low. Therefore you may make frequent and long exposures without having to worry about the state of your batteries.

As soon as you switch to "bulb" the "M" appears again in the lower left corner of the LCD to remind you that the automatic exposure control is inactivated. This is logical, of course, as the length of exposure is solely determined by depressing the release button. It follows that the aperture ring on the lens may not be locked in position "A". It is hardly likely that you will

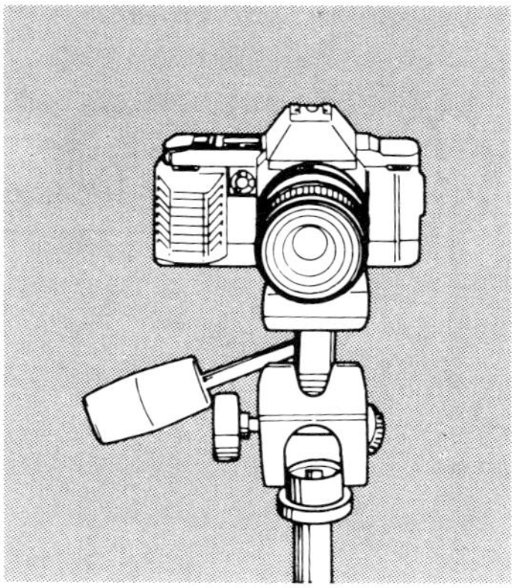

The camera has to be attached to a tripod for long exposures with shutter set at "B".

require the aperture to be set to the smallest opening when making long exposures. On the contrary, it will usually be the case that a large aperture comes into effect to keep the shutter speed down to a manageable time. The red "M" flashes in the viewfinder as the only display, even if the aperture ring has been left in "A".

The use of a tripod is an absolute MUST for long exposures. I would also recommend the use of a cable release, as this is the only way to ensure vibration-free shutter release. A cable release with locking facility is useful here, so that you need not hold the release down for the entire duration of the exposure. Contrary to other cameras, it is not possible to connect the release directly to the T70. You will need a special adapter for this simple device which is available under the designation T3. The adapter is screwed into the remote release socket which is situated in the handgrip of the camera under the grooved cover.

The Canon Remote Release 60T3 presents a much more elegant solution and costs about a third more than the adapter. This is the "electronic remote release" version which is also connected to the remote release socket.

Just how long you have to keep the shutter open when set to "bulb" to obtain a reasonable result under poor lighting

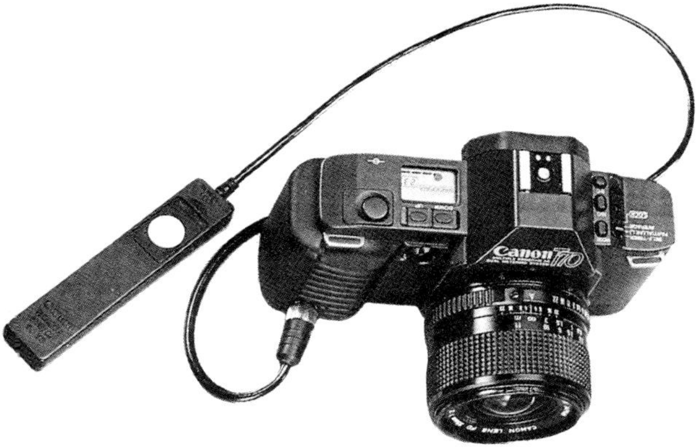

The Canon remote release 60T3 is an electronic cable release and is attached to the remote release socket in the hand grip.

conditions will have to be estimated, or you will need a good separate exposure meter. One can never be certain of the results of such long exposures and I would recommend you to take several at different times. Even if you measured the available light with a high-performance exposure meter, it still does not guarantee correct results. This is due to an effect which is called low-intensity reciprocity failure and was discovered by K Schwarzschild.

After about 1 second exposure, photographic emulsions become "lazy"; the effect of a short exposure to bright light is not the same as the quantitatively equivalent amount of less intense light over a longer period. The film is less effectively exposed during longer exposure times than one would expect from the meter reading, an effect which increases the longer the exposure time. The result is underexposure. Unfortunately it is not possible to state a rule because each manufacturer's products and film types react differently. For colour film there is the added problem of a shift in colour balance because the three emulsions of the film lose speed to different extents. A slight misrepresentation of colours usually has to be accepted in amateur photography to keep the expense of processing to a reasonable level. For perfect results these colour shifts have to be counterbalanced by correction filters. If you are in the habit of frequently using long exposures, then I would write to the manufacturer of your film to obtain information on its characteristics with regard to correction factors during exposure.

The T70 is the first camera to offer a kind of built-in stopwatch. In long exposure mode the frame counter box disappears in the LCD and a seconds counter appears instead. It counts to thirty. After the first 30 seconds one of the horizontal bars, normally used for film transport control, appears and the counter again starts counting to 30 if the exposure continues. After the second 30 seconds the second bar appears and after that the third, which means the total elapsed time is 90 seconds. The clock can count another 30 seconds after this so the total that can be timed precisely is thus 120 seconds. This facility is unique to the T70. For shots in very dim light it may be necessary to use a torch to see the LCD display, but you can leave your own watch at home.

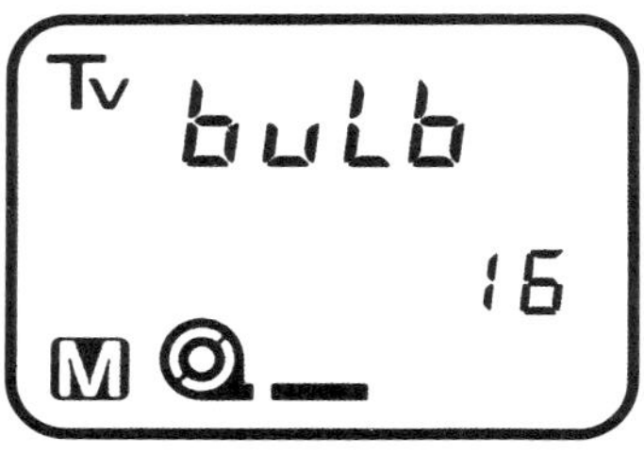

The T70 will keep count of your long exposures. The LCD display counts to 30 seconds. After the expiry of the first 30 seconds the first horizontal bars representing the film now indicates 30 seconds elapsed and the display carries on counting. In this way it is possible to count up to 120 seconds, i.e. three bars and one figure 30.

As mentioned previously, the self-timer function cannot be used for long exposures outside the range of normal shutter speeds. Therefore it is not possible to cheat by using the self-timer instead of a cable release.

A favourite application for long exposures is in photographing fireworks. This can be achieved much easier than you might have thought. Set up the camera on a firm tripod and release by cable release or remote release 60T3. Don't let anyone tell you that you need a particularly fast film, quite the contrary. Using a normal speed film you will find that you have to stop down to quite a small aperture. For Kodachrome 64 (ISO 64/19°) you should try aperture f/8, for a film of ISO 100/21°, as for example Kodacolor Gold 100, aperture f/8 or f/11 should be large enough to bring the spectacle brightly into the picture.

If possible choose a position where you have enough foreground and background in the frame. Just the display without any reference point can look a bit lost and will lack proper scale and impact. A shorter than standard focal length, perhaps 35mm, would bring a lot more into the frame, and in upright format may cover the full flight of a rocket. A certain amount of inclination of the camera could help as well; only if the foreground is very bright should you keep the camera level. Set the distance setting on the lens to infinity and you are ready. Wait for the show to start and then press the release. As soon as some (not too few) rockets have recorded their tracks on your film, unlock the wire release. That's it. You should take more than one shot; the display changes all the time and is usually particularly spectacular towards the end, so make sure you've got enough frames left.

Command Back 70

A special accessory that makes your T70 65g heavier and 3.4mm thicker is the Command Back 70, or data back. At the cost of such a negligible increase in size and weight it offers an amazing range of facilities. It can be interchanged with the normal camera back by a few simple manipulations.

To start with, the Command Back 70 has a quartz clock. Once you tell it what time it is, it will continue to keep count for ever, or well until 2029 at any rate, the only thing you have to do is invest in a battery every four years. It is programmed until that date to take account of months with 31 days and those with 30 and 28, and it even knows which years are leap years. The

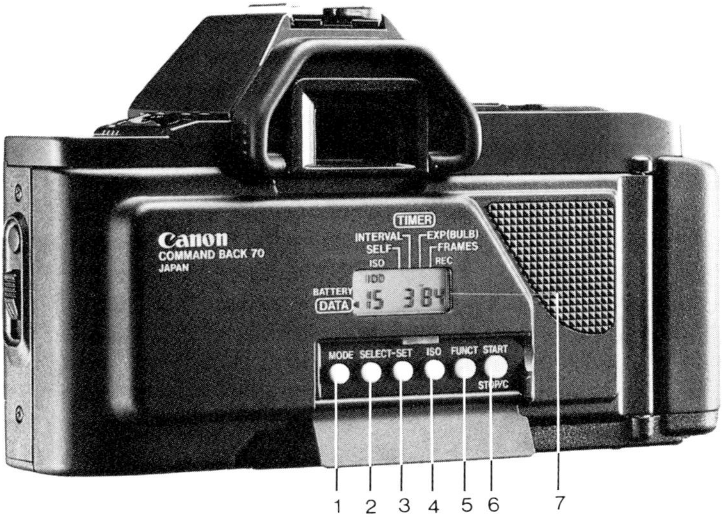

Command Back 70 for the Canon T70

1 Shooting mode selector
2 position selector
3 number selection
4 film speed setting
5 Date/Time switch
6 start/stop/delete key
7 liquid crystal display (LCD)

date can be read off the LCD display at the back. If you depress a button you can see the time, which can be exposed onto the film frame instead of the date if required. The automatic recording on film of time or date is the main function of the databack.

Most of us would find it very useful to know the date when a picture was taken. No one can remember all the events the camera recorded; "Was it the year we . . .?" "No, you are wrong, Emma was only five years old when she had the big teddy for Christmas." It is surprising how quickly we forget the sequence of events and it would be so nice to be able to sort out a backlog of photos in their proper order. Of course it is possible to write the date on the back of the print, but who does? And unless you are really consistent your family album will be in a muddle. Let the Command Back 70 take care of it.

The mode of date display, and consequently the way it is printed on the photograph, may be determined by you. There is the sequence of year/month/day, or you can switch to the more usual sequence of day/month/year. The date appears in orange letters in the bottom right corner of the print, if the photograph was taken in landscape format. If taken in upright format the date might end up at the top right corner if the camera was turned by 90° to the left. But if the camera is held such that the right thumb is on the release button, a position which is much more comfortable because of the fully integrated motor, then the date will appear vertical in the bottom left corner of the print. This is usually better as the figures are not obliterated by an excessively light background in this section of the frame. An orange background is the worst because it will camouflage the numbers altogether.

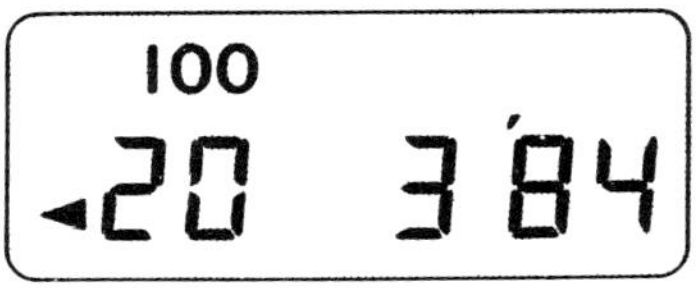

The date may be printed on the negative in the English convention of day-month-year.

Apart from the date you can also print the day, hour and minute. Or you can print a code up to six digits long. And finally there is the possibility of recording the exposure number, and this can be up to four digits long. (Changing the film would not affect the exposure counter, the Command Back discounts the blank exposures used in loading the film).

All these functions correspond more or less to those of any other data back with quartz clock. But the Command Back 70 is particularly well designed to fit smoothly and elegantly onto your T70, hardly noticeable as an accessory. However, its functions are not just limited to exposing useful data onto film. As its name suggests, it can take care of certain useful control functions, especially in the long exposure range. For example, you can program the camera from the Command Back to expose from 1 second to 23 hours, 59 minutes and 59 seconds. Or you can program to repeat one particular shot for a required number of times at set intervals, or perhaps a long exposure of a certain duration within the above-named period. Finally you are able to program up to 99 shots, after which the camera will switch itself off. And if all this is not enough, you can choose individual functions and combine them with others and the same holds true also for the exposure of data. Both groups of functions can be used in any combination.

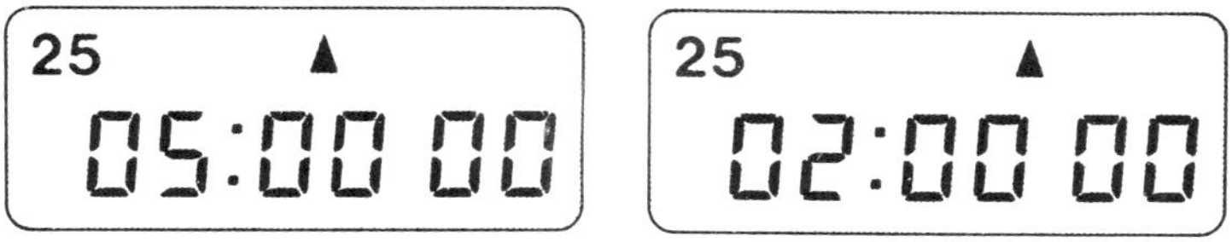

The photographic unit is programmed to take a shot every 5 hours (left). The display on the right shows a long exposure of over 2 hours.

Can I help with some examples? Program your camera to take a shot every 2 hours, 15 minutes and 30 seconds; or that it takes a shot every 5 minutes and 30 seconds; or that the shutter remains open for 4 hours and 15 minutes; or that the camera switches off after 12 exposures. Or have fun with one of 52 possible combinations.

If you are taking automatic long exposures you will have to use the rubber eyepiece cover, which is accomodated in the anti-slip pad in the shoulder strap. It is necessary to prevent external light from entering through the eyepiece because it would cause incorrect exposure. The cover may be pushed onto the ocular mounting after the eyepiece rubber shield has been removed.

The Command Back 70 attaches without cable to the camera back and need not be removed. If you don't wish to expose the date, simple pressure on a button will suffice to inactivate the system. The quartz clock is always on standby.

The databack is therefore not simply an accessory that you take out occasionally, once attached it is part of the equipment.

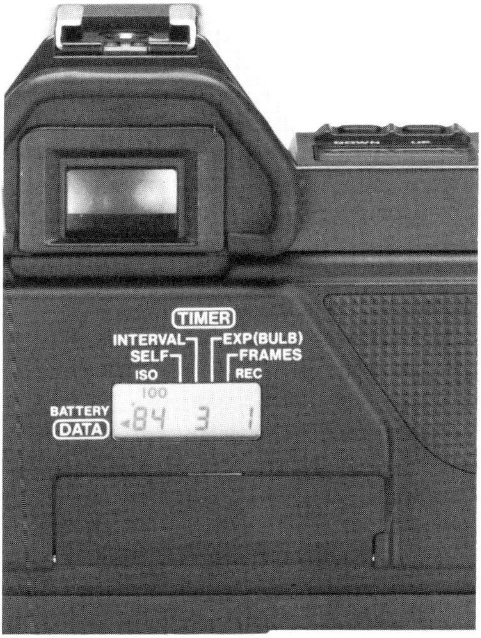

The cover for the programming panel on the Databack 70 is held in place magnetically. The total thickness of the Databack is only 3.4mm.

The New Era of Flash Photography

Flash photography has undergone some major changes in recent years. One of the most important developments has been the internal flash control by a separate metering cell integrated into the mirror box. The cell is orientated backwards so that it measures the flashlight reflected from the film surface (together with the general illumination). This system, which has not been adopted by Canon, was praised in advertising, and by the press in particular, as it allows the use of any selected aperture. Reading between the lines you will expect my next comment to be that as ideal as this is, there are limitations. Yes, you may stop down the aperture to obtain great depth of field, but in doing so the flashgun used will have to produce sufficient light because the small aperture will allow only a small amount to enter. There you have it! You can only use powerful TTL flashguns, as they are called, in order to make use of this facility. Most flashguns of average output reduce the possible range of apertures for different distance settings to those offered by normal computer flashguns (with external flash illumination control).

The internal flash control has some further advantages. It not only measures the brightness produced by the flash, but also the daylight if the flash is used to fill-in shadow areas. If you are using a filter or any other accessory in front of the lens, the metering cell would not be bothered at all, it simply meters the light that is reflected by the film surface, which is exactly that amount which exposes the film. Therefore it is not surprising that most manufacturers have now opted for this system. Canon fans must have felt a bit disadvantaged in this respect as "their" make did not take part in the development.

Canon's design engineers have been working on their own concept of how to overcome this problem and with the appearance of the T50 presented to the world the first electronic flash, to be based on an entirely new principle. The Speedlite 244T emits a short infrared flash when the release is slightly depressed. This flash is used to measure not only the distance of the subject, but also its reflectivity. Based on this comprehensive information, never before available on conventional flashguns, the flashgun is able to select a suitable working aperture for the set film speed and, to top it all, it also sets it on the lens. Therefore it is able to meter not only the light produced by the flash, but also that from other sources.

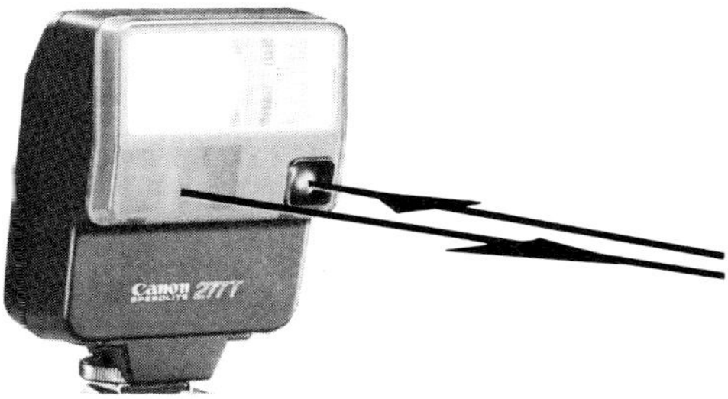

Before releasing the flash, the Speedlite 244T and 277T measure the distance and reflectivity characteristics of the subject by bouncing a brief infrared flash off it.

This method has brought revolutionary improvements to flash photography and may be said, without exaggeration, to introduce a new concept of ease and perfection. Canon have introduced an improved and more powerful flashgun for the T70, the Speedlite 277T, which is also suitable for fill-in flash, and boasts outstanding operational convenience.

The Speedlite 277T

The Speedlite 277T is an exceedingly compact and handy instrument for its guide number of 25 at ISO 100/21°. It connects without cable to the T70's accessory shoe. The illumination angle covers the angle of view of a 35mm lens. The wide angle reflector, which is supplied with the instrument, extends the illumination angle to cover that of a 28mm lens.

The Speedlite 277T is powered by four AA size alkaline 1.5V batteries, or the equivalent nickel cadmium batteries. The illumination time ranges from $^1/_{700}$ to $^1/_{50000}$ second, depending on subject distance and reflectivity conditions. Using a lens at f/2 and a film speed of ISO 100/21° the instrument will illuminate adequately within the range of 0.5 to 12.5m. The flash range for new alkaline batteries varies between 0.5m and 8m. A set of batteries should produce between 200 to 1700 flashes.

To start with, the film speed has to be set at the back of the flashgun. This may be done within the range of ISO 25/15° to ISO 400/27° in one-third stops. A selector switch provides a choice between program flash mode or variable flash mode, the latter bearing the legend "F NO.SET". When switching over, a luminous yellow-green mask covers the selected legend so it stands out quite clearly. The ready indicator serves also as a manual release. The only display element on the flash is the aperture scale from f/2 to f/22, where, in variable flash mode, the selected working aperture lights up. If the flash is used in program flash mode, then the automatically selected working aperture will be illuminated. If a red dot illuminates to the left of aperture f/2, it means that the instrument is over-extended. That means the subject is too far away or the reflectivity of the surface is too low. The luminous display is ideal as it is easily legible and there is no need to search for pertinent data, only the relevant value is illuminated, the others are dead.

At the front of the instrument, below the flash reflector, is an unusually large window for the metering cell. This switches over automatically, on receipt of the reflected infrared, to metering and control of the main flash. The light that is metered covers not only that from the reflected flash, but also the general illumination, as would be the case when fill-in flash is used in daylight shots. The infrared flash is behind the slightly transparent area next to the metering cell. It can be seen for a short time when the release is tapped and the instrument is ready to shoot.

Canon tried to adjust the flashgun's styling to complement that of the camera by inclining the flashgun slightly forward. The steamlined effect suits the functional form and appearance of the camera.

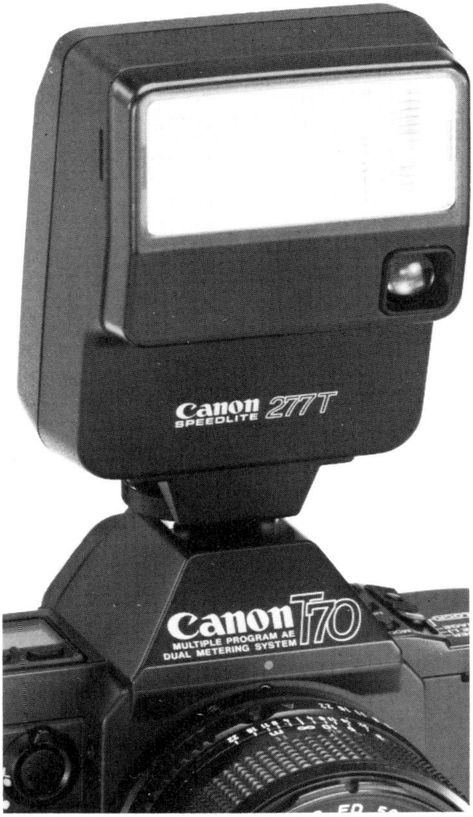

The Speedlite 277T used with the T70 means ease and convenience in flash photography.

Program Flash Mode

This is a new term in Canon literature and should not be confused with any other system under the same description used by other manufacturers for their program-controlled flash mode. Canon does it as follows.

To start with, "program" does not stand for a specific program mode. The T70 does not mind at all which of the

The photographer's actions in program flash mode are limited to the initial film speed setting. The flash will automatically cover the considerable range from 0.5m to 12,5m, insofar as the film speed is 100/21° and the lens has a speed of at least f/2.

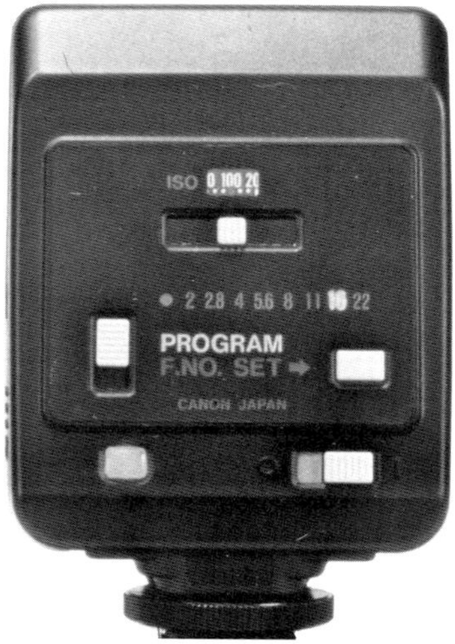

program functions are selected, as long as the program is not switched off. Therefore you can use the shutter speed priority mode and the T70 won't complain. Simply push the flashgun into the accessory shoe and secure it by tightening the knurled ring. Ensure that the film speed setting on the flashgun is correct. Then push the left-hand switch at the rear of the flashgun up until the PROGRAM legend is yellow-green. Switch on the flash and you have fulfilled all your duties. I shall assume, of course, that the FD-lens is set to "A" because you will shoot in manual mode only very rarely.

The great advantage of program flash mode is that the camera undertakes the choice and setting of working aperture all on its own. Using an ISO 100/21° film, this allows for the full range of aperture settings from f/2 to f/22. This means real progress, even against the most modern flash systems, such as the type of TTL flash mentioned above. In TTL flash you are still required to select and set the working aperture, and this can be done only after you have ascertained, after focusing,

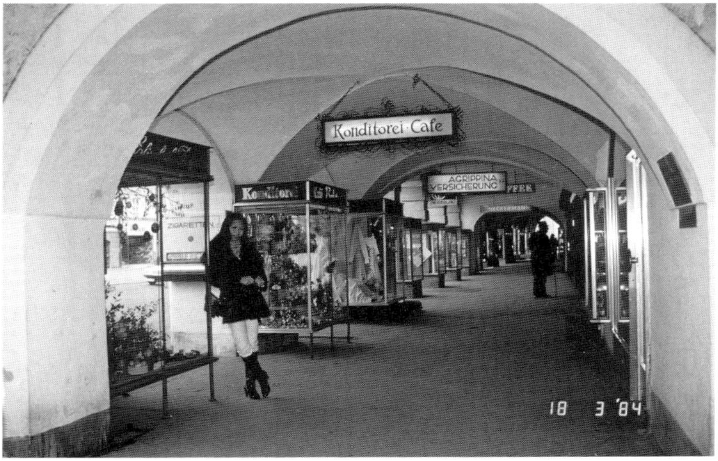

The Speedlite 277T is also suitable as a fill-in flash.

what apertures are available to you for the distance focused. The Canon speedlite 277T does all this for you and simplifies the most demanding flash photography to focusing and releasing.

The "flash ready" signal illuminates in the viewfinder, and only then the flash symbol. At the same time the aperture value, which was probably flashing up to this point as the available light is usually insufficient for an unassisted shooting, changes to the working aperture ascertained and set by the flashgun. The LCD display on top of the camera also changes at this time to the synchronisation speed of "90" (i.e. $^1/_{90}$ second), as this is always the shutter speed selected by the exposure program for flash photography. Longer synchronisation times are not possible. Only on "bulb" is it possible to synchronise the flash for a longer shutter opening time.

If the largest available aperture value flashes in the viewfinder then the distance to the subject is too great. This warning is most useful, saving you a lot of spoiled pictures. All other flash systems, without the facility to assess the situation by infrared flash before the actual exposure, are only capable at best of telling you after the shot that the conditions were insufficient. But then it's too late, and the warning can only be taken as an invitation to repeat the shot with different settings. The Canon T70, together with the Speedlite 277T, is definitely superior in this respect.

You will generally focus first, then choose the required frame, and then depress the release lightly. The flashgun determines at this point the working aperture suitable for the subject and will warn you, if appropriate, by flashing the greatest aperture value to get closer to the subject. Be careful not to simply advance closer to the subject while still holding the release button. As long as it is depressed, the working aperture selected originally will be remembered. It is therefore logical to let go the release button when receiving an alarm, then change the distance to the subject and then to repeat the whole process. If one of the available aperture values remains lit, then the conditions are satisfactory and you can release. If the aperture value continues to flash, you will have to go even closer and repeat the process. In any case this method ensures that you are given sufficient indication of suitable conditions before it is too late. And this is how it ought to be. Other systems, however, have certain technical hurdles which cannot be overcome. You have to consider the Canon program flash mode for the T70 with 277T Speedlite flash in this light in order to appreciate how definitely superior the Canon solution is to other systems.

Another important aspect is fill-in flash. It happens only too often that heavy shadows without any detail spoil an image because the film is unable to cope with the wide range of contrast between the darkest and the lightest parts. Automatic fill-in flash is as easy as pie. The 277T works perfectly in daylight – unless of course the daylight is extremely strong. If the available light exceeds exposure value 16, then it is very likely to produce an overexposed image. But this happens very rarely indeed. On the other hand it is logical that the warning for too great a distance setting (flashing of largest aperture value) does not come into effect. The daylight would confuse the metering system. This warning is therefore limited to pure flash shots where the basic brightness of the scene does not exceed exposure value 8.

Variable Flash Mode

Canon means here automatic flash for a pre-selected aperture. Again this is pre-selected on the flashgun. If you switch the Speedlite 277 to "NO.SET" then aperture f/5.6 will illuminate on the rear of the flashgun immediately after the instrument is switched on. If you want to use a different working aperture you have to depress the key on the right where the arrow next to the legend "NO.SET" is pointing. The illumination of aperture values moves down the scale until it reaches f/2 and starts again from f/22. The "flash ready" display in the viewfinder will illuminate and, as usual, the flash symbol and the selected working aperture. Should you have tried to select a larger aperture than is available on the lens, then the largest aperture value flashes in the viewfinder. The aperture ring on the lens has to be set to "A", as the setting of the aperture is again performed automatically.

The infrared flash will not function in variable flash mode as you are taking the decision of what working aperture to use. And what good is it then? Well you could be ambitious and decide to take an active part in creating your image. Your choice of aperture will influence the depth of field. Perhaps I can

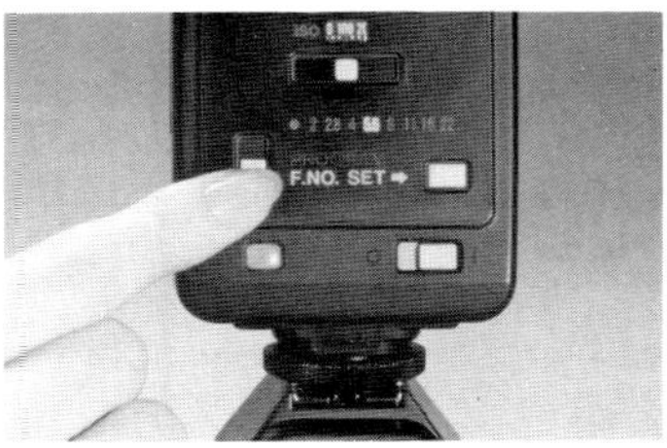

In variable flash mode the required aperture can be keyed in on the flashgun.

illustrate this by the following example. You have loaded an ISO 100/21° film and the lens has a speed of f/2. Taking a subject distance of 3m, you may choose between five working apertures, namely f/2, f/2.8, f/4, f/5.6 and f/8. You will remember our discourse on aperture and depth of field and know that the final result will be quite different if you are using aperture f/2, compared with aperture f/8. This is what provides your scope for creative photography in variable flash mode.

Another aspect could be of interest. You may need for some purpose as fast a flashing rate and most rapid repeats as possible. You can choose a relatively large aperture so that the flashgun will have to expend less energy. The flashgun does not have to expend all its energy and re-charges quicker for the next shot.

The overall distance range that the Speedlite 277T can cover in variable flash mode is identical to that in program flash mode: 0.5m to 12.5m at ISO 100/21°. This makes nonsense of Canon's recommendation to switch to variable flash mode to extend the distance range.

One disadvantage in practical use is that it was not possible to state the automatic range for variable flash mode on the 277T. This compromise in favour of compactness seems to be excessive and unnecessary. To my mind it is unacceptable to be forced to cut out the range table from the flashgun manual and have to carry it around all the time in order to refer back to what working apertures are usable for different distances. Unfortunately I cannot provide you with any other solution than to carry a table with you, otherwise the whole variable flash mode is good for nothing. I often wondered how many good ideas failed because of a minor flaw; how easily the cleverest engineers can fail on a minor detail because the impetus did not last until Friday evening. It would have been possible, just, to include a table on the side of the flashgun.

In case you no longer have the table for aperture ranges in variable flash mode I shall state them below for film speed ISO 100/21°:

f/2	1.5m-12.5m
f/2.8	1.0m-8.8m
f/4	0.7m-6.2m
f/5.6	0.5m-4.4m
f/8	0.5m-3.1m
f/11	0.5m-2.2m
f/16	0.5m-1.6m
f/22	0.5m-1.1 m

Flash with Canon Speedlites

It would not be very wise to use a flashgun other than a Canon T-series Speedlite with your T70. However, if you already possess an A- or G-series Speedlite then it might be of interest to use this on the T70. This is possible, but flashguns such as the 177A, 188A, 533G or 577G will not change automatically to synchronisation speed $^1/_{90}$ second as soon as the flashgun is

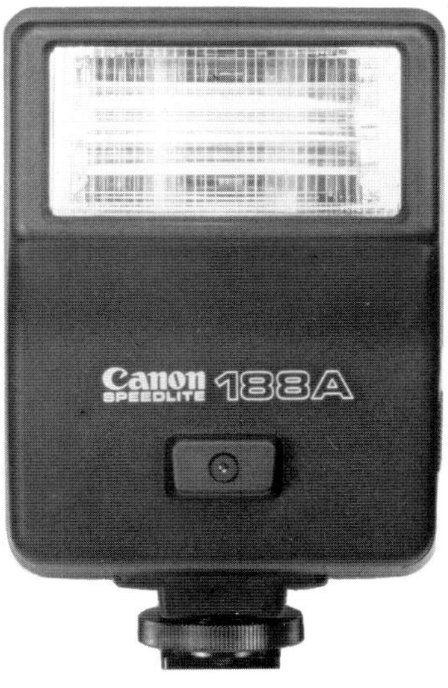

The Speedlite 188A is a very handy electronic flashgun in the Canon range, having a guide number of 25 at ISO 100/21°.

The Speedlite 199A offers a guide number of 30 at ISO 100/21°, which is quite a powerful output for a flashgun attached without cable. Disregarding the hammerhead flashguns, this is the most powerful flashgun offered by Canon.

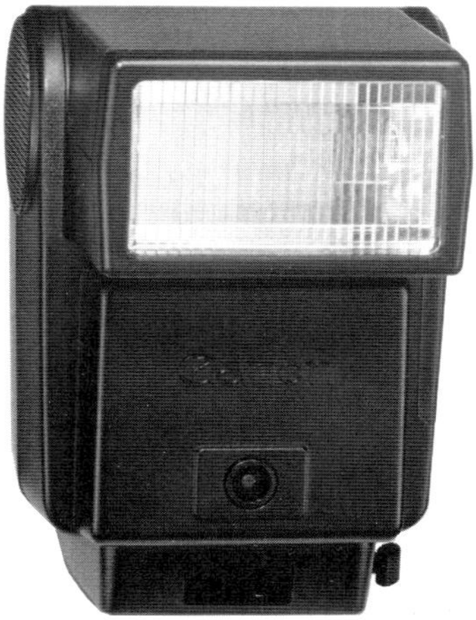

operational. It makes no difference what automatic program has been selected on the T70. The ready-to-shoot display and the flash symbol will appear in the viewfinder, but the warnings for exceeding the automatic range will not appear, which is logical.

Canon warns against using flashguns from other manufacturers as the T70 could be damaged because of its special circuitry. If you do risk it, you have to switch to "Tv" and select 1/60 sec.

Picturesque shadows due to the side lighting, the main subject being arranged off-centre and seen from an upward angle, and the diagonal arrangement of lines lend this view of the "Rock Cupola" in Jerusalem its special interest. The building is shown in direct relation to its surroundings. This and all the following colour plates come from the author's portfolio.

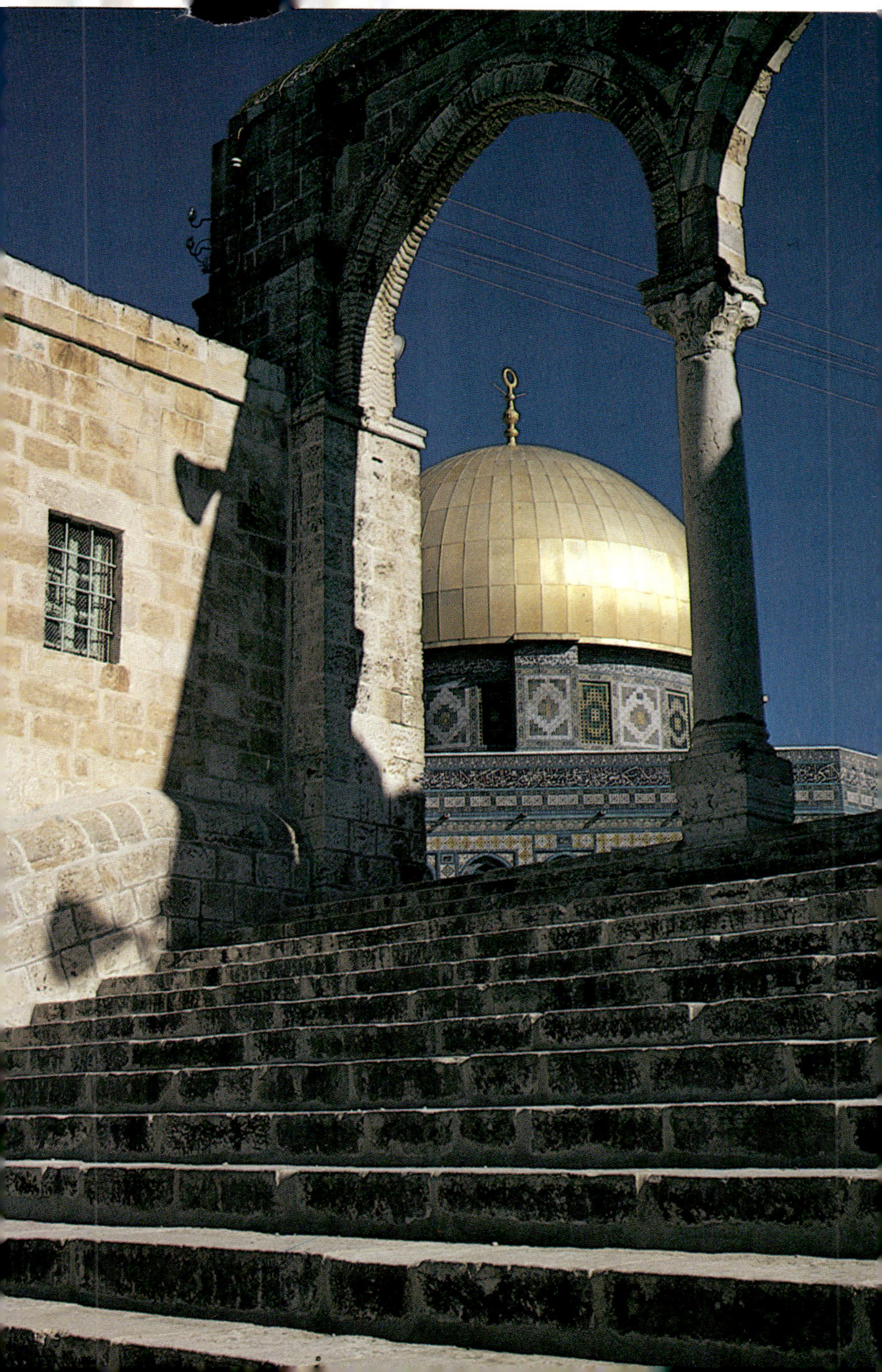

Practical Tips

There is no doubt the T70 is an excellent camera. Together with it and one of the FD lenses you are guaranteed needle-sharp and generally correctly-exposed pictures. What is the difference then between technically perfect and photographically effective pictures? The answer is not difficult to find. The saying that a good tool can only produce excellent results in the hands of an expert holds true in photography. Don't worry, though, there are only a few basic tricks to learn which separate good photographs from the run-of-the-mill snaps. Once learnt they will soon become second nature and you will see your subject with different eyes, not as you normally perceive it, but as the two-dimensional view of the lens as projected onto a defined frame.

I shall point out a few things in the following pages and illustrate my point by some representative shots. If you study these pictures you will see that a successful image is the sum-total of all these little tricks I will have mentioned, even if I may have pointed out only one particular one at the time.

Close-up is Best!

You must have witnessed scenes like this. Uncle Bill wants to take a picture of Aunt Sarah. He cocks the camera and steps back, further and further, although Aunt Sarah could have fitted into the frame much closer up! Only when she has merged into the general background does he press the release.

And now you know why so many pictures look so miserable. You pay for every millimetre and then you throw most of it away. Get up close, allow your subject to fill the frame. The result will astonish you by its immediacy and impact. The two pictures below say it all. Both were taken with a Canon FD 80-200mm f/4. The subject was caught unawares in the bustle of the Munich carnival. The long lens allows you to bring the subject

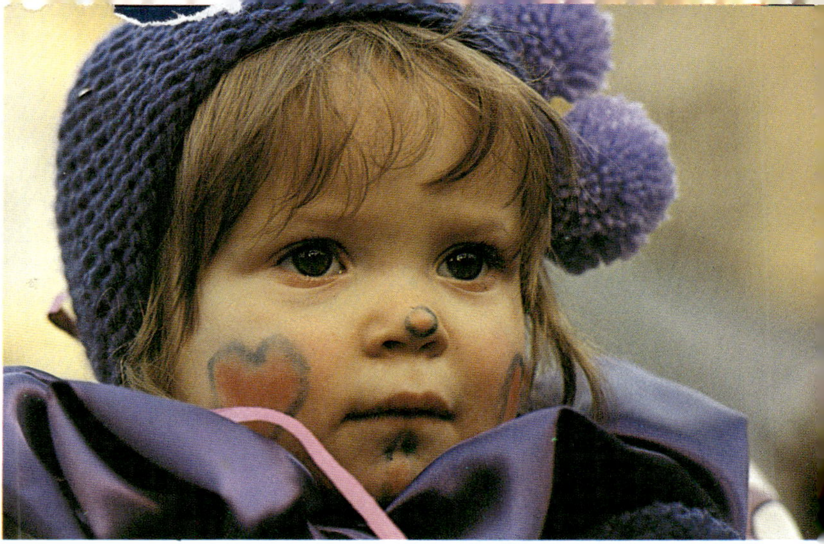

Don't be timid about cutting off part of a subject occasionally. It is not always necessary to show it all.

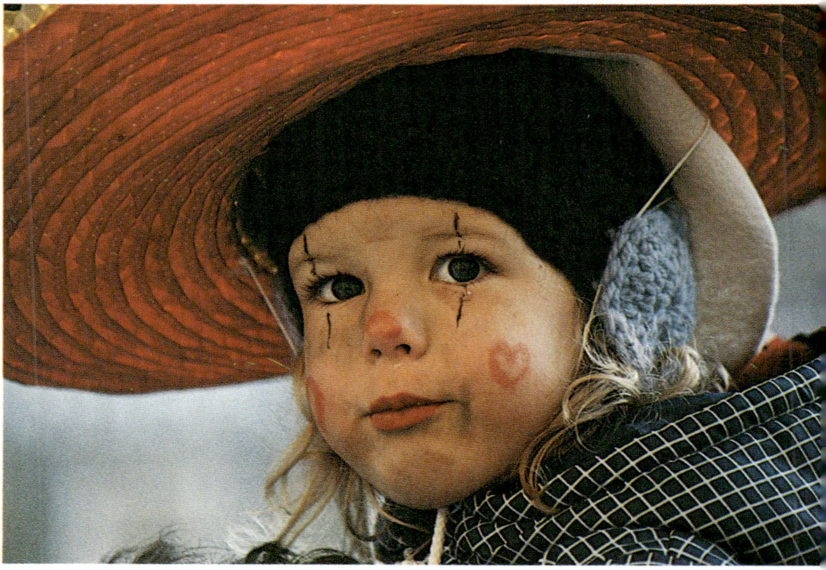

The oblique view from below presents a pleasant, natural perspective for portraits. Always go for the low viewing angle!

close from a suitable distance, without embarassing the model.

A further effect becomes clear when looking at these pictures. Whether you use a standard lens or a long lens to bridge the physical distance to the subject, the large reproduction scale brings about a sharp decline in the depth of field, provided you used a large aperture. Always focus on the eyes. The decline in sharpness behind the subject works in your favour and blurs any background which otherwise would only distract from the figure.

Another thing to consider with portrait photographs is the angle at which you look at the subject. Look up into your model's face! If you look down onto your subject the effect is somewhat patronising and the perspective unnatural. Risk a few shots by first taking some comparative frames from eye

Diagonals need not be absent, even in fully frontal shots. The arrangement of the puppets and the curtain form them in this picture.

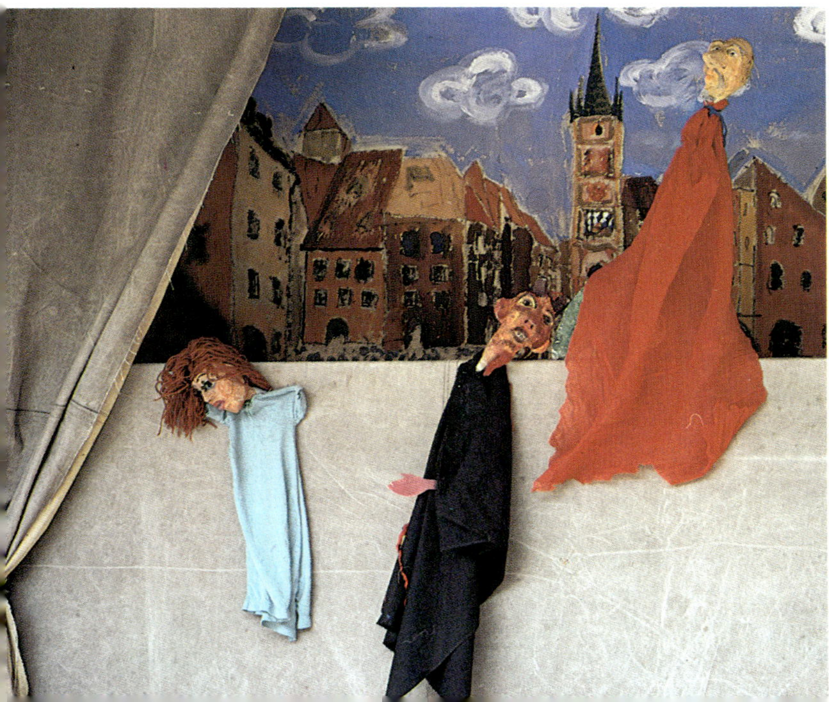

level, then from below and from above. A comparison of the final pictures will demonstrate the astonishing differences.

The Essential Diagonal

When you look at good photographs you should be able to identify recurring compositional structures that provide the interest. An uninitiated viewer will not be able to put his finger on it. He will see that the picture is effective, but not why.

One of these special features is the diagonal which, as a generalisation, should not be missing from any picture. As a rule diagonals are easy to find. They are the result of a suitable viewing angle, or the way the structural elements in the image have been arranged in relation to the chosen frame. Whether

The ribbon of the bright road leading into the distance is the diagonal in this picture.

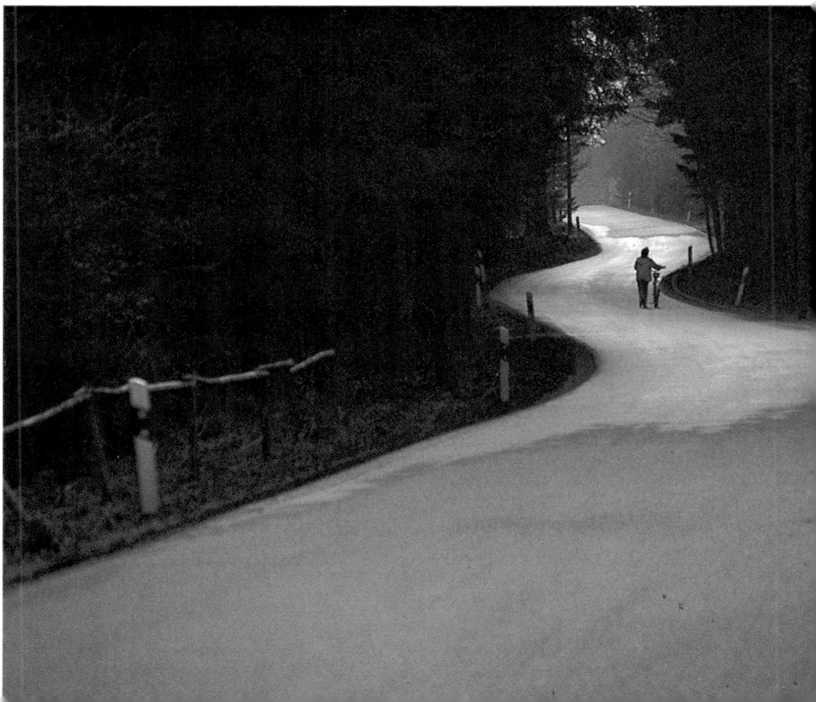

you take up a fully frontal position to your subject, or step aside a couple of paces to introduce a diagonal movement into the view requires the same effort, only the final effect is different.

Which elements in your picture are used to form the diagonal does not really matter. In the picture below it is the puppets which form one diagonal leading to the top right-hand corner of the picture, and the second is the curtain framing the scene on the other side. The road leading away into the distance forms the diagonal in the second picture. I used selective metering on the brightest part of the road to submerge the wood into a neutral darkness and thus to emphasise the bright band of the road snaking away from the viewer. This photograph serves as a further example of how the Canon T70's selective metering, together with memory lock, can help in creating just the image you had in mind.

Whatever you are photographing, it is usually advantageous to try and arrange either the whole subject or elements of it diagonally in relation to the frame. The frame can be chosen quite simply and easily in the viewfinder; it only requires careful study of the subject. After a few rolls of film you will develop a feel for creating your images and be able to introduce or seek out exactly those elements which create interest in your pictures.

Light for your Pictures

There are many situations which we have to accept as they are. Nevertheless, we often have scope to influence the settings. A subject, viewed just a few steps to the right or left may reveal quite different aspects. Only too often we notice fellow photographers in front of a memorable sight; out with the camera, finger on the trigger, and it's all over.

In trying to capture the moment, the photographer often forgets one most important point. The direction of the light and its overriding effect on the final result. Let's assume the sun is behind us. The scene is fully illuminated. The contrasts will be

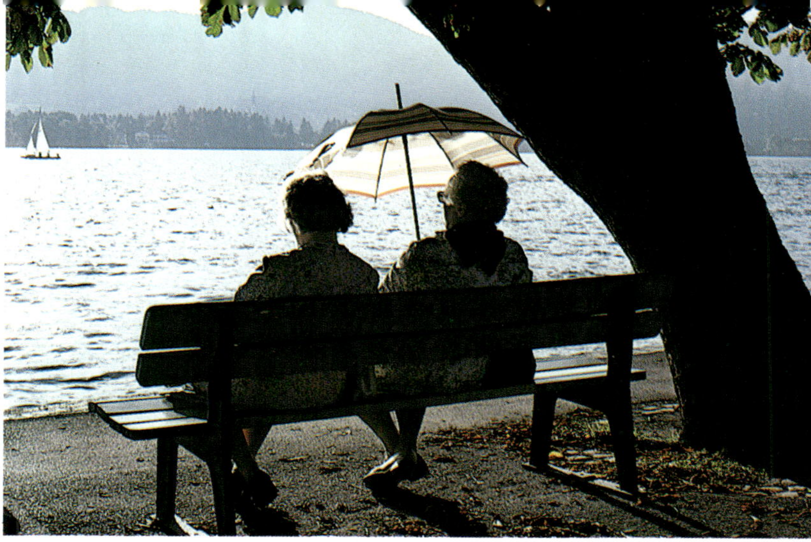

Side lighting brings out even the smallest unevenness; it is the ideal light to add interest.

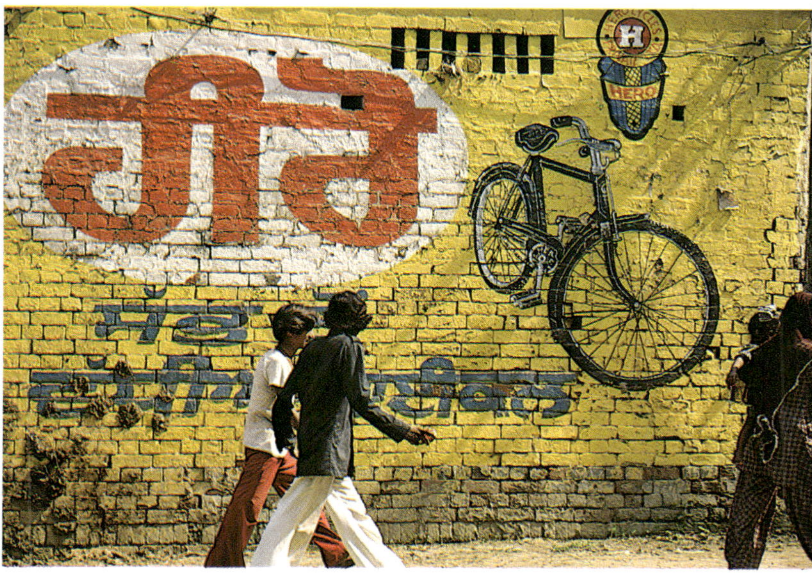

Shots against the light are wonderful for a mood-creating effect. Using selective metering and memory lock it should not be too difficult.

low and the film will be able to cope quite easily to show all details. But this image will lack impact. There will be no shadows, objects in the background will be covered and invisible. Frontal illumination is therefore the shortest and safest way to boring pictures! Avoid it whenever possible!

On the other hand lateral light livens up the scene. The sun creates highlights and shadows, follows contours in hidden crevices and brings depth to a scene. The slightest unevenness is outlined and even flat surfaces look interesting and full of shapes. Always look for this type of light, it is ideal in most situations. The only situation where this type of light ought to be avoided is for portraits; heavy shadows on the face can be most unflattering.

Backlit shots are for "postgraduate" photographers. Magic and romance may be captured in a successful against-the-light view. It requires careful assessment of the situation. Switch your T70 to selective metering. In a situation such as that depicted below you would place the metering circle to cover about half the light umbrella and half the dark person. This may be done in a matter of seconds. Then you can choose the frame and release.

Variety in Detail

Close-ups, for which you do not necessarily need special equipment, serve not only to extend the scope of your photography but will also train your eye to see detail. You can play to your heart's content by arranging your subject in a certain frame; a little more surround, a little less. You can change the distribution of objects, create definite lines and diagonals, draw attention to individual items.

The term close-up should not be defined too rigidly. It is quite possible to create many successful still-life pictures even with a standard lens. A lens such as the FD 80-200mm f/4, used for the photograph on the left, is ideal in many situations. Used at the close range setting of 1m this focal length makes

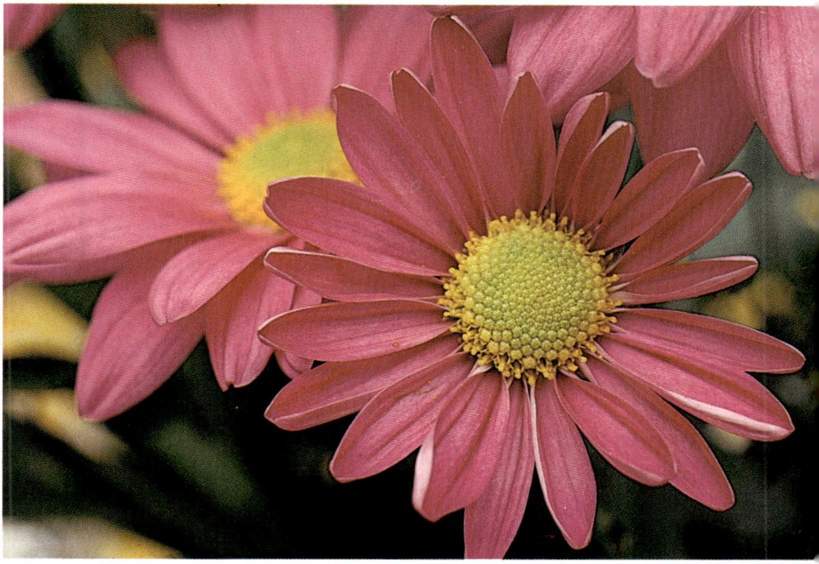

A natural still-life at the side of the road. The scene observed diagonally in side lighting, taken with a FD 80-200mm f/4 lens.

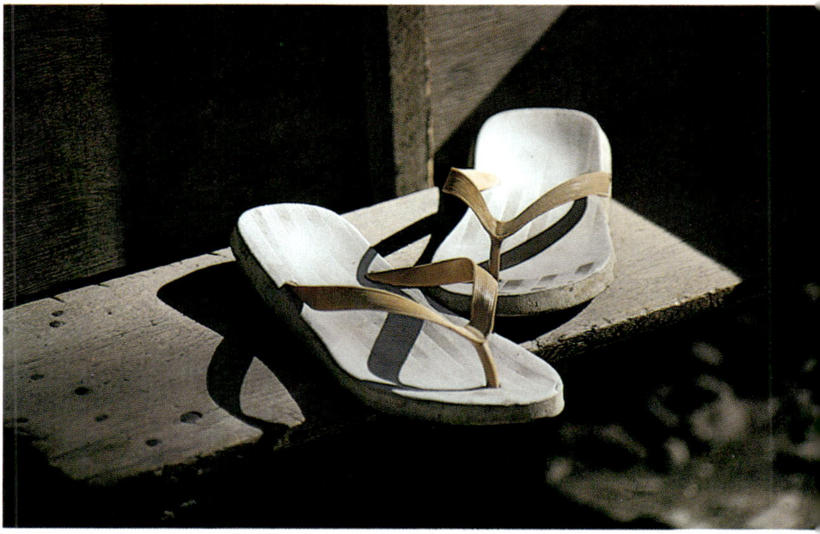

The front bloom arranged off-centre and the clear separation of distance planes due to the sharp decline in depth of field increases the effect of this shot.

feasible quite a large reproduction scale. All I had to do was to allow the light to illuminate the sandals from the side, arrange the bench obliquely to the frame and take the picture. The exposure was metered selectively on the brightest parts in the centre of the frame.

The flowers were taken with a FD 50mm macro lens. This picture demonstrates the suitability of diffuse light for macro photography. If you find that the lighting conditions are unsuitable for large subjects, you may look for close-ups. The decisive factor in producing an effective image is the asymmetrical arrangement of the elements of the subject and a pleasingly controlled decline in depth of field towards the top left corner, although a relatively small aperture was used. You must not forget that the depth of field declines rather more sharply in the close-up range. This difference in sharpness shows the second flower as background and increases the

Massive objects are sometimes suitable as foreground if they are still included in the depth of field. You will need a small aperture.

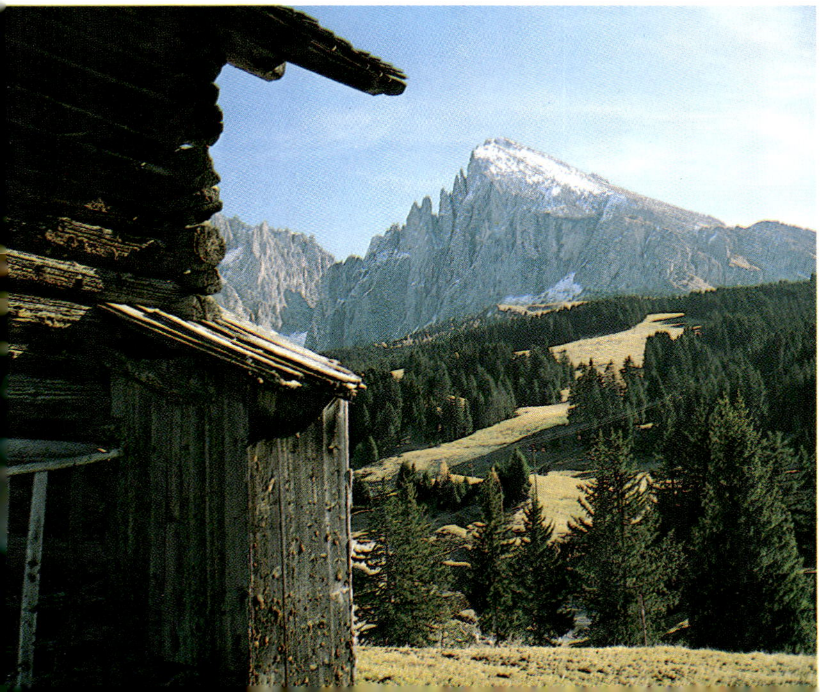

three-dimensional effect by the clear differentiation between the distances of the two flowers. A small depth of field has its advantages in situations like this when it may be used to create effects and moods. Controlled unsharpness is an excellent means to picture creation.

Foreground for Depth

All tricks towards good pictures have one aim in mind; that is to compensate for the fact that our photographs have to satisfactorily depict our three-dimensional reality in only two dimensions. The significance of this difference can be demonstrated quite easily. Cover up one eye and look at a scene. What appeared to be an impressive subject is suddenly just a confusion. Lines merge into each other, planes at

A tree or even a twig will be sufficient to lend depth to your shots. If it is rather close then it could be shown unsharp.

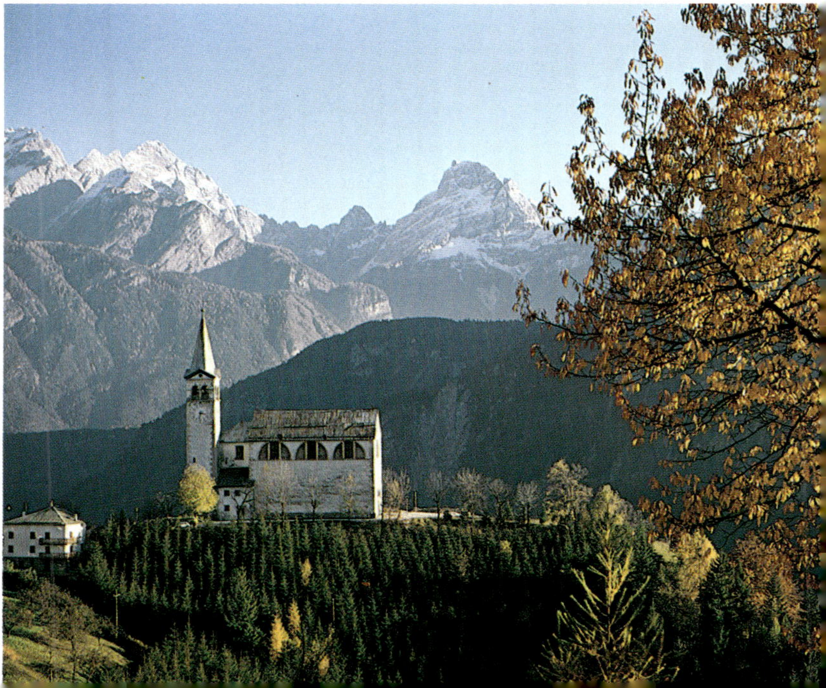

different distances are indistinguishable. If this happens you should look for another position from which to take the picture; the view seen by one eye is the acid test for your final picture.

In landscape photography the foreground becomes the scale by which the viewer may compare familiar objects with distant features. In this way the picture attains depth because the eye's movements from near to far features produce a pseudo 3-D effect. You can use a tree, a branch, a path leading obliquely away or a fence for this purpose. The only important criterion is the amount of contrast between near by and far away, and not between light and dark as we usually mean by this term in photography.

For a solid subject, such as in the picture on the left, you will need to extend the depth of field from close-up right to infinity, that means you will need a small aperture. In this case a wide-angle lens is particularly suitable as it offers a very large depth

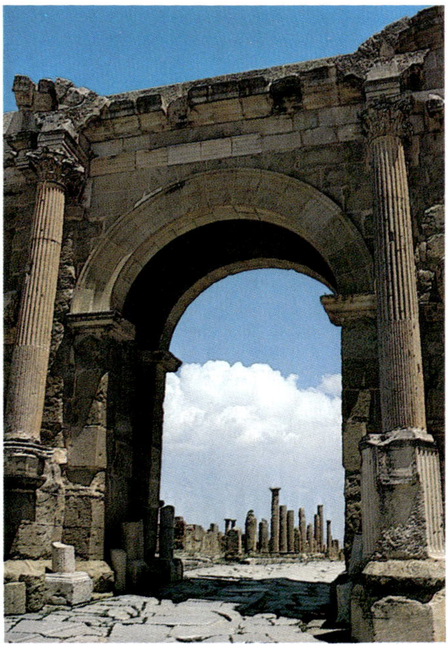

The wide-angle lens forces you to incline the camera to capture the full height of the building and this in turn leads to converging verticals. The distance between the arch to the columns in the background is relatively long.

of field at small apertures. If you are using a telephoto lens then the foreground has to be in the middle distance to still be in sharp focus. Branches framing the scene can be blurred as this could be quite pleasing with individual leaves turning into soft patches of colour. With a long lens you could shoot straight through the foliage. The final effect is rather romantic and dreamy. Whether sharp or diffuse, it is the foreground that makes your picture.

Manipulating Perspective

If you think a wide-angle lens simply manages to show more on the 35mm frame than a standard or telephoto lens, then you know only half the truth. Every focal length has its characteristic method and manner of representing things.

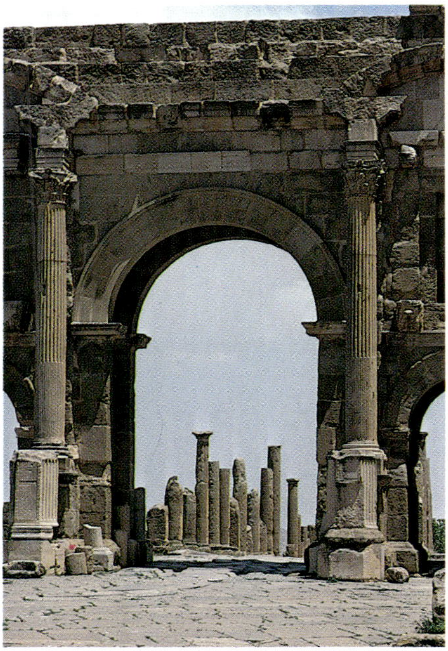

The same view taken with a medium telephoto from a greater distance. The perspective is more natural, and a small inclination of the camera does not matter. The white cloud at the top of the picture is just visible, the middle and far distance are not so far apart.

Consequently two pictures of the same scene, one taken close-up with a short focus lens and the other from a greater distance with a long focus lens, will look quite different.

The two pictures below demonstrate this quite clearly. If you want to utilize the large viewing angle of the wide-angle lens on tall subjects fully you will have to move up close and tilt the camera to accomodate the height of the subject. This will result in converging verticals; the building will seem to fall away at the top because the bottom, being closer, is represented larger than the farther away top and the view seems to broaden towards the top; natural parallels become converging lines.

If you have enough space to step back then you would be better advised to use a longer lens. The picture on the right shows that the inclination of the camera is not so noticeable with the smaller viewing angle of the telephoto lens. You need not give away any foreground and you can represent the building in a more realistic manner. This is not all, the relationship between foreground and background changes as well. In the picture on the right the white cloud, just visible above the building line, has moved behind the massive arch. The distance between arch and columns in the background is noticeably shortened. The representation of the scene is quite different in character.

This play with perspective, made possible by interchangeable lenses, offers you many creative possibilities. Use it to the full; you wouldn't use your T70 to its full capacity if you neglected all these features.

Integrating or Selective Metering?

As long as the distribution of brightness within the subject is relatively uniform, and extremes of bright and dark are not present, then you will be served best with integrating

The most difficult scenes to cope with are snowscapes. Automatic metering and program mode is unsuitable. Selective metering is the answer. Aim the metering circle partly on a dark and partly on a bright area for a good result.

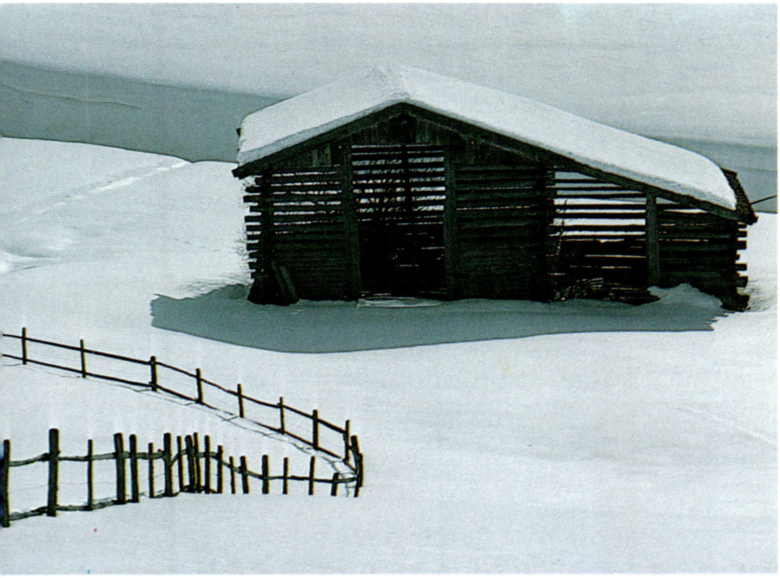

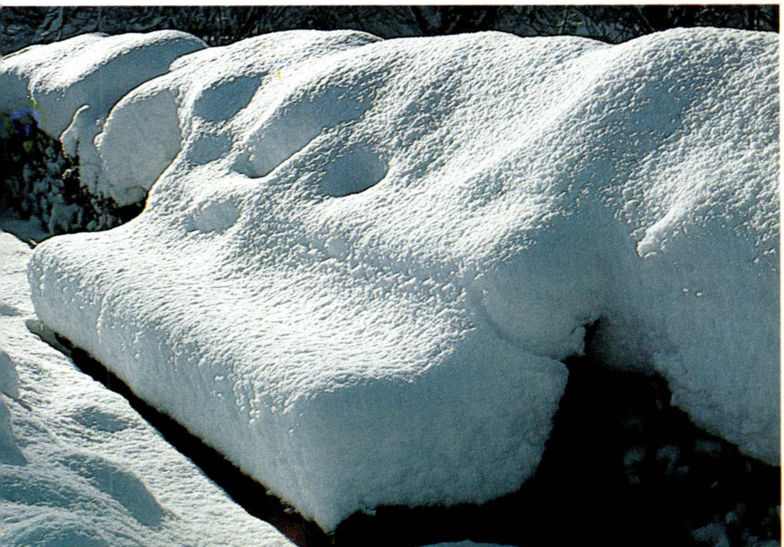

metering. The method of metering also saves you from having to decide on which particular point within the chosen frame would be the most representative for selective metering. Therefore it is the best method for the fast shot in either program or shutter-speed priority mode.

Integral metering is at a loss in situations with high contrast. The two examples opposite demonstrate how the distribution of light and dark can be extreme in some situations. The examples here show one of the most extreme situations you will ever come across, namely snowscapes. If you meter these scenes, or rather allow the camera to do it for you, you can be sure that the result will be underexposed. Your T70 has no way of knowing that the subject in front of its lens is nowhere near the standard subject of 18% reflectivity. Therefore you have to switch to selective metering and point the metering circle in the viewfinder so that half its area covers some of the bright areas, and half the darker, shaded parts. In the top picture you would point the metering circle to cover part of the shed, a little shadow and some bright snow. It would be just as wrong to expose purely for the dark shadows (in particular with slide film). For the bottom picture I would choose the left top corner of the picture as the most suitable spot for metering because it represents the best average between light and dark.

Selective metering becomes truly useful only in conjunction with the memory lock. It is sufficient to point the camera at the required metering spot, depress the release button lightly to take the measurement, and then keep the button depressed to retain these data in the camera's memory. The frame can then be realigned to the required view and the shutter released.

Don't Forget your Telephoto!

If you are hunting animals with your camera you will welcome a long lens, and this does not include the popular 135mm. The fun starts with 200mm. But you have not really arrived until you have put a 300mm, a 400mm or an even longer lens on the

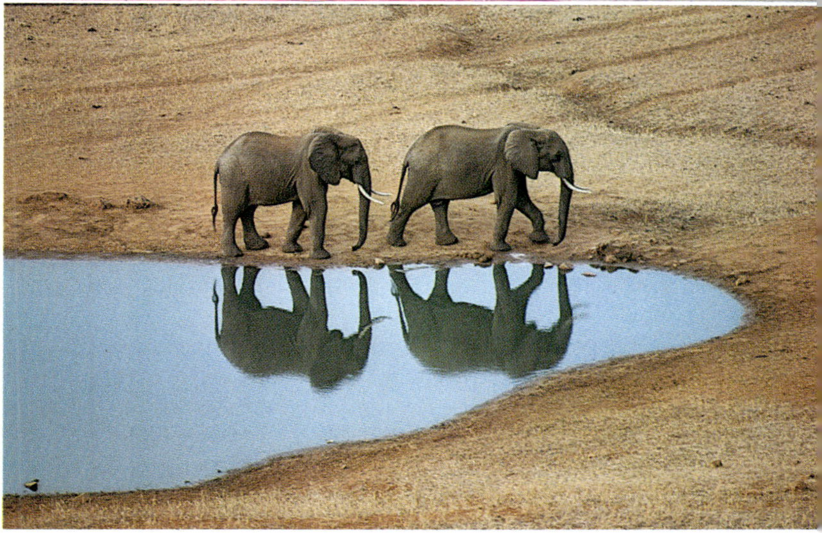

To get this shot I used a FD 300mm f/4L and increased its focal length of 600mm by use of a FD2X-A teleconverter.

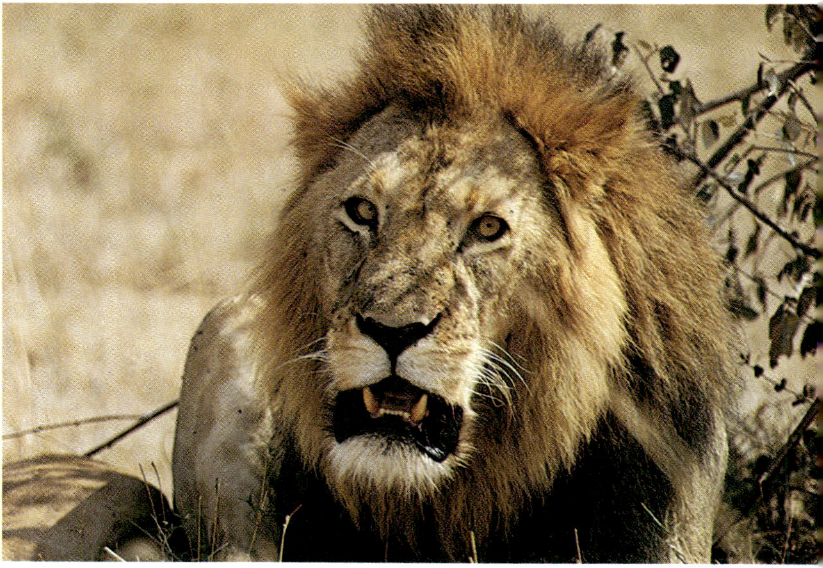

Leo was in a bad mood and could only be taken safely from the Safari bus by a FD 300mm and 2X converter.

front of your T70. These long lenses are primarily necessary to cover the "flight distance" in the wild (but who will flee, you or the wild creature, is not stated). These long lenses come in useful in a safari park to avoid all the man-made intrusions and so produce a realistic image. The long lens is ideal to bring the subject close to the viewer and eliminate any distracting features.

The reference to 300mm and 400mm should not discourage you if you think you would not be justified in investing in such long lenses. How about a Canon teleconverter, or Extender, as Canon prefers to call it? The FD2X-B, for example, extends the focal length of the lens used to twice its length. Using this converter turns a FD 70-210mm f/4 into an impressive FD 140-420mm f/8. You will have noticed one thing, the compromise lies in the lens speed. But for comparison, the mirror lens 500mm f/8 would not offer any more lens speed. The converter, on the other hand, may be used in conjunction with several lenses and in doing so forms a very economical alternative. To save the situation you will have to use a fast film. This in turn means that you are limited to working within these restrictions, unless you have a second camera which is always loaded with a fast film. Another solution is to use a monopod, which could provide you with sufficient support. By the way, both pictures on these two pages were taken hand-held; in the one on the left I supported my hand on my knees, in the one on the right I used the roof of the safari bus to support myself.

Fresh Memories

Most of us use our cameras mainly on our travels abroad when we are unshaven and far from home. This is not a bad thing; after all we are particularly interested in retaining on film the strong impressions we have gained in unfamiliar surroundings and to recreate the wealth of detail at a later time in order to relive the wonderful experiences.

For this type of photography I would urge you to invest in a

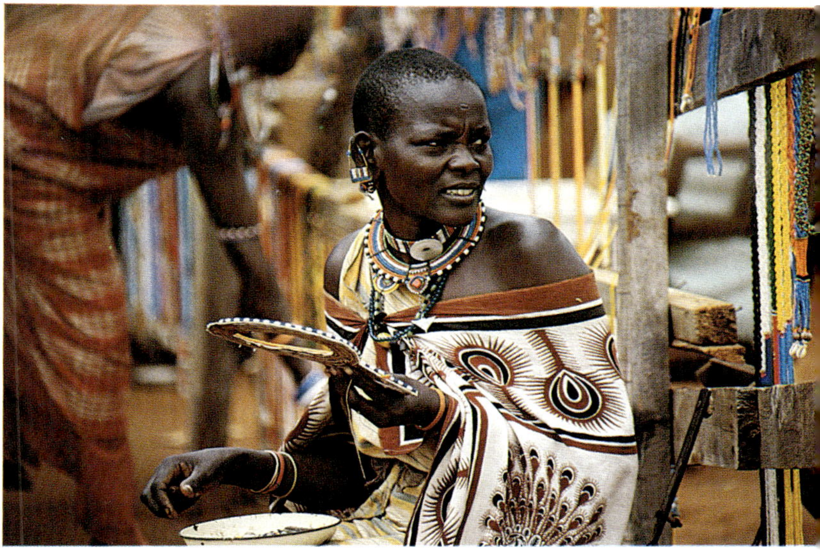

The FD 80-200mm f/4 will give you good opportunities, even where the models are rather disinclined to pose for you.

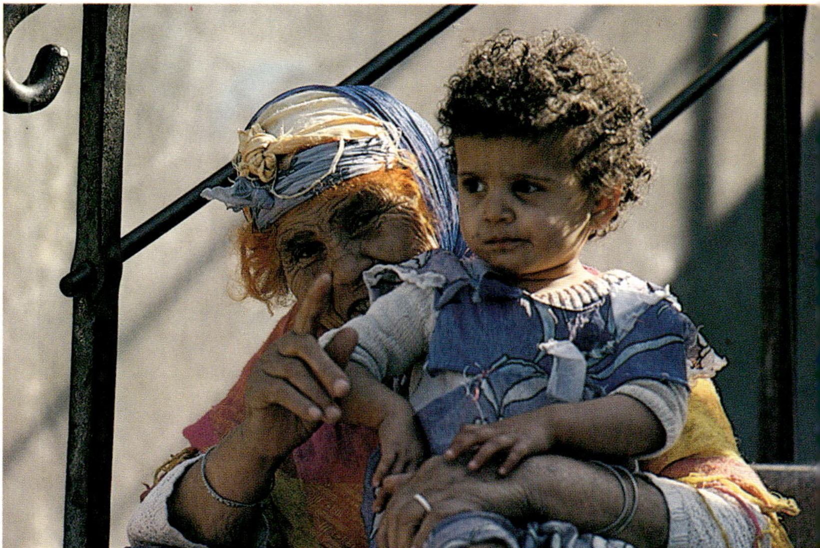

The moderately long focal length of the FD 135mm f/2.8 makes it easier to catch your subject unawares.

telephoto lens or a long zoom lens. Focal lengths between 70 to 200mm are ideal. A variable focal length lens offers you the widest range of possibilities as it allows precise selection of the required frame by a simple twist or axial shift of the focal length ring. It is possible to make corrections up to the last moment; perhaps the focal length needs to be slightly reduced, to get just the right section into the frame.

If you are travelling in a group, move away from the others now and then. Observe them as they run after their subjects with their standard lenses while you can wait for just the right moment to catch that magic instant with your long lens. The subject will hardly ever be aware that you are stalking it. Such pictures are more natural than those posed smiles directed into the lens. This is a further argument in favour of the telephoto lens, perhaps more than one. The easiest solution is to use a variable length telephoto lens.

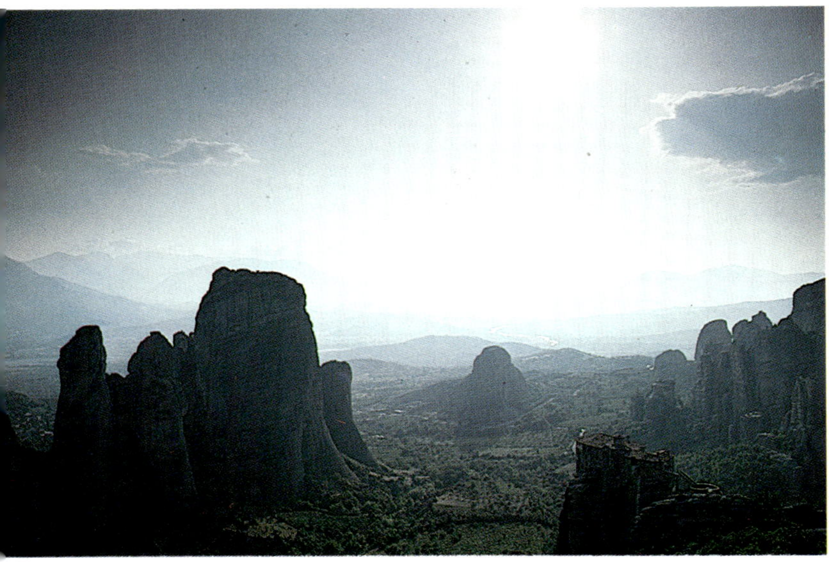

The sun is often included in shots with the super wide-angle. A grey graduated filter allows the sky to be emphasised.

It is essential to support the camera with a long lens properly. Going down on one knee and supporting the elbow on the other is ideal in many situations. The low camera position often increases the impact of the picture. In any case, you should never be higher than the eyelevel of the person you are photographing.

The Sky also Belongs in the Picture

People who have never taken a picture generally disregard the sky altogether as if it did not exist; the emphasis is on earthly objects. The photographer on the other hand learns to consider sky and earth as one unit, because that is the way it is represented on film.

We have identified therefore another source of common

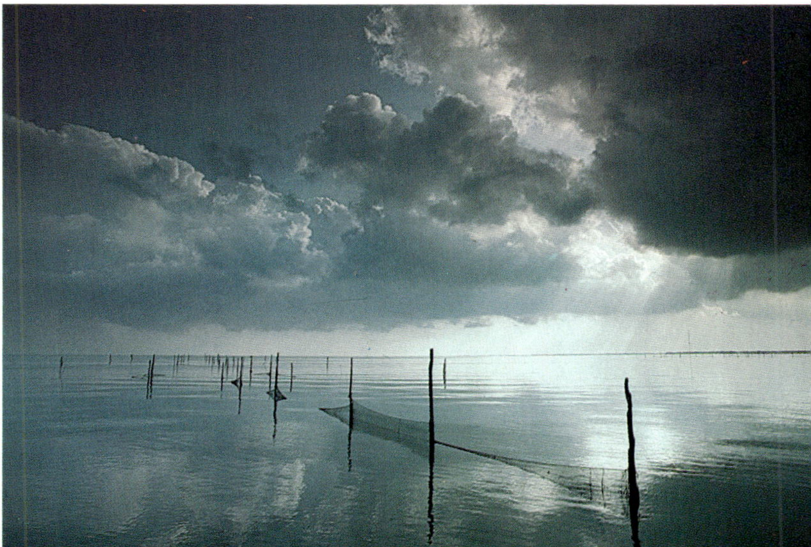

The FD 20mm f/2.8 lens is ideal for capturing open scenes. The sky was subdued by a grey graduated filter.

mistake. Disregard for the sky when taking the picture becomes only too apparent when we look at the resulting print. If there is a lovely cloud formation, don't hesitate to include it in the frame. A polarizing filter is ideal to intensify the blue of the sky and make light summer clouds appear as fluffy cottonwool balls. The effect of the polarizing filter depends on the position of the sun. It is strongest at right-angles to the sun. It will suppress some of the specular reflections in a landscape, and all colours will appear fresh and glowing.

The two photographs below were taken with a grey graduated filter. However, it is necessary to switch off the automatic mode when using such a filter. The exposure has to be metered selectively before the picture is taken, the setting is then retained and the filter put in place. The much too bright sky is toned down and the contrast reduced to a manageable level. The choice of a graduated filter, grade 1 or 2, allows you to control the effect on the sky, to show it to better effect and to dramatise the entire scene.

Another thing to look out for is that the horizon does not run through the exact middle of the picture, cutting it in half. If the line of the horizon is positioned in the lower or upper third of the frame, then it puts a certain emphasis on the larger section and increases the impact of the picture and helps the viewer's understanding of what you are trying to convey.

Close-up Shots – No Problem

You would not believe what a pleasant change a few close-ups can mean to your picture collection, and there are more subjects than simply flowers to enthrall you. There are thousands of subjects to delight you in close-up, regardless of where you are. You only need to sharpen your perception and pick out exactly that item from the confusing wealth of detail that will create particular interest. This will require a little practice. Nature has equipped us with a safety device; we notice only a fraction of all that is going on around us so that we can concentrate on the most important matter of the moment. This subconscious selection process protects us against an overload of impressions with which we would be unable to cope.

Are we supposed to disregard such a useful habit suddenly and learn to see all these little details, just for photography's sake? You will be astonished at how much fun and real excitment you will get from just that little bit of seeing, and how many interesting and beautiful things you will discover. Even so, you are still passing by thousands of details. But the amount of detail you have learnt to see will delight you and give you a feeling of real enrichment.

There is another aspect to consider. We have lost our eye for small things, the minute world. And often it is just these ordinary but small things that reveal unsuspected beauty. The camera, with its framed view, manages to convey surprising details at close range.

If we talk of close-up or macro photography we generally think of a large reproduction on film. Some would not allow this term to be used for a scale of under 1:1, that is less than actual size, but this is not so. Always remember that your negative measures only 24x36mm. This relatively small format, which is so handy in respect of weight, size and flexibility of equipment, is never used in the final picture. We either see it printed as an enlargement, or projected onto a screen at many times its original size. If the negative is enlarged to postcard size the original reproduction ratio of 1:1 results in nearly a four-times magnification in the print. If the same 1:1 reproduction ratio is projected onto a screen one metre wide, then the magnification is 28-fold.

There is another important point. The larger something is represented on film, the smaller is the recorded section of the subject. In other words, you show more and more of less and less. You soon arrive at a point where the concept of the whole is lost in sectional detail; you no longer recognize what you are looking at. Such large reproduction ratios are useful for the expert in a particular field because it allows him to study detail in depth, but for the normal person the aesthetic value is lost. You may have seen such photographs presented as riddles in magazines. Large reproduction ratios in pictures of common articles are often so strange that they are puzzles and often nothing else.

All these arguments should help you overcome your fear of this supposedly difficult type of photography. In general amateur photography you need not worry about too many gadgets. It is possible to master the technique, within reason, much more simply and without too many problems. If you find that you do develop a special interest in the field of macro photography you can then invest in some of the accessories offered in the Canon range.

One term that we often meet in connection with close-up photography is "reproduction ratio". The exact definition of this term is difficult for the novice. But it is quite easy once we look at it this way; an object taken at a reproduction ratio of 1:5 is represented at $^1/_5$ of its actual size on the negative or slide. You only need to think of the ratio as if it were written as a fraction. A scale of 1:2 represents the subject at half its actual size on film, and a scale of 2:1 means that the subject is shown twice its size.

Close-up Lenses

The first step in close-up photography is the close-up lens. You

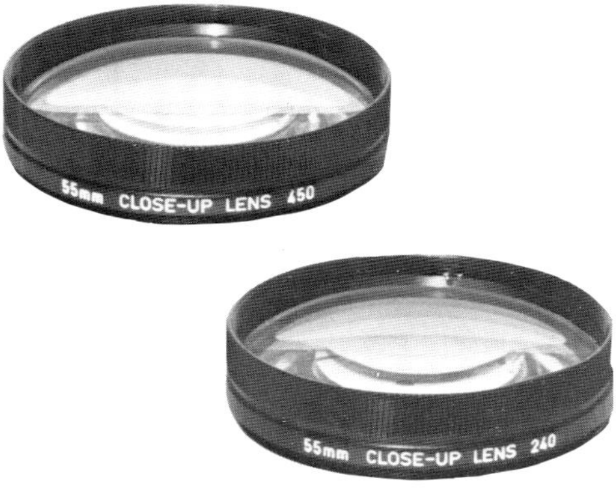

The Canon close-up lenses, available in the most-used diameters, are well corrected achromatic supplementary lenses.

provide your camera with a pair of spectacles by putting on one of these lenses. Canon close-up lenses are available in several diameters for FD lenses. Two types, 240 and 450, are available. The two numbers represent the shortest close-up range in millimetres at the infinity setting on the lens. The lens field is only 68x103mm with a close-up lens 240 when using it with a FD 50mm f/1.4.

Close-up lenses are screwed into the lens thread in the same way as a filter. Their great advantage lies in the fact that they shorten the focal length of the lens without having to increase the extension, as is generally the case when a larger representation on film is required. The basic lens remains entirely unchanged in all its functions. In other words auto diaphragm, metering at open aperture, and shutter speed priority are all totally unaffected.

The 52mm diameter Canon close-up lenses are so-called 'supplementary achromat' lenses. This means that they are not just simple supplementary lenses, but special, corrected, two-element lenses which improve the reproduction characteristics of the lens in the close range. One thing that needs to be remembered is that the normal lens has not been designed for the close-up range. It will have been corrected for infinity to satisfy the conditions generally applicable in most photographic situations. If we disregard this proviso and move close to the subject, thus creating entirely different conditions for the lens, we will have to reckon on some loss in quality. This is an optical fact which all manufacturers are governed by. Only the so-called 'macro lenses' are an exception to this rule; as their name suggests, they are corrected for the close-up range.

Using a simple close-up lens you will have to stop down perhaps to f/11. If you use one of these achromatic lenses, on the other hand, then stopping down to f/5.6 will usually suffice. This allows you a greater range for the shutter speed, an important consideration for hand-held shots where you need as fast a shutter speed as possible to guarantee sharp pictures.

Another factor that applies to all close-up supplementary lenses is that the speed of the base lens is unaffected. This is another important point. If the lens extension is increased, then the light has to travel a longer distance within the camera to arrive at the film plane, and this in turn means a loss in light intensity. If we insert some accessory between the lens and the camera, thus increasing the extension, then the aperture value engraved on the lens, say f/4, is reduced to a smaller effective aperture of f/5.6 or even f/8. This is a great disadvantage from which close-up lenses are free.

Close-up lenses can be used with other focal lengths, not only the standard lens. If used with longer lenses they can be used to particularly good effect. The important consideration is that their use is simple, adds hardly any weight or bulk to the equipment, and requires no extra skills. As long as macro photography is not your overriding interest you will be well served with one or perhaps two of these close-up lenses.

Disengaging the Auto-Diaphragm

Now that we have exhausted the close-up lens's ability to make the camera see better at close range, we are left with one other means of achieving a greater reproduction ratio on film; that is by increasing the extension. Regardless of how this is done, and I shall discuss this shortly in more detail, it usually means that the communication between lens and camera is broken. Hence the T70's normal exposure program is inactivated because it depends on the transfer of data between lens and camera. The loss of program mode is no hardship as it is of little use in close-up photography. The very practical shutter speed priority, however, is replaced by another form of exposure program which is better suited to close-up application, namely the aperture priority mode. Also, as the severing of the coupling function no longer allows open aperture metering, we have to meter at the working aperture.

If the accessory that you are using does not bear the legend "FD", then you have to lock the auto-diaphragm lever at the back of the FD lens before inserting it in the camera. This is to allow the aperture ring to act directly on the aperture blades. To do this you have to move the auto diaphragm lever against the spring action to the opposite stop and push a small plastic adapter, which is available as an accessory, into the guide in this position. Only the 50mm and 100mm macro lenses are slightly different; their auto-diaphragm levers have a strong click-stop position at this location and there is no need to use the plastic adapter. As soon as the auto-diaphragm lever is secured in this position, the required accessory can be inserted. Under no circumstances should you attempt to attach the lens with the

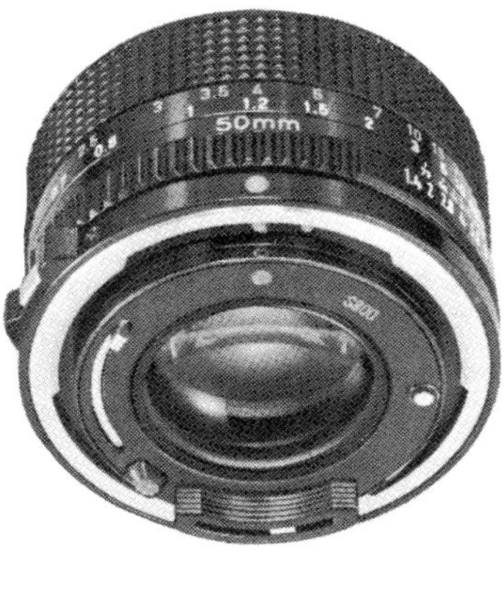

The auto diaphragm of normal FD lenses can be inactivated by a plastic adapter which is available as an optional accessory.

plastic adapter in position directly onto your T70! (This applies also to the automatic bellows and bellows FL, described in later chapters.) The camera would not be able to function like this and you might even damage it.

If you lock the auto-diaphragm lever of one of the macro lenses, 50mm or 100mm, by engaging the lever at the opposite end of the movement range, then this lever has to be released again before the lens is attached directly to the T70. Otherwise the camera will not function.

Working Aperture – Aperture Priority Mode

We have talked already about working aperture and aperture priority modes. Used in combination, these two functions result in a very practical and easy-to-use exposure program for close-up photography with the T70 and uncoupled accessories. The working aperture priority mode becomes effective only after some accessory or lens is attached which does not have the FD coupling elements or does not activate the auto-diaphragm. In this group, besides the close-up accessories, are also the Canon 7.5mm f/5.6 fisheye lens, the mirror reflex lens RF 500mm f/8 and the lens for perspective correction TS 35mm f/2.8.

Using such a lens, or lens accessory combination, you first switch to working aperture mode by depressing the MODE key and one of the UP or DOWN keys. In this mode the LCD display will show an aperture symbol on the left-hand side of

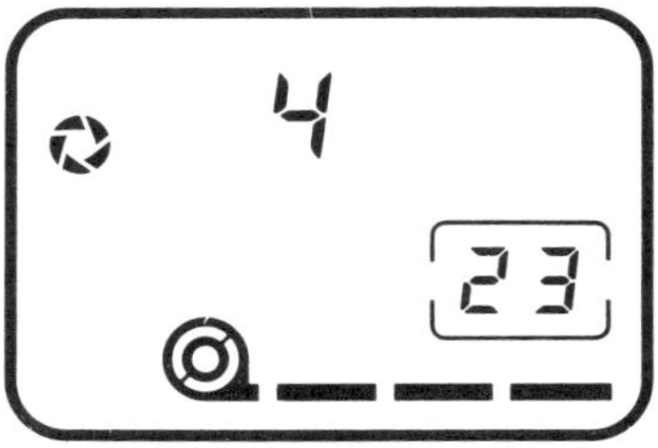

The working-aperture mode is indicated in the LCD display by the aperture symbol. It is possible only with lenses or accessories without FD facilities.

the display. First you select the frame and focus, only then do you select the working aperture manually, when you do so the viewfinder image will dim. At the same time you can assess the depth of field in the viewfinder. Now you can slightly depress the release button and the shutter speed automatically selected for the aperture will be illuminated in the viewfinder. However, one peculiarity has to be considered; the shutter speed value in the viewfinder is displayed in the position normally reserved for the aperture. The aperture value requires only two digits, the shutter speed up to four. This is the reason why the shutter speed is displayed only up to $^1/_{90}$ second, i.e. as 90. Shorter times are indicated by two codes for two different time ranges: HL (presumably an abbreviation for HIGH LOW, whatever that is supposed to mean), covering the times from $^1/_{125}$ to $^1/_{350}$ second, and HH (probably for HIGH HIGH), for $^1/_{500}$ to $^1/_{1000}$ second. If you need to know exactly, you will have to look at the LCD display, which shows the shutter speed in half stops.

In case of danger of overexposure the "HH" will flash in the viewfinder and the "1000" in the LCD. In this case you should turn the aperture ring to a smaller aperture value until the flashing stops. In case of danger of underexposure, a "2" will flash in the viewfinder and in the LCD, indicating that the automatic exposure range has reached its limit. In this case you have to go for a larger aperture. If you have already arrived at the largest possible aperture value, then you have no other choice but to use a flashgun. Canon has a special macro flashgun, the Macrolite ML-1.

Extension Rings

The simplest way to increase the reproduction ratio is to increase the lens extension. Up to a certain point the focusing range of the lens does this for us. But only to a certain degree of course, as manufacturers usually endeavour to keep the dimensions of their lenses as compact as possible and,

The Intermediate Ring Set M may be combined in a number of ways and thus allows a fine adjustment to suit the conditions. The diagram here shows how a standard 50mm lens and various combinations of rings cover the reproduction ratios between 1:10 to 1.2:1 in intermediate steps.

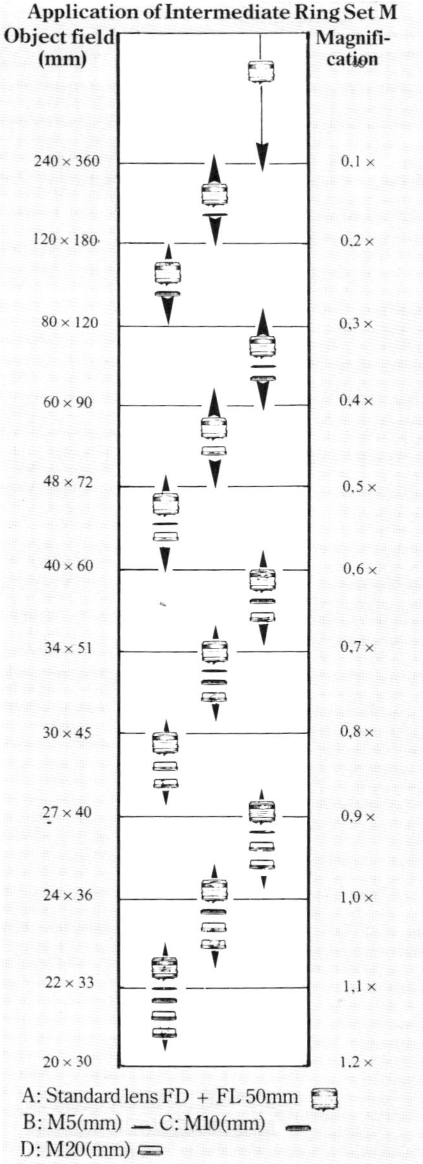

moreover, a long focusing helix would increase the cost of the lens. On the other hand it presents no problem to a single-lens reflex camera to insert a tube between the camera and the lens. This is where the extension ring or tube comes in.

The simplest form of extension rings for your Canon T70 is provided by the Intermediate Ring Set M. This consists of two 20mm rings, one 10mm ring and one 5mm ring. These offer a wide range of combinations, in 5mm intermediate steps. Each ring has front and back fittings suitable for the Canon bayonet.

These rings interrupt the communication between lens and camera and it is therefore necessary to lock the auto-diaphragm as described in the previous chapter. You will generally have to stop down to f/8 or even f/11 when using these rings in order to retain lens performance at these short distances.

If you wish to retain the facility of open aperture metering, then you could invest in a set of automatic extension rings FD15U, FD25U or FD50U. Using these, you retain not only open aperture metering, but also shutter speed priority. (I shall disregard program mode as it is hardly suitable for macro photography.) Due to mechanical difficulties the automatic extension rings should not be used in combination as this could

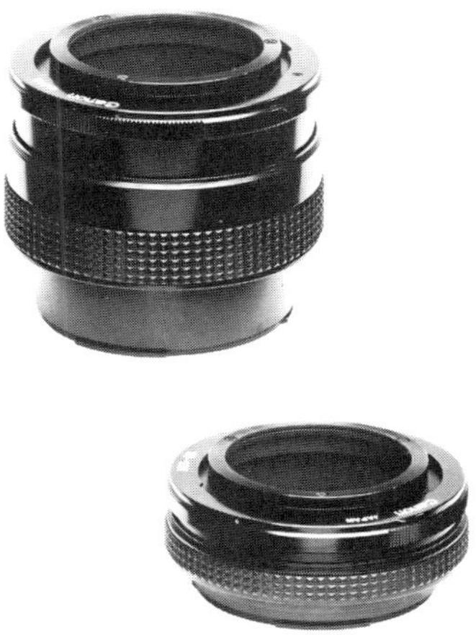

Vario Intermediate Rings have their own focusing helical focusing mechanisms and therefore offer continuous increase in extension.

lead to difficulties in the aperture data transfer. The extension length of the rings is identical to their description, only the FD25U is actually 25.8mm long.

Variable extension rings represent a halfway stage between continuously adjustable extension by bellows and the fixed interval extension by ordinary extension rings. These are available as M15-25 and M30-55, and have their own focusing helix permitting continuous adjustment of the extension. However, these do not offer data transfer between camera and lens and have to be used with working-aperture priority mode.

Continuous Extension by Bellows

The heart of the entire Canon Close-Up System is the Automatic Bellows. This is a powerful optical bench with two adjustable standards and an additional focusing rail with three fine adjustments, providing the greatest possible versatility for close-up photography.

First, I should like to clarify a possible misconception. The description "automatic" is not strictly correct. Despite the promising name, it is not possible to use open aperture metering and therefore no automatic aperture mode is possible. However, the auto-diaphragm may not be inactivated when the bellows are attached.

The basis of the automatic bellows is the dovetail track which guides the two standards during rack and pinion focusing. The setting screws for all movements may each be separately locked. On top of the focusing track are two scales. One of these scales is subdivided from 0mm to 175mm and indicates the extension of the bellows. The shortest possible extension is 39mm. The second scale shows magnification factors for a 50mm macro lens. The inner set of values refers to the lens in its normal position; the outer set for the lens in reversed position. The magnification factors are dependent on the focal length of the lens and therefore apply only to 50mm lenses. The extension scale and the magnification factors refer to the

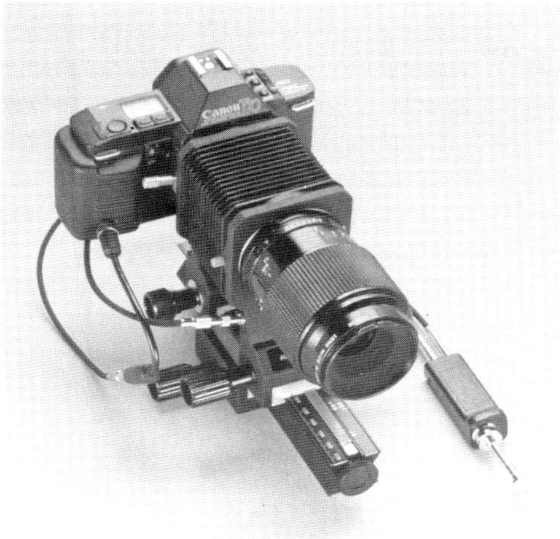

The Automatic Bellows form the heart of the Canon close-up system.

setting of the front edge of the housing standard at zero.

The two scales on the focusing track are provided to aid the photographer in setting the extension needed to obtain the required magnification. When using a 50mm macro lens and with the housing standard set to zero it will suffice to turn the focusing screw of the lens standard until the plastic indicator of that standard points to the required magnification factor.

If you are using lenses with different focal lengths you can first ascertain the required extension by referring to a table supplied with the bellows. This may then be set by aligning the plastic edge of the lens standard to the appropriate position on the scale.

The plastic piece mentioned, retains its validity as the setting index even when the lens standard is turned around for the reversed position. It is a peculiarity of the automatic bellows which facilitates an increase in performance by reversing the lens. The lens standard can be attached by a few simple manipulations to the focusing track in the reverse position, thus allowing the lens to be used in its reversed position without the need for a special reversing ring. The auto-diaphragm remains operative even in this configuration.

Having attached the lens unit centrally on the focusing track, the bellows extension read from the table is added to the value which is indicated on the scale by the front edge of the housing standard. The plastic edge of the lens standard is then set to the resulting value. Let's assume the housing standard points to 60mm and the required extension is 50mm, the calculated required point to which the plastic edge of the lens standard is to be set is then 110mm. If a 50mm macro lens is used, then the process is much simpler. The front edge of the housing standard is set to a certain magnification factor; the magnification factor required for this shot is added to that factor and the plastic edge of the lens standard is then set to the resulting magnification value.

To change from horizontal to upright format, the camera is turned by 90 degrees to the left, as seen from behind, where it will engage. The same simple manipulation will return it to the normal horizontal format position.

For focusing, you start by choosing the desired magnification. The camera is then set to the required setting distance to produce that magnification. Next the extension is read off the table which is set on the scale on the focusing track. For fine focusing the entire unit is turned on the setting track by the setting knob, which is then fixed in the final position by the setscrew.

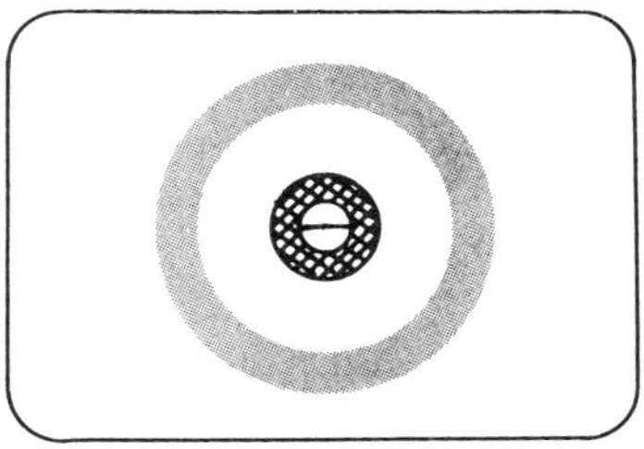

Focusing is best done on the shaded part of the focusing screen for large reproduction ratios.

A twin cable release is supplied with the automatic bellows. One end fits into the lens standard, the other into the cable release adapter T3, which in turn is screwed into the remote control socket in the handgrip of the T70. If you are using a FD or a FL lens, a slight pressure on the cable release will stop down the aperture, full depression will release the shutter. The first stage therefore allows easy checking of exposure data and depth of field on the focusing screen. As the lens standard is reversible, the auto-diaphragm functions remain fully operative with the cable release and the lens in the reversed position.

For close-ups it is generally advisable to focus first and check the exposure afterwards. This, as we have mentioned previously, is due to the fact that the length of the extension has a considerable effect on the amount of light that will arrive on the film plane. With respect to correct exposure I would like to remind you that the distribution of brightness across the frame is of considerable importance with this type of photography. A small, bright object against a large, dark background will definitely require selective metering. Even then it may still be necessary to make a certain minus correction if the selective metering zone covers some of the background also. Such correction can easily be made by adjusting the film speed setting. If the basic setting was 100 ISO and you need to obtain an exposure correction of -2/3 stops, then you set it to 160 ISO. Don't forget to reset the film speed to the original value!

Close-up shots generally require long exposure times and it will therefore be necessary to provide a firm camera support. The same restriction applies to the subject taken; it too has to remain still. The slightest draught and the petal or butterfly wing will move, taking it out of the depth of field, and the movement will make it even more blurred.

Because of the extremely shallow depth of field it will be necessary to place all important details within the plane of acceptable sharpness. Even at a magnification factor of only 1:2 and the relatively small aperture of f/16, the depth of field is only +/- 4mm! If you are more ambitious and wish to obtain a magnification factor of 2, you are left with only +/- 0.5mm!

Slide Copier 35

If you own automatic bellows you have the possibility, with the aid of a Slide Copier 35, to copy your slides. This useful accessory is screwed to the front of the bellows. If you are critical with respect to quality then you should use a 50mm f/3.5 macro lens for the reproduction of your slides. This will produce a reproduction scale of 1:1 to 1.4:1 for 35mm film, allowing sufficient tolerance to produce a limited enlargement of 8 mm in the vertical and 12mm in the horizontal direction. You can even reproduce pocket camera-sized slides onto 35mm format by using the macro lens in retro position. This will require a reproduction scale of 2.1:1. Again, it will be possible to make certain sectional enlargements as you are able to obtain a reproduction scale of 3:1 in this configuration.

A diffusing screen will distribute the light evenly across the entire picture; the light source, however, has to be provided by you. Generally speaking there is no real alternative to electronic flash. Daylight changes its intensity and colour characteristics too often and too quickly.

It will be necessary to make some trial exposures to ascertain the correct distance to place the flash from the diffusing screen. The density of the original slide will also have some influence and it may be necessary to make some corrections to the standard values, once these have been ascertained.

To make duplicates from negatives you will have to use a film roll holder.

The Macro Table

This accessory was developed as an object holder for the camera together with the automatic bellows and is attached at the front. The macro table has four feet for safe support of the equipment in the vertical shooting position. Two table clamps hold flat objects down securely. An opal diffusing screen is also used to hold down flat objects and is necessary for macro shots by transmitted light. The macro table can be used, among other things, to duplicate slides up to 4.5x6cm format.

Bellows FL

Bellows FL are the predecessors of the automatic bellows and still very popular. This is a very strong, precise and versatile instrument, offering coupling to the auto-diaphragm, but not with the cable release. It is necessary to reset a lever to open the aperture again every time the release is activated. This means that the whole setting process is performed at fully open aperture; the exposure on the other hand, is controlled by working aperture mode. The bellows allow continuous extension from 34.5 to 142.5mm.

Bellows FL offer three setting facilities. Not only are the lens and camera standards adjustable by rack and pinion, but the entire unit can be moved on the base tube by means of a separate setting track. This allows easy adjustment of reproduction scale and fine focusing, without having to move the tripod.

For vertical shooting I would recommend a Macro Support, which is attached to the base tube and can be extended from there. It helps to support the unit and thus prevents you from moving the unit inadvertently. The Bellows FL have a transfer mechanism for the auto-diaphragm of the lens and therefore it must not be put out of action before the unit is attached. However, it is important to move the aperture ring of the lens from the automatic "A" position, as it is impossible otherwise to attach the bellows. Furthermore it is important to depress the aperture cocking lever on the bellows before the lens is attached to establish the connection to the lens stop-down lever.

The length of the extension may be varied continuously by two setting screws. The setting screw of the housing standard and also that of the lens standard acts on the toothed rack in the centre of the base tube. On the opposite side to the setting screws are the clamping screws. To lock the movement of the unit the screws have to be turned to the back, as seen in the shooting direction.

Retro Position

We noted previously that normal lenses are corrected for infinity. This is quite logical as most subjects are to be found at a reasonable or far distance. What happens when you extend the extension by various accessories more and more to be able to get closer and closer to the subject?

The distance between the optical system and the film plane gets larger and larger; that between the front element and the subject smaller. This constitutes a complete reversal of the conditions for which the lens has been constructed. Generally, the distance between film plane and lens is small and between front element and subject is large. This led to the idea of reversing the lens to get closer to the original conditions. Attached in the reversed position, the front element has to look a relatively long distance backwards towards the film plane and the subject is relatively close to the rear lens element, thus shooting in the reversed position is practicable. But nothing is as simple as all that. After all, the filter thread does not readily fit into the camera bayonet fitting. This presents no great problem; Canon provide reverse adapters in 52mm, 55mm and 58mm sizes, which fit into the bayonet fitting on the camera and the lens may then be attached on their front. They are also equipped with a focusing helix to allow fine focusing to accomodate the use of other non-adjustable extension accessories.

All coupling elements are now looking to the front. Canon supplies also a macro diaphragm which, in effect, is a cut-open lens rear cover. And just like a rear cover, it is put on the lens bayonet and locked. It is the duty of this "diaphragm" to set the lens as if it were properly inserted into the camera. Only then is it possible to effect manual setting of the aperture. It also protects the delicate coupling elements and acts as a lenshood.

The reversed position is useful even for macro lenses for reproduction scales greater than 1:1. But, as the coupling elements are pointing the wrong way, they are now inoperative. In other words, the auto-diaphragm has first to be inactivated in order to allow the aperture ring to act directly on the iris diaphragm. This makes aperture priority with working aperture possible.

Macro Lenses – the Universal Specialists

This type of lens has become restricted to a specialist in close-up photography by the word "macro", a concept which is hard to break and quite untrue. These lenses are true universal objectives. If you labour under the preconception that macro lenses are useful only for close-up photography, then you are quite mistaken. The description "universal lenses" would suit much better as these lenses can achieve the same, or sometimes even better results, than the normal lenses, always comparing the appropriate focal lengths. There is only one disadvantage; they are generally not as fast as the normal lenses. In most cases this will be no disadvantage. As a reward these lenses present you, without exception, with the choice of taking subjects from infinity to about half life size (and this is continuous) just by turning the focusing ring. Quite an advantage, if you think about it. You are suddenly free; the limitations in the close-up range have dropped away and you will notice with delight how many wonderful subjects that you missed before you are now able to exploit.

The macro lens is a valuable and exceedingly useful lens in its focal length. It also offers particularly good correction of reproduction errors which are not dependent on reproduction scale, as is the case with normal lenses. The macro lens does not let you down to the same degree in the close range and is

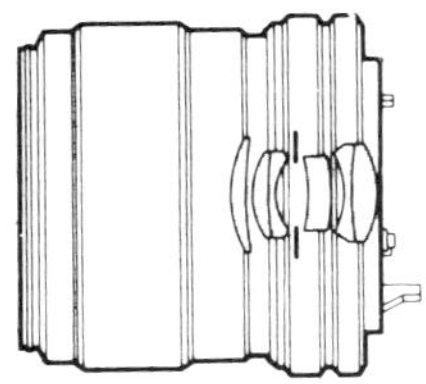

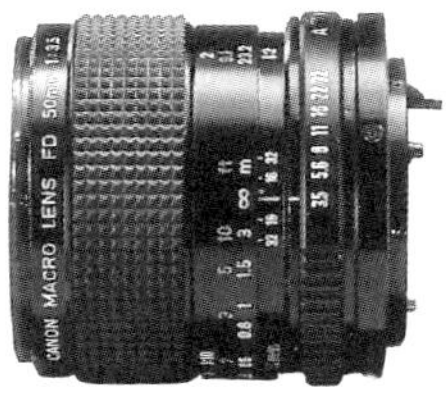

The FD 50mm f/3.5 macro is an excellent universal lens of standard focal length.

able to produce particularly sharp reproductions at short taking distances, and this to the very edge of the frame. You cannot expect the same correction characteristics from a normal lens. A macro lens therefore is an exceedingly useful addition for general photography, in particular the 50mm lens. It is also very suitable for duplicating slides.

Canon offers three macro lenses for the T70: a 50mm, a 100mm and even a 200mm macro. These lenses are quite different in their performance and application. The ranges offered indicate that each is dedicated to a different application range. The FD 50mm f/3.5 macro lens may be considered the universal standard lens par excellence. Compared with the usual standard lenses its speed is not exactly amazing, but this is the only disadvantage. Comprising 6 elements and with almost symmetrical construction, it produces excellent reproduction quality and exceedingly good sharpness to the edge of the frame. The focusing helix allows focusing distances down to a reproduction ratio of 1:2, that means you can show your subject up to half life size. This covers, as we have seen, the entire uncomplicated, hand-held close-up setting range to a taking distance of 23cm (to the film plane). If you also use the extension ring FD25, which is part of the equipment, you are able to get down to reproduction ratio 1:1, i.e. life size. With this arrangement you may avail yourself of all conveniences such as coupling to automatic aperture, metering at open aperture and shutter speed modes.

The longer the focal length of a lens, the longer the

extension. Comparing the 50mm and the 100mm macro lenses, the FD 50mm f/3.5 manages to achieve a reproduction ratio of 1:2 with the shortest extension. On the other hand it offers the shortest working distance. Both these factors make it an ideal instrument for reproductions on a stand or tripod, for reproductions generally and for slide copying. Larger repoduction scales may be achieved with the least expenditure on additional equipment to increase the extension.

The FD 100mm f/4 Macro, on the other hand, requires twice as long an extension to achieve the same repoduction ratio of 1:2 because it has twice the focal length. This necessitates a larger construction. The taking distance too is doubled, to 45cm from the film plane, to be precise. The larger taking distance makes it easier to illuminate the subject, but for ordinary home photography you will come across some restrictions. This lens is therefore better suited for outdoor photography where the larger taking distance presents an advantage rather than a disadvantage. Moreover, this lens will be useful as a small telephoto lens, particularly in outdoor photography where the 100mm focal length is particularly useful. The exceedingly well-designed construction of this lens, with its five elements arranged in three groups ensures

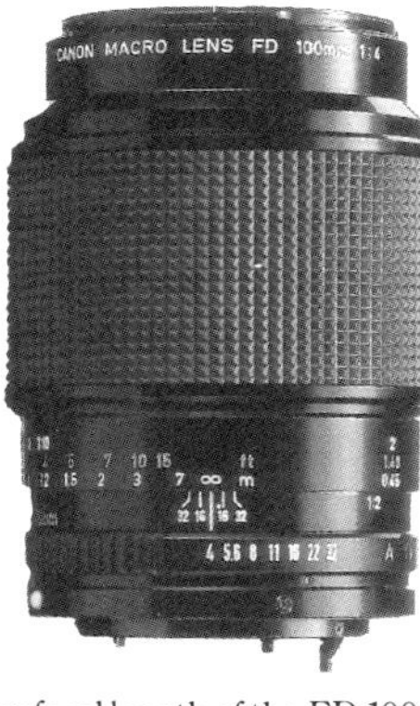

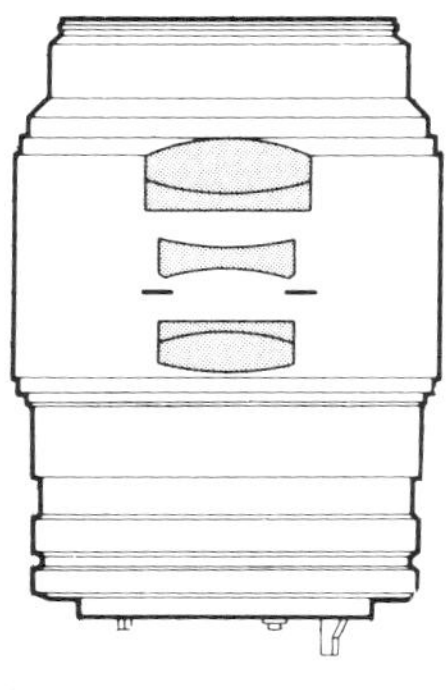

The longer focal length of the FD 100mm f/4 macro offers a larger working distance.

excellent reproduction quality in the far range. This lens may be considered a small telephoto of particular excellence by virtue of the continuous focusing range down to 1:2.

Here too, an extension ring may be used to get down to reproduction ratio 1:1. Because of the longer focal length it has to achieve twice the extension, i.e.type FD50.

Finally we shall consider the FD 200mm f/4 macro lens, which occupies an altogether special position. So far only very few macro lenses have been available in this range. Canon have opened up new technological ground with the introduction of this macro lens.

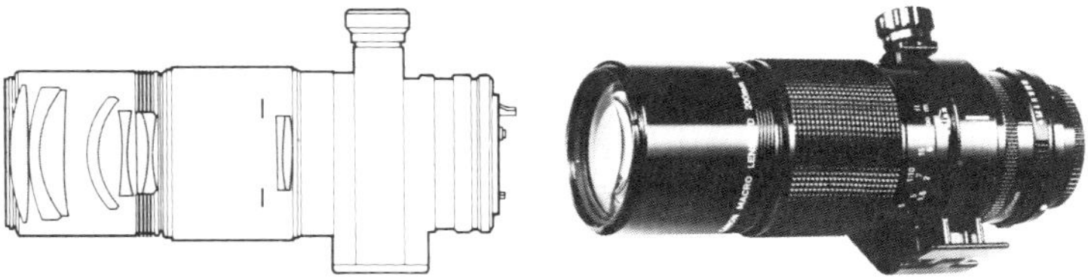

The FD 200mm f/4 macro manages continuous focusing from infinity to 1:1 with an extension of only 38.6mm.

As we have seen, the extension of the lens has to be increased to achieve a larger reproduction ratio. A focal length of 200mm therefore would require a 400mm long mechanical construction to achieve a scale of 1:1. In other words, conventional structural methods don't offer a feasible solution. The method that Canon has devised is unique. The first and second elements of the FD 200mm f/4 are moved relative to each other for focusing. This revolutionary optical trick offers completely different conditions. The very short focusing movement produces a surprisingly large measure of change in reproduction ratio. The focusing helix is incredibly short, allowing focusing across the full range from infinity to 1:1, and measures only 38.6mm. For the two other macro lenses with conventional focusing helix this is 50mm and 100mm respectively. This macro lens has a considerably shorter extension than even the macro lens of standard focal length! Incredible! And it can even manage to do without the extension ring for the range between 1:2 and 1:1, as is necessary for the other macro lenses.

This differential focusing, as Canon call their new method, allows the construction of an entirely new concept of macro lens with excellent performance, a lens speed of f/4 which is very good for the 200mm focal length, and weighing only 790g without the tripod ring. The filter screw fittings measure 58mm; its structural length at infinity setting is 182.4mm, and it offers also an integrated, extendable lens hood.

This lens is obviously the ideal instrument for nature photography. For a reproduction scale of 1:1 the taking distance would be 31.6cm from the front element (58cm from the film plane). The nature photographer is usually very thankful for this larger taking distance as it is often physically impossible to get any closer to the subject, or the subject would be scared away if it was threatened by the photographer bearing down on it. Just think about small creatures in the wild who would be gone like the wind if you came too close. This lens makes it possible to take large-scale shots of creatures that are quite capable of getting rid of the undesired attentions of the photographer by a well placed sting or bite. And last but not least, the larger taking distance allows sufficient and satisfactory illumination of the subject in its natural surroundings and attitude. This is exactly where lenses with shorter focal lengths suffer from limitations in the larger reproduction ratios. The subject is too close to the lens and cannot be illuminated properly, and close-ups are no longer possible due to the physical, rather than optical limitations.

There is one aspect in the choice of macro lenses where you need not worry. The depth of field is identical for all focal lengths, as strange as this may sound thinking about the general rules applicable to standard lenses. However, this applies only to the close range. One often hears the argument that the shallow depth of field at close range is even further reduced for the longer lenses. But this is not true. The optical impression may change. After all, the longer lens has a smaller viewing angle and covers therefore a smaller section of the background. The details in the background are represented larger and so present a more diffused view.

To return to the FD Macro 200mm. An incidental feature needs to be mentioned. Because of the differential focusing method and the resulting minimum increase in lens extension, the loss in lens speed is much less severe than in conventionally built lenses. Taking a 200mm lens and extending this to 400mm to obtain a reproduction scale of 1:1, the lens speed would be reduced to an almost impossible degree. All the marked f/numbers would be doubled meaning an exposure increase of x4. The new FD 200mm f/4 requires only a one-stop (x2) exposure increase under the same conditions.

Micro Objectives

Micro objectives are corrected for the very close range, but their practical usefulness generally ends with 1:1 reproduction ratio. There is still a considerable gap between these scales and those used in microscope photography. Canon developed micro lenses FD 35mm f/2.8 and FD 20mm f/3.5 to cover this range. By looking at them you can see their similarity to microscope objectives. These lenses are particularly small, with a physical length of about 20mm. The manner of coupling is also similar to those of microscope objectives, and they possess a standard thread of 20.32mm similar to microscope objectives. Connection to the camera is by an adapter accomodating the lens in its plastic mount and fitting into the Canon bayonet.

These lenses are corrected for reproduction ratios in excess of 1:1. The optimal performance of micro lens 35mm f/2.8 lies at 2:1 reproduction scale, the 20mm f/3.5 at 5:1. These lenses have no focusing ring, but are intended for use with extension bellows. Using bellows and perhaps some additional extension

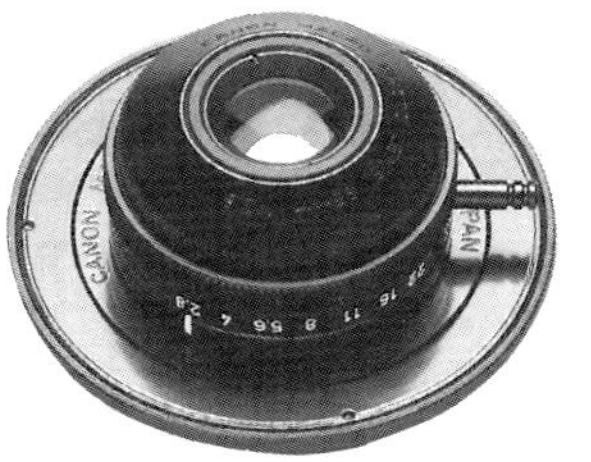

A microscope lens such as this 35mm f/2.8 is an excellent and reasonably-priced system for large reproduction scales.

rings these lenses will give large reproduction ratios. Using the Automatic Bellows with micro lens 35mm f/2.8 reproduction scales from 1.96 to 5.84 times actual size are attained and the 20mm f/3.5 micro gives 3.93 to 10.72 times life size. By using suitable means for further extension even a 20-times magnification is possible. This appears to be the limit as it is no longer possible to introduce any light between the subject and the lens. To make lighting at all possible at these close ranges the front bezel is conical to allow light to enter at an angle.

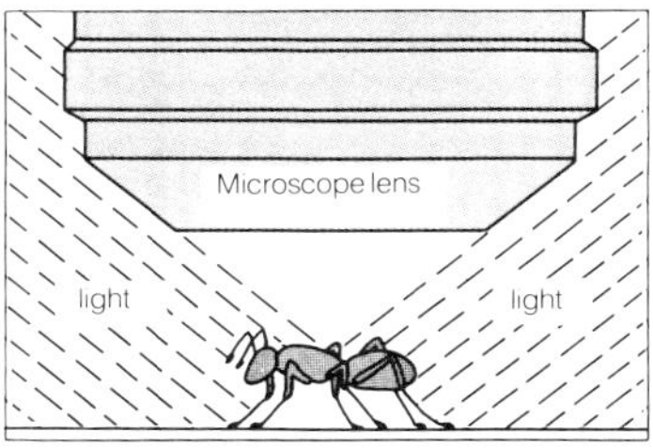

The front bezel of the two Canon microscope lenses is conical to facilitate illumination from above at very short taking distances.

Aperture setting is manual for both lenses; the smallest aperture is f/22. Auto-diaphragm is not feasible with such a specialist lens. These micro lenses are modestly priced top quality systems for the macro photography specialist and enthusiast.

Other Accessories

The electronic flash Macrolite ML-1 was designed for close-up photography, and in particular for use with the FD 80-200mm f/4 zoom lens. It consists of three parts: a ring fitting with two integrated laterally-arranged flash reflectors, which may be attached directly to the lenshood bayonet of lenses with filter diameter 58mm and via an adapter also to those with filter diameter 52mm; a control unit which is fixed in the camera accessory shoe and connected by cable to the reflector, with centre contact and automatic contact for flash synchronization; and finally a power source in the form of two Battery Compartments D contained in a bag with shoulder strap and connected by cable. The guide number of the flash unit is 16 at ISO 100/21°. Three aperture settings are possible if both flash units are activated simultaneously: from about 0.5m to 2.8m at aperture f/5.6, from 0.5m to 1.5m at aperture f/11 and from 0.4m to 0.72m at aperture f/22.

The three Canon macro lenses are also suitable for use with the Macrolite ML-1. However, if lenses with focal lengths 50 and 100mm are used, some corrections have to be made with regard to the different reproduction ratios. Aperture setting has to be manual via the lens aperture ring when using the Macrolite ML-1. The synchronization time of $^1/_{90}$ second is selected automatically.

There are two reproduction stands in the Canon programme, Model 4 is thought to be useful for the amateur and Model 5 was designed principally for the professional. The column of Model 4 is 617mm high, and the camera arm is adjustable in height. The base plate has a working area of 280x420mm, which is quite sufficient for originals up to A3 format.

The useful area of Reproduction Stand 5 is 475x595 mm. Magnetic paper clamps hold the original in place. The 900mm high, rectangular column has a scale with 5mm graduations. A counterweight inside the column ensures that the height adjustment is uniform and easy over the entire range.

The Canon focusing rail was developed together with the Reproduction Stand 5 and as such forms a particularly secure support for the camera and allows precise turning of the unit through 90 degrees. Furthermore, it is possible to shift the entire unit axially by 85mm, a fine focusing aid that is particularly useful when working without the aid of bellows, as the integrated focusing rail offers the same facilities. The focusing rail is also suitable for use with Reproduction Stand 4.

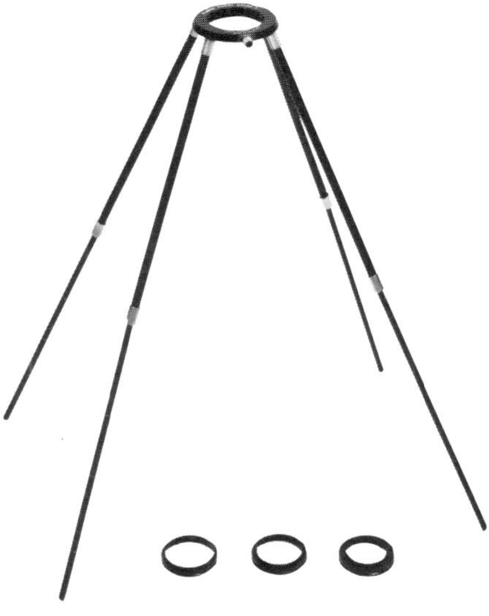

Repro stand F has extendable legs and can be used to focus on all important document formats, making reproduction easy and without the need for extensive preparation.

Finally there is Repro Tripod F. It can be folded up by a few simple manipulations to a very compact size and is very useful for tabletop photography. Using a standard lens, originals with sizes from 128x199mm to 257x397mm may be copied. However, you will have to do without open aperture metering and shutter speed priority as the intermediate ring M5, supplied with this equipment, inactivates the coupling elements. But as we have described already in some detail, this presents no particular hardship as the T70 can cope quite easily in working aperture automatic mode.

Canon FD Lenses for the T70

A camera such as the Canon T70 will only achieve its full potential if it is used together with a range of lenses. If you possess different lenses for your camera then you should use them as they were intended. Change them as and when the situation requires and the Canon bayonet is sturdy enough to cope with that. Overcome your inborn laziness and make use of the advantages offered by different focal lengths; only then will you be able to make full use of the equipment that cost you so much.

The choice of Canon lenses for the T70 is quite bewildering and you will find it difficult to make a choice. On the other hand it is good to know that your camera system provides you with a good range of optical equipment. I cannot imagine anyone needing all the lenses offered in the FD programme, and that is not the intention of the manufacturer. The choice on offer seeks to cover the needs of a disparate assortment of amateur and professional photographers in a variety of situations, including jobs such as the reproduction of precious originals, photographic assignments from close-up to far-off, or optical manipulations for effective advertising features. Canon now offer more than 50 units in their FD programme and as such may be counted amongst the very best in this field.

I do not intend to list here resolution in lines per millimetre in describing one or other lens. I have never used my own lenses for counting lines; I find them useful only for taking pictures, and I don't think you would find it particularly useful either. The quality of Canon lenses is always excellent and need not be specially mentioned. You could convince yourself of this fact by reading the various publications in which different makes are compared. You will soon find that Canon are generally counted amongst the very best. With this in mind I can assure you that you need not worry about the performance of the lens as a criterion in the choice of which lens. (Even Canon, against the background of their own excellence, offer some particularly sophisticated units which are designated by the letter "L").

Based on the foregoing we may start with the assumption that the lenses we are considering are always of constant high standard so we can concentrate on more practical aspects in our choice of lens, such as weight, size, lens speed and price. All Canon lenses will fit all single-lens SLRs in the Canon programme, and you are thus assured of complete interchangeability should you decide at a later stage to buy a second camera but prefer it to be a different model.

All Canon lenses bearing the description "FD" have an aperture simulator and so they are suitable for open aperture metering and program mode. The Canon program offers only a few lenses that are not fitted with such an aperture simulator and therefore require working aperture metering. As examples I would like to mention the 7.5mm f/5.6 fisheye lens, the mirror lens RF 500mm f/8 and the special lens for perspective control TS 35mm f/2.8.

The World of New Perspectives

We read in books and articles that interchangeable lenses, and hence changes in focal length, will give us different perspectives. But this is only a half-truth. As long as you change only the lens and not the camera position you will only obtain a different size section of the scene; the perspective will remain the same. You can demonstrate this fact by enlarging a section from a wide-angle shot and comparing this with the original picture of the same section taken by a longer lens. The perspective in both these pictures will be exactly the same, but not the quality of course, as any enlargement will by necessity have caused a slight deterioration in quality.

How then can we achieve a change in perspective? Not by a change in focal length, but only by a change in viewpoint. You may put this to the test. Take a person close-up with a short lens. He or she will be shown rather dominant against a retreating background. Take the next picture with a standard lens but move back to show the person in the same size within the frame as before. Now the distance between figure and background will be more "realistic"; it will appear more as it does to our naked eye. Now take a third shot with a long lens. You will have to step back to show the person to the same height. The spatial distance between figure and background appears to be even further reduced. There is another effect to be considered for the subject chosen in this example. Because the main subject is relatively close to the camera compared with the distant background the person will be depicted in sharp relief against a blurred background, because of the limited depth of field of the longer lens in the close and medium ranges. Depending on focal length, the background and the foreground between camera and main subject will be anything from slightly to totally blurred; only the figure will be sharp.

If you own more than just a standard lens for your T70, and you would not get any true idea of what your T70 is capable of if you only had one lens, you could try a few "dry runs". Change your position and perhaps the lens as well and experience the different perspectives through the viewfinder. Always keep in mind that good photographs are the result of some effort. If you want others to see your own special view you will have to move around the subject to find its best side. Just changing the lens alone will usually not bring the desired results; some footwork, a bent knee, a raised position, all will help in producing a different perspective. Examine your subject carefully from all sides and view it through the viewfinder, or better, learn to do it in your mind's eye.

Remember that the perspective from normal eye level is usually that of the commonly-observed view and can easily be very dull. But the worm's eye perspective, a view seen from a low position and the camera pointing up, or the bird's eye perspective, a high position with camera pointing steeply down, can reveal new images. Generally it is possible to increase the dynamics of a view by adopting an unusual viewing angle or at least avoiding the general eyelevel viewpoint. From a photographic point of view I would recommend you to stray from the straight and narrow and to be more adventurous.

Coating for Good Pictures

You will know what I mean when we talk about reflections on glass surfaces. Part of the light is reflected where glass and air meet. This is a phenomen that has to be avoided in the construction of lenses. Even makers of some quite expensive ones have not managed to cure this problem. The lens is supposed to allow as much light as possible to find its way to the film plane, and secondly to eliminate stray light from the system which reduces image contrast.

The glass-air interface of a non-coated surface will reflect about 4% of the incident light. If you consider that some modern high-performance lenses are constructed of six or even more elements you will find that ten or more glass-air interfaces are no rarity. A simple calculation will show how much light is really arriving at the film plane and how much is free to cause flare in the system. It will show how, not only is the speed of the lens reduced, but it will demonstrate also that modern lens designs cannot do without expert coating to reduce unwanted light reflections. To achieve this, very thin layers are evaporated onto the surface in a very high vacuum. In this way reflection can be reduced to the best possible theoretical value of 0.2%. These coatings can also incorporate a colour factor which is useful for colour corrections. The particular combination and construction of the layer gives each lens its own particular colour characteristics, whether warmer or colder in tone. The coating therefore is often used by the designer for balancing colour reproduction. You may have come across the expression "colour balance of lenses" in some photographic literature. This explains why some lenses have a slight blue sheen, whilst others tend towards brown or purple.

These days almost all Canon lenses are multi-layer coated by the Canon Super Spectra Coating (SSC) method. Multicoating is a relatively modern procedure in which each individual element is coated with several different layers. The correct application and choice of individual layers is the important point here. The effectiveness of the method depends largely on the

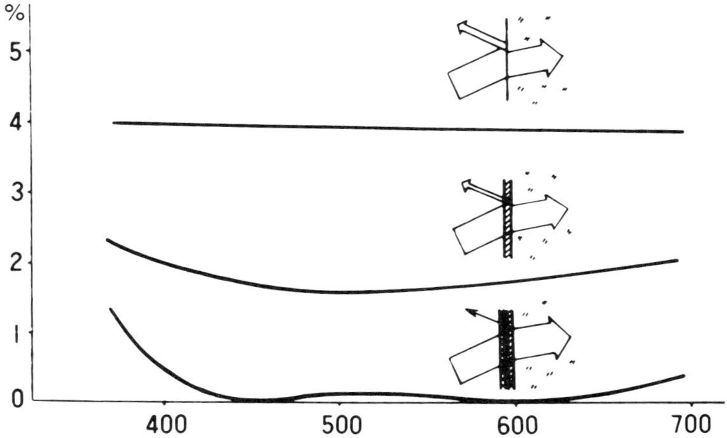

About 4% of the incident light is lost as reflection at uncoated glass/air surfaces. A good single layer coating will reduce this reflection to 2%. An effective multi-layer coating can reduce this even further to a fraction of one percent. (wavelengths are indicated in nanometres)

type of glass used, its refractive index, the radius of curvature of the lens element and its position within the construction. A lens is constructed of different elements and types of glass, each requiring different coatings. The structural characteristics therefore decide to a large extent the number and type of coatings of individual surfaces.

Optimum Correction for Close Range

We shall examine one more structural principle employed by Canon. This is to maintain the reproduction quality of certain lenses which would otherwise decline considerably for close focusing distances. I mean the so-called automatic correction balance, often referred to under the description of "floating elements" or "floating focusing". For certain types of lens construction, primarily the wide-angle and the super wide-angle lenses, reproduction quality declines sharply for close focusing distances, remote from the infinity setting for which most lenses are designed. To counteract this decline in performance, Canon uses a construction technique which allows certain elements within the optical system to move with respect to each other during focusing, i.e. the air gaps between the elements within the system are changed. Depending on the type of lens the moving part within the system may be the rear element, or even a whole complex of elements within the system. The effect of this type of construction on overall sharpness to the edge of the frame is quite remarkable and makes the extra expenditure worth-while.

A Measure of Progress – Internal Focusing

A further example of the progressive engineering of Canon FD lenses is internal focusing. All Canon lenses from 200mm incorporate this feature.

What does it mean? Looking at an ordinary lens you will note that it gets longer the more you turn the focusing ring to focus on a shorter distance. In other words, focusing on shorter distances requires a longer extension. The construction is based on a focusing helix which moves the entire system away from the film plane. For focal lengths up to middle range telephoto this extension remains within manageable limits. But for longer focal lengths the extension gets larger and larger the closer the subject. If you examine very long lenses you will find, that the extension can be quite considerable. This leads to difficulties. A relatively large and heavy system, using a conventional focusing helix to increase the extension has to move quite considerable masses. The lens gets too large, too heavy and cumbersome, and the centre of gravity is noticeably displaced.

Canon was the first manufacturer to introduce a long lens

The principle of Canon internal focusing. Only one rear element is moved for focusing.

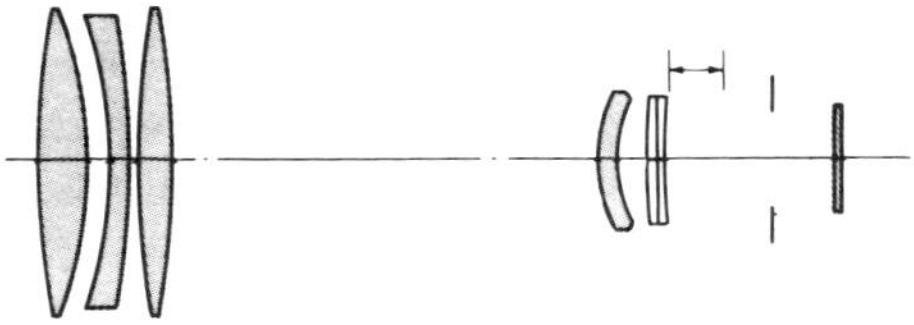

with internal focusing for SLR cameras, namely the FD 400mm f/4.5. The barrel of this lens, which we shall consider only as an example, remains rigid during focusing. Only a small rear element within the barrel is moved. The advantages of this form of construction are considerable. It is no longer necessary to move large masses, and focusing is achieved by a smaller focusing mechanism, which in turn leads to a much lighter construction. The diameter of the barrel can be much smaller; the centre of gravity of the unit does not change appreciably during focusing, and the shifting of the rear element allows much closer focusing distances than in conventional constructions. Finally it is possible to correct for reproduction performance at close ranges with internal focusing. But all this was not enough for Canon; they added a further advantage. Focusing adjustment of some lenses is extended beyond infinity to make it easier and more precise to focus on objects just short of infinity.

Considering all these advantages we may regard internal focusing as the measure of the technical standard of a lens series. If you investigate the market you will note that Canon is the only manufacturer who offers as many modern telephoto lenses of this high quality. The next rival is Nikon.

The Special Lenses

Most lenses used on modern cameras are so-called achromats. These are lens systems which correct colour aberrations for two light wavelengths. Achromatic correction is achieved by a combination of elements of flint and crown glass.

For medium focal lengths this correction is sufficient. But as soon as we reach the longer telephoto range a residual error of colour correction, the so-called secondary spectrum, becomes more and more noticeable as this secondary spectrum is dependent on focal length.

These errors in reproduction caused considerable difficulties in lens design in the past. But it has been possible to develop new types of glass, such as the Canon UD glass, which produce abnormal partial dispersion. This glass does not disperse the colours such that individual wavelengths are spread far apart thus producing multiple sharp images at different points. The same effect can be achieved using calcium fluoride (fluorite) crystals. Canon were the first optical manufacturer to be able to grow these in sufficient size and purity for grinding into lens elements.

Fluorite elements and the UD glass elements give the lens designer the possibility of correcting for a third colour, which at the same time achieves a better reproduction quality for the intermediate wavelengths. Such systems go under the description of "apochromatically corrected". The FD programme offers a considerable choice of these high quality lenses in the long focal length range. These bear the supplementary code "L". (Canon also includes lenses with aspherical surfaces in the group "L".)

Apochromatically corrected lenses are particularly excellent as they are able to cover a wide contrast range and give true-to-life colour representation. As you might expect, the great manufacturing cost is reflected in the price, and most of these systems will be used mainly by professional photographers.

Variable or Fixed Focal Lengths?

When extending his equipment the amateur photographer is always faced with the choice of additional lenses which would be most suited to his purpose. There is no general answer to this question. The decision of what to buy depends on the particular purpose the lens has to fulfil. If the photographer is particularly interested in animal photography he will have to decide on a completely different set of lenses from someone whose main love is, say, landscape or flowers. However, I can give you some basic advice which will help you in making a decision.

Variable focal length lenses are becoming increasingly prominant in 35mm photography. They are most tempting. The focal length can be continuously varied within a certain range, simply by a small movement. In this way one variable focal length lens can replace a whole set of fixed focal length lenses. Not only do they replace the fixed focal length lenses, they also cover the ranges in between the generally offered focal lengths. The zoom lens will bridge the gaps between 100, 135 and 200mm, smoothly and continuously. If you have ever used a 8mm cine camera or video camera you will be quite familiar with this facility. The frame most suitable for the picture is selected quite easily by a simple twist or pressure on a button, and the same is possible with a SLR camera and a zoom lens. But what are the disadvantages?

One powerful argument has lost its justification. When zoom lenses for single lens reflex cameras were introduced, their optical performance was much poorer than that of fixed focal length lenses. But now this difference has been reduced to such an extent that it is hardly possible to distinguish. You need not worry any longer about quality. However, this statement should not be taken as a generalization; I am talking about Canon lenses and the same is not true for all makes. Some lenses on the market still show a considerable deficiency in quality. We still have to consider the greater weight of the zoom lens, and that fixed focal length lenses are usually easier and faster in operation. On the other hand, carrying three or even more individual focal length lenses makes the camera bag quite bulky and heavy.

We are left with one important point which you will have to consider when buying a zoom lens; the compromise lies in the lens speed. The lens diameter for a certain speed has to increase with increasing focal length. Not even the most ingenious engineer can do anything about this fact. If you examine the table of available Canon lenses you will note that the speed of the lenses decreases with increasing focal length. There are a few special constructions, but these end up as heavy glass blocks. It follows that a zoom lens has to be provided with the best possible speed for its upper focal length limit. Let's take as example a Canon zoom lens with relatively long focal length range, the FD 85-300mm f/4.5. The speed of f/4.5 is quite acceptable for the 300mm setting, for 200mm this is no longer earth-shattering and for 150mm down to 85mm this would be altogether unacceptable for a fixed focal length lens.

What advantages and disadvantages can we list for the fixed focal lengths? Because of the increased use of zoom lenses the fixed focal length lenses are increasingly considered for specialist use. This applies in particular to the lens speed. The hand-held shot is often only possible with a fixed focal length lens because the longer the focal length the faster the shutter speed required to avoid camera shake. Now for a lens with focal length 200mm we cannot use a slower shutter speed than $^1/_{250}$ second and the difference in lens speed between f/4 and, say, f/2.8 may decide whether the shot is feasible or not. On the other hand, the photo-chemical industry is aware of this and produces increasingly faster films with the same reproduction quality to compensate for this fact, unless you consider these advances as a means for extending the limits of photography.

A further advantage of fixed focal length lenses is the possibility of special applications. A macro 100mm lens, for example, can never be replaced by any type of zoom lens. Here the fixed focal length and conventional rigidity are an advantage.

To conclude this comparison we should consider the price. A relatively complicated zoom lens is naturally more expensive than an individual focal length lens. This means a larger investment at one particular time, against several smaller

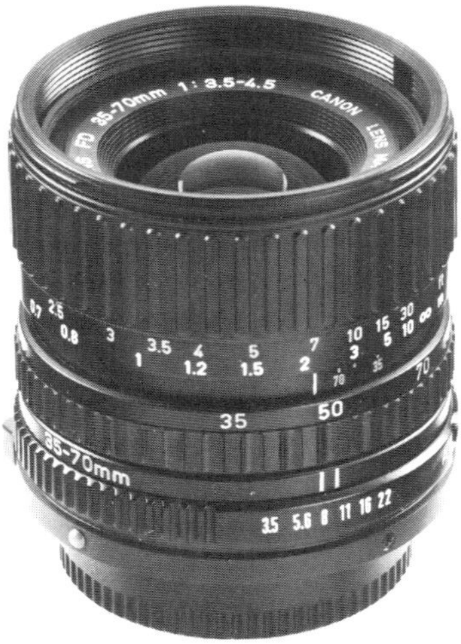

A real competitor for the conventional standard lens: the FD 35-70mm f/3.5-4.5.

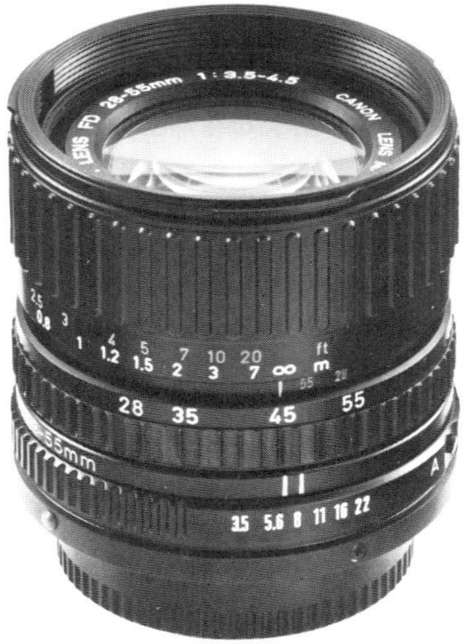

If you tend towards the wide-angle you may choose the FD 28-55mm f/3.5-4.5.

outlays as and when this fits more easily into your budget.

The ranges covered by variable length lenses have been considerably extended over recent years. Not so long ago it seemed quite impossible to construct a variable length lens from wide-angle to telephoto, but technical advance has made this quite possible. If you own a lens such as the FD 50-135mm f/3.5 you have a standard lens that extends into the very popular short telephoto range. But the price you pay for this versatility is a relatively large and heavy lens which is always attached to your camera. Only if it is indeed always in place and ready for use will it replace the conventional lens, I can see no sense in carrying it around in the bag. Think about these pros and cons before you decide to buy.

Variable focal length lenses covering a smaller range around the standard range are generally much better in this respect. Here again Canon were pioneers in the market, they were the first to introduce the FD 28-55mm f/3.5-4.5 and the FD 35-70mm f/3.5-4.5. Both these lenses are compact and light and can suitably replace the conventional standard lens with hardly any disadvantages as compared to the fixed focal length lens. The use of these lenses increases your chances considerably, even though the range does not seem to be that great. The possibilities offered from a moderate wide-angle of 35mm to a short telephoto are considerable, only the speed of these lenses cannot compare with that of a fixed focal length lens. But in view of the modern film material that has become available this should not present too great a problem.

A few years ago many amateur photographers chose the 35mm when considering a wide-angle lens. This situation has changed in recent years because of considerable technical advances. Today you can choose between 28mm, 24mm and even shorter lenses, all of excellent quality, and we find that these so-called super wide-angle lenses are extensively used by many enthusiastic amateurs. To start with I would recommend the well-tried 35mm, or perhaps even the shorter 28mm. Still shorter focal lengths present interesting possibilities, but they are no longer of general use and are therefore only to be regarded as a second, special wide-angle for particular applications. If you are specially interested in this field I would recommend combinations such as a 35mm together with a 24mm, or a 28mm together with a 20mm or even a 17mm super wide-angle.

On the long side I would recommend the 135mm as a very good telephoto compromise in the hands of almost any amateur, if you intend to buy only one long lens. Many committed photographers consider the 85mm a very useful lens, but this can hardly be considered a telephoto in the present sense.

When talking about wide-angle lenses I said that many changes and advances have taken place in recent years, and the same applies, at least in our basic attitude to additional lenses, to the longer focal lengths. The modern amateur photographer has extended his interest not only to the wide-angle, but also to the telephoto lenses. This is quite logical as the possibilities of a SLR camera are in no way exhausted as soon as 135mm is reached. A 200mm lens can still be used quite easily for hand-held shots and, together with the excellent viewfinder of the T70, this becomes an ideal snapshot instrument which is a lot more versatile and easy to handle than may be generally assumed. You should certainly consider the purchase of a 200mm lens. Only if you go beyond this limit will you find that the applications become more limited, the use more difficult, and the price less attainable.

Standard Lenses

In SLR photography the focal length of 50mm has come to mean the normal length. These standard lenses, as they are known, produce images that are closest to those seen by the human eye. They are thus the most suitable as a starting point for equipment that may at a later stage be extended according to taste and finances. And you will bear with me if I assume that you, as proud owner of a powerful Canon T70, are going to buy additional lenses.

Most SLR cameras are still offered together with a standard 50mm lens, but the tendency now seems to be towards supplying them with a variable length lens covering that length. The production runs of standard lenses are usually quite large and they can therefore be offered at a very reasonable price. Considered in this light, and also that it usually offers the fastest speed, the standard lens is no bad investment. The high

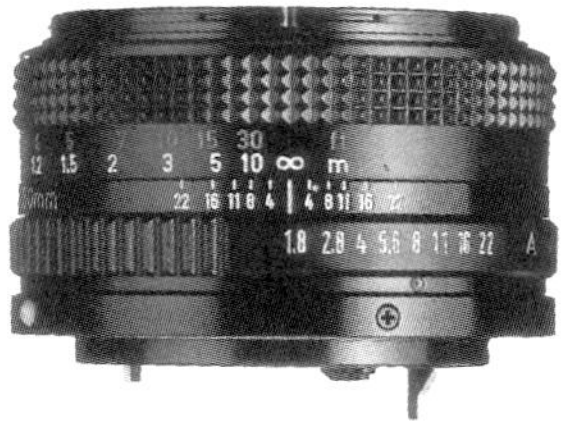

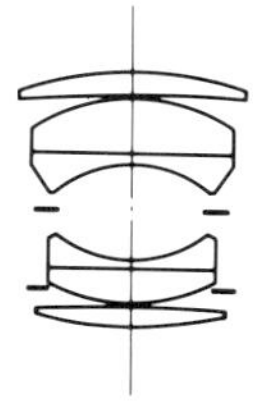

The smallest FD lens is the extraordinarily powerful FD 50mm f/1.8.

lens speed is one of the greatest advantages that the standard lens has to offer and which no other equivalent lens is capable of producing and thus it may be used as a very valuable backup in situations when the lighting conditions are unfavourable.

Added to this is the real objectivity of the 50mm lens. Optically it adds nothing to what is presented. On the other hand, wide-angle and telephoto lenses impose their own character. They introduce an element of cheating, whilst the standard lens presents things as we are used to seeing them with our own eyes. Thought of in this way the standard lens is an essential part of the equipment for documentary reportage.

Within the FD programme you have the choice between the very favourably priced FD 50mm f/1.8, the smallest of the FD lenses, and the FD 50mm f/1.4, which is half a stop faster. The phrase "half a stop faster" should help you in your decision. Ask yourself whether you will really utilize this half-stop advantage and if the extra expense is worth it. If you have to go to the very limit, you will choose the FD 50mm f/1.2 which is very compact considering its enormous speed which it manages to produce with a normal filter diameter of 52mm. Compared with its predecessors in respect to lens speed, the former 55mm lenses, this lens is suitable for being always attached to the camera as it is easy to operate and, despite the high speed, excellent in performance; you need not worry about a drop in quality even at fully open aperture.

As an alternative choice you may decide on a macro lens of this focal length. These lenses do not offer the same speed, but they compensate by offering exceedingly high performance for almost every conceivable subject from infinity to 23cm in front of the film plane, but we have already discussed this type of lens at some length in previous chapters.

Wide-Angle Lenses

In SLR photography the focal lengths 35mm, 28mm and 24 mm are considered wide-angle lenses, while distortion-free systems with 20mm, 17mm and even 14mm focal lengths are referred to as super wide-angle lenses. Lenses within this range offer great depth of field, always referred to from the same shooting position, increasing with decreasing focal length. These wide viewing angles are often preferred in landscape and architectural photography where a sharp representation of as large a spatial expanse as possible is of importance. But, as with every rule, this should not be applied too rigidly. Sometimes a long lens is the right one for these situations, it always depends on the photographic intent.

A look through the viewfinder of your T70 has particular import in the use of short focal lengths. The world seen through a super wide-angle lens looks quite different to that perceived with the unaided eye. It is only natural that you will need a little experience to get used to the different conditions and to apply a different shooting technique. The exessively steep perspective emphasises the expanse of the view, making the inclusion of a foreground even more necessary than with a standard lens. Shots with super wide-angle lenses generally require a fairly imposing foreground to help emphasise the depth of the view. On the other hand interior shots are often only possible with short lenses. This technique is often used in advertising, belying reality in presenting a spacious image of a hotel room which is really quite small and unassuming.

Wide-angle and super wide-angle lenses will show up the slightest inclination of the camera from the vertical if a building is included. The viewers of your pictures will not accept that you are in fact showing the world as it is. You could pretend that these failures are to be considered as modern art, but you will not get away with it for long. This rules does not apply in landscape photography; there you may take some liberties and incline the camera to shift the horizon to the top or bottom half of the frame, and none will be the wiser. Under certain circumstances you may employ the steep viewing angle to the top or bottom. These unusual perspectives are particularly popular for high buildings and lend them a special dynamic quality. If this is the only way of showing the entire height of an imposing church, for example, then you would probably be right to adopt this method as a very effective solution.

The very short lenses present special problems. Starting with a 24mm you often wish that you could jump over your own shadow. The large viewing angle covers a great deal, often more than you would have wished for. Using these short lenses you will have to check whether your own shadow is intruding and if you cannot find a better position you will be well advised to forget about this particular shot.

Another point that needs mentioning; don't insist on taking your portrait sessions with one of these wide-angle lenses. If the model is to be shown at a reasonably large scale you will have to go quite close. The result will be image distortions which are not due to a faulty optical system. You will end up with large noses and distorted heads and limbs more suitable for the carnival than a portrait.

Lenses with large viewing angles are not only suitable for inanimate objects. They are excellent as snapshot instruments at short range. Because of the large depth of field you can preselect a distance setting at which you expect a reasonable shot which will be in sharp focus for the resulting working aperture and then you need only wait for the right moment. All you need to do is press the trigger and you will have caught your subject completely unawares.

Apart from the technical aspects there are structural limitations to be considered which I would like to explain to you. As practical as a single lens reflex camera is, it has its limitations with short focal lengths. The folding mirror in the camera body, which makes the principle of a reflex camera possible, needs a certain amount of space. This presents the optical designer with the problem that he cannot move the lens close enough to the film plane. Initially it was solved by folding away the mirror and locking it in this position. But our wonderful reflex camera then no longer functioned as such. Then another technique was invented to overcome this mechanical problem by an optical solution, namely the so-called "retrofocus" construction. This structural principle allows even extremely short focus lenses to be built with a back focus distance which is sufficiently large, i.e. the distance from the last lens surface to the film plane. All short lenses used with the T70 are built according to this structural principle, so that your reflex camera remains a reflex camera.

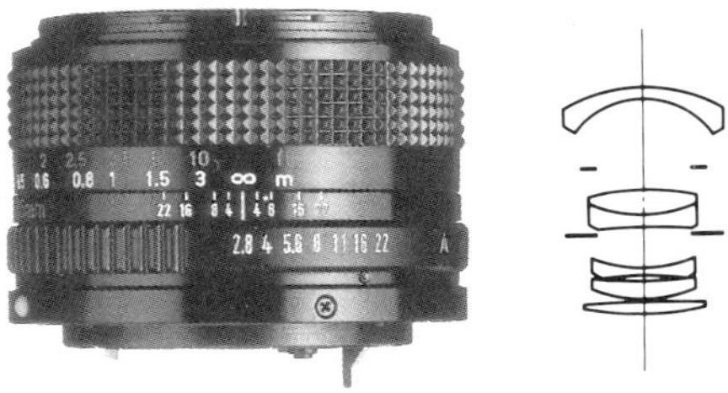

A very well priced and good wide-angle lens, the FD 35mm f/2.8.

In the moderate wide-angle range Canon offer two lenses, the very favourably priced, compact and highly efficient FD 35mm f/2.8 and the very fast FD 35mm f/2 which would be suitable as a standard lens for those who tend towards the shorter focal length for this application, and this lens is comparable in speed to the 50mm lenses. Both lenses cover a 63° angle of view.

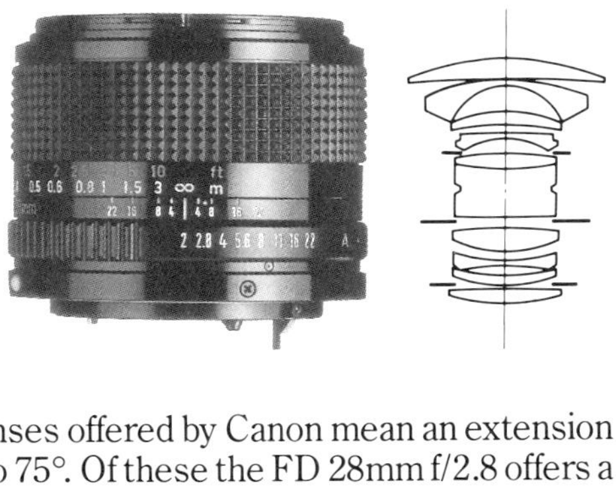

Like all fast wide-angle lenses by Canon, the FD 28mm f/2 has automatic correction compensation.

The two 28mm lenses offered by Canon mean an extension of the angle of view to 75°. Of these the FD 28mm f/2.8 offers a particularly compact construction, weighing only 170g and having an overall length of a mere 40mm. The other 28mm, the FD 28mm f/2 is again a fast lens. Just like the fast 35mm lens, the FD 28mm f/2 offers automatic correction compensation and maintains its high performance across the entire focusing range down to the close-up limit of 0.3m.

Similar facilities are offered for the 24mm focal length. The FD 24mm f/2.8 is complemented by the faster FD 24mm f/2. At this focal length this is quite a remarkable speed. One should not forget that wide-aperture systems require more and more technical expenditure the more they differ from the standard focal lengths. The angle of view of the 24mm lens is a remarkable 84°. Another useful feature applying to all the described lenses, down to the 24mm, is that they manage with a filter diameter of only 52mm. There is another 24mm lens available which is even faster. This lens is described in the chapter for aspherical lenses.

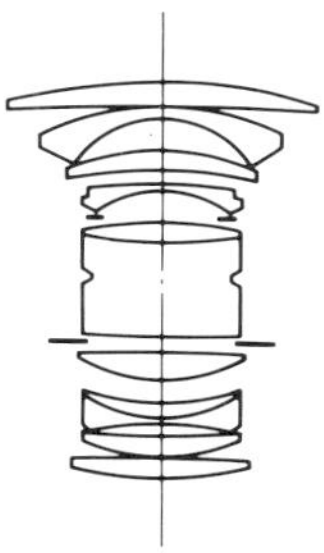

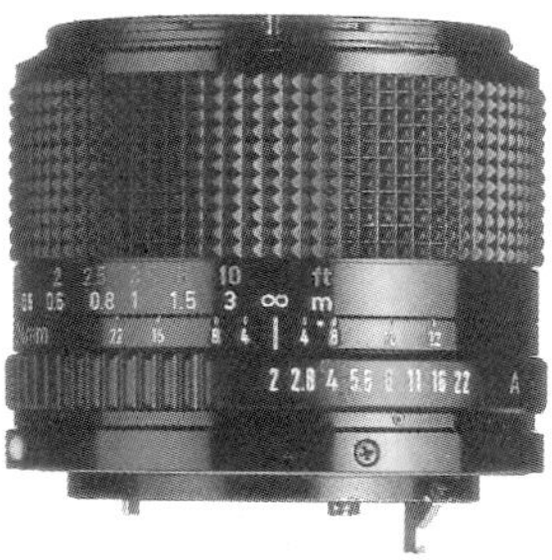

The FD 24mm f/2 embodies the considerable optical complexity necessary to produce great lens speed at this focal length.

The FD 20mm f/2.8 is a star amongst super wide-angle lenses with an angle of view of 94°, a considerable speed and excellent performance. The necessary retrofocus construction makes it a rather expensive optical system, but I am sure you will understand that such a high level of correction of reproduction errors for this extremely large angle of view and lens speed cannot be achieved with moderate means.

The FD 17mm f/4 with an angle of view of 104° gives what is

A very versatile super wide-angle, the Canon FD 20mm f/2.8.

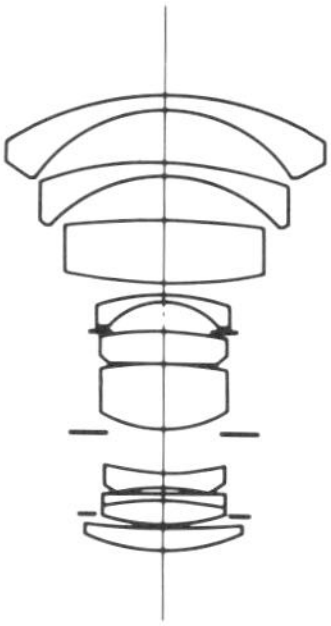

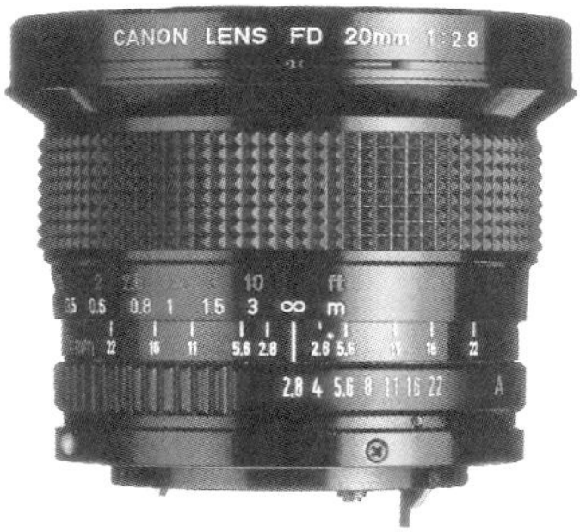

known in photographic circles as very steep perspective at close viewpoints. Despite the truly enormous angle of view the residual distortion of this lens is less than 1%. Here too, automatic correction compensation is employed to maintain the high reproduction performance down to the shortest focusing distance of 25cm.

I just mentioned the term "residual distortion". This requires a little further explanation. (It must be remembered that super wide-angle lenses whose focal lengths approach those of the fisheye lenses, by necessity represent the images according to different optical principles.) In photographic terms projection of an image without distortion is called 'rectilinear projection' Straight lines are shown as straight lines even at the edge of the picture. A certain residue, usually barrel distortion, is still apparent even with modern wide-angle lenses, but this is of no consequence in pictorial photography.

Although wide-angle lenses down to a focal length of about 18mm can be produced that are free from detectable curvilinear distortion, there is always what is called, 'wide-angle' distortion that is not the fault of the lens. In fact, a

Distortion aberration: a square or rectangle shows barrel (centre) or pin-cushion distortion.

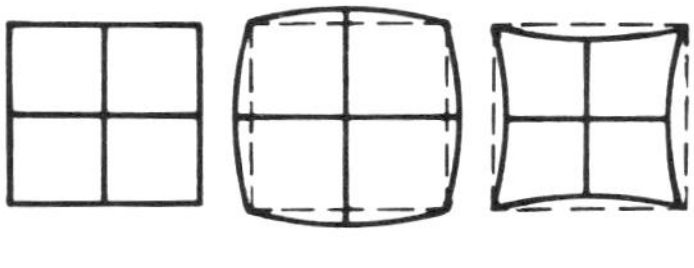

pinhole produces exactly the same distortion. It is seen by the elongation of the shapes of objects falling towards the corners of a picture. This is very apparent with spherical objects that are pulled into almost sausage shapes, the further they are from the lens axis the greater the distortion. The simple geometry of projection by a lens shows that such wide-angle distortion is inevitable at the edges of the field because the image is projected onto a plane surface and not on a strongly-curved one as is the case with the eyes which do not give such distortion. This type of distortion has to be accepted if one wishes to take pictures with such extreme lenses.

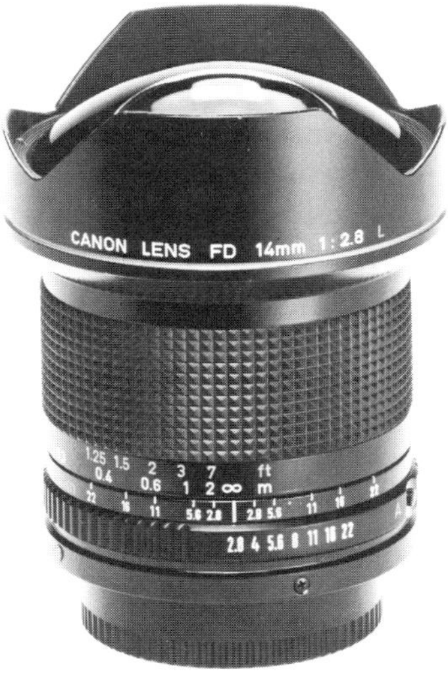

At present the smallest, lightest and fastest 14mm super-wide-angle in the world: the Canon 14mm f/2.8L with a diagonal angle of view of 114°.

The most powerful wide-angle lens in the Canon series that is still able to represent without aberrations is a veritable treasure, at a price to match, which will not come as a surprise I am sure. I am talking about the FD 14mm f/2.8 super wide-angle with aspherical surfaces. This lens covers an angle of view of 114°. You cannot imagine the breadth of the view of this lens until you actually experience it by looking through the viewfinder. This optical masterpiece has true high performance construction, a physical length of only 83.5mm and weighs 490g, and that at a speed of f/2.8! This specification makes the FD 14mm L the top-performing lens in its class on the market. But please remember that the extraordinarily extreme angle of view requires very sensitive handling and great expertise. Only a limited number of subjects will be suitable for the excessively stretched representation. But then this is the lot of many a lens that has pushed forward the limits of photography.

Essential – the Long Lenses

The logical consequence of long focal lengths is that the smaller the angle of view, the smaller the section of the subject represented on the 24x36mm negative format. But smaller angles of view mean that the subject is brought closer. Long lenses can bridge distances to far away subjects, or they can represent closer subjects at a larger scale than standard or wide-angle lenses.

To start with I would like to point out that long lenses are of almost unlimited versatility and, if you pardon the apparent contradiction, an essential luxury. Some people labour under the misconception that a telephoto lens is quite useful to bring a far-away subject closer to the viewer, but is otherwise only rarely needed. Moreover, it compresses the background, and distorts the perspective and so should not be employed as a general lens. All wrong! He who has discovered the magic of the long lens and how in so many situations it presents the best and quickest way to the most successful pictures, will be totally dedicated to its use. The effect starts with 85mm. the FD 85mm f/1.8 looks more or less like the fast standard lens, but already it presents your images in quite a different way. In addition it is almost equivalent in lens speed to the standard

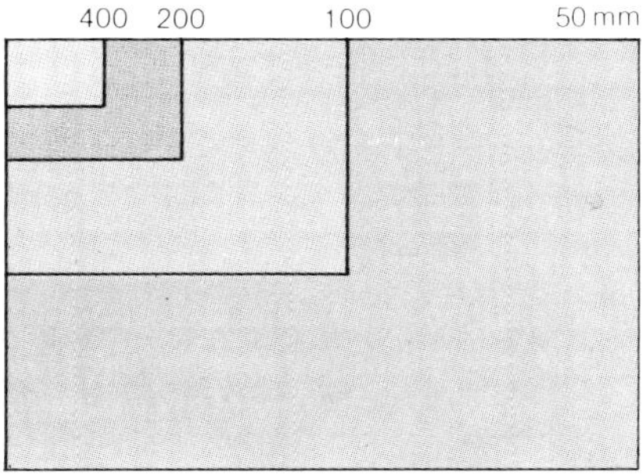

Comparison of the coverage of different lenses with the 50mm standard lens: 100mm, 200mm and 400mm, all taken from the same position.

lens, being only half a stop slower than the FD 50mm f/1.4. The combination of lens speed and moderately long focal length makes this an excellent universal lens. An added advantage is that it is often very handy not to have to approach the subject closely because a little distance can increase the naturalness, the longer focal length helps to cut-out unwanted background and to compose the picture more precisely.

The long lenses are veritable impact makers. The ease with which striking details may be picked out and isolated from the surroundings results in scenes which are often best seen in large format. Let's say you have a 200mm lens on your camera. You will have to show subjects in your immediate surroundings as sectional details in large format. Suddenly you see the head of your subject at an astounding closeness and scale, the background dissolves into a hazy fog, increasing the presence of the main subject. The depth of field of the long focal lengths is very shallow, an effect which increases with larger apertures, and this can be a wonderful tool in creating the desired effect.

One thing becomes quite clear. People, portraits and long focal lengths make an ideal combination. The FD 85mm, for example, would be the ideal instrument for portrait sessions at home. The FD 135 is even better, and the FD 200mm better still if you are looking for your subjects outdoors.

But people and snapshots of scenes are only one application.

The long lens is just as much at home in landscape photography. General rules ares that it is important to provide the proper frame and give depth to a view by including a suitable foreground. By using a telephoto lens you can find this foreground in the middle distance. In this way your long shots need not lack the foreground to give depth to your view. The viewfinder of the T70 is an ideal instrument in picture creation. You can assess the effect of the final picture exactly on the focusing screen. It is therefore quite easy to find the suitable foreground to enhance the long view.

Telephoto lenses are also ideal for detail studies in the close and medium range. A well-chosen detail shot often says more about a landscape, a scene or its mood than a good overall view. The corner of a window; a shadow tracing the outline of an uneven wall that is illuminated by side lighting to give a sculptured effect; a row of bright flags in the wind; reflections on a whitewashed wall. One basic photographic premise becomes almost obligatory when using long lenses: 'less expresses more'.

If you ever tried your hand at animal photography you will know that the long lens is absolutely essential. In the animal kingdom the lenses between 300 and 500mm are king. It makes no difference whether you stalk your prey in the open or try to catch an effective view in the zoo. In the open you need the long lens so as not to startle the animal into flight; in the zoo you need it to isolate your subject from its background and to present it as an entity in its own right.

The suitability of the long lenses for use at close range should not be ignored. By reason of their internal focusing, a sophisticated structural design offered by Canon even with the FD 200mm f/2.8 and the FD 200mm f/4, the conditions for unusually short focusing distances are quite favourable. A further advantage is that the telephoto lens allows a greater shooting distance than could ever be achieved with a standard lens, even when you need to show a very small object at a large scale, and for small creatures it is usually essential to keep one's distance.

Telephoto Lenses

Canon offers a wide selection of universally applicable telephoto lenses. To start with there is the FD 85mm f/1.8 with a length of 53mm and weighing only 345g which, by virtue of its small size, may compete in many situations with the standard lens. But contrary to the standard lenses, this focal length only covers an angle of view of 29°, compared with 46° of the 50mm lens. The 85mm may be used with fully open aperture and its longer focal length provides ideal conditions for working with selective depth of field. Another advantage; all these lenses have a uniform filter diameter of 52mm.

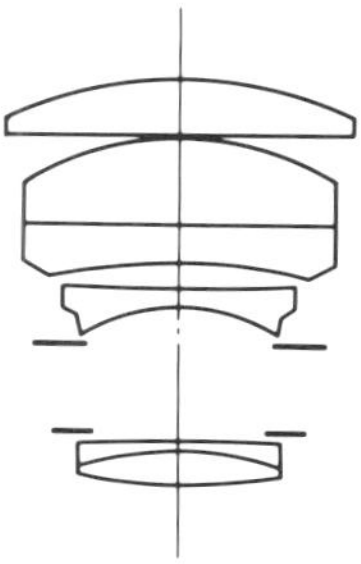

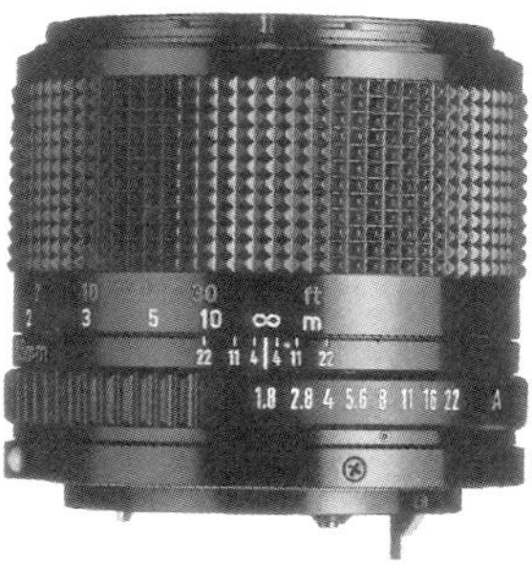

The FD 85mm f/1.8 lens is suitable as an alternative standard lens for photographers who prefer the longer focal lengths.

There are two further lenses in this focal length in the FD programme and I shall introduce these to you in the chapter on super-fast aspherical lenses. The FD 85mm f/2.8 SF is another specialist lens. In its basic position this lens is a normal, high definition 85mm lens, but a second, completely separate focusing ring causes spherical aberration to be introduced, producing soft-focus images. A feature of special value is that the degree of soft focus is continuously variable.

The next focal length offered by Canon is the FD 100mm f/2.8, having the same short structural length as the 85mm and weighing only 270g. If lens speed is of importance you can choose the FD 100mm f/2. However, the larger aperture is

Considering its focal length of 100mm, the FD 100mm f/2 offers unusually high speed.

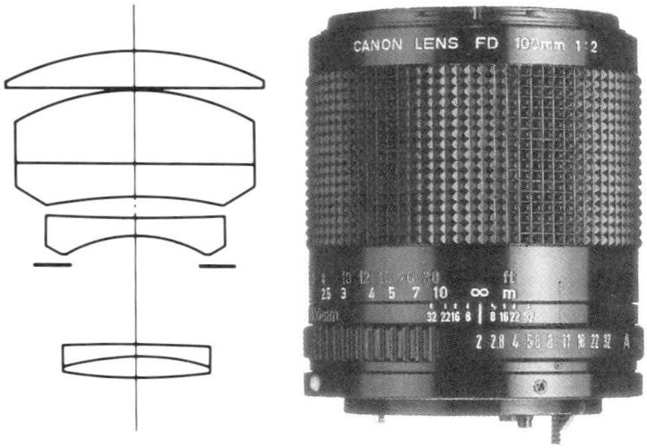

accompanied by greater cost. Even so, both lenses have been kept to a filter diameter of 52mm.

The choice gets harder for the most popular telephoto length of 135mm and Canon offer three lenses of this specification. To start with there is the FD 135mm f/3.5, a particularly well-priced model with relatively simple optical construction. Next you could consider the FD 135mm f/2.8, which, possessing a more sophisticated construction, is even shorter. This is a most compact and light lens, again with filter diameter 52mm.

On the other hand, the FD 135mm f/2 is quite chunky,

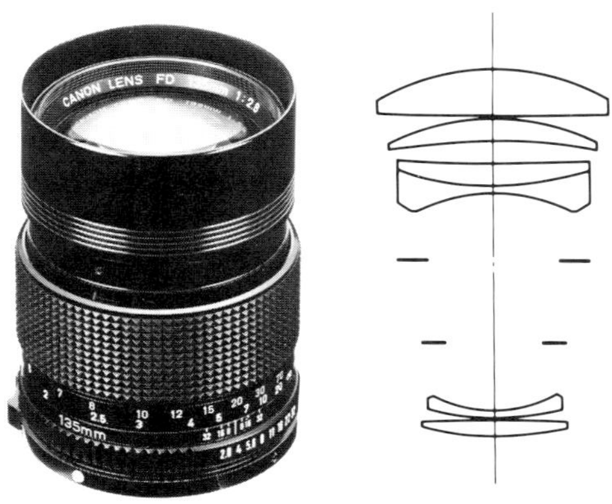

Excellent performance, compactness, high speed and a short close focusing limit combine to make the FD 135mm f/2.8 a very popular lens.

demonstrating the fact that at larger focal lengths the size increases if the performance and lens speed is to be maintained. This lens weighs a hefty 670g and has a filter diameter of 72mm. The great technical refinement is also reflected in the price. Should you be forced to photograph at a distance under poor lighting conditions then you will be grateful for the extra stops offered by this lens. Just as with the other two 135mm lenses this model is fitted with an extensible lens hood which Canon includes as part of the equipment from this focal length upwards.

At a focal length of 200mm we reach the limit of what may be considered universally applicable lenses. Both lenses of this focal length in the Canon programme offer something very special; the FD 200mm f/4 is the first Canon lens in that range of focal lengths offering internal focusing. For this reason it occupies a very special place in the photographic market. Internal focusing allows not only smooth focusing without displacement of the centre of gravity, but also better conditions for the short focusing distance of 1.5m. This is the longest Canon FD lens with a filter diameter of 52mm.

Its faster brother, the FD 200mm f/2.8 has also been converted to internal focusing. This lens consists of seven

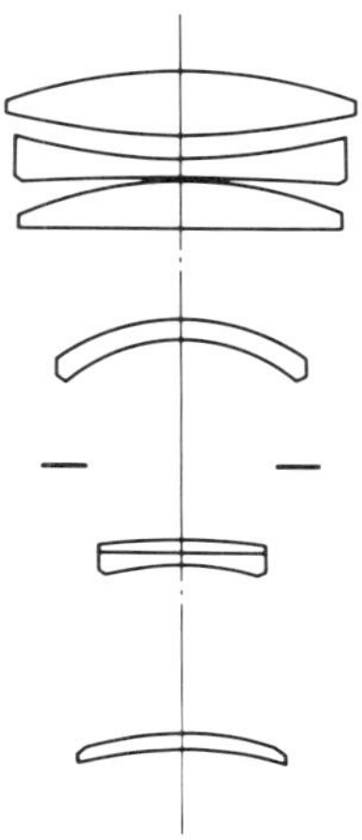

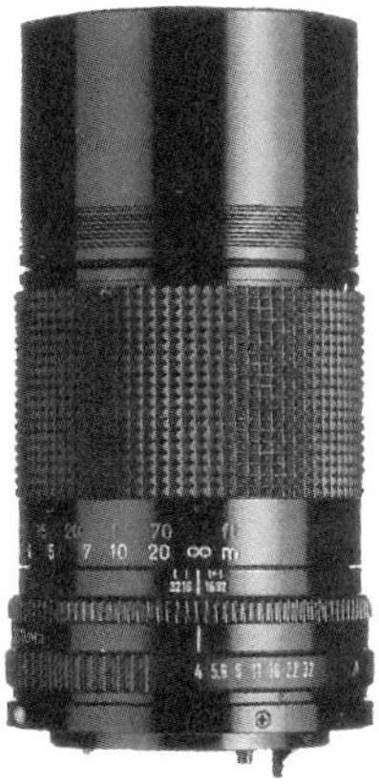

The FD 200mm f/4 is the first FD lens on Canon's scale of ascending focal lengths that has internal focusing as standard. Canon excels in this respect compared with other manufacturers.

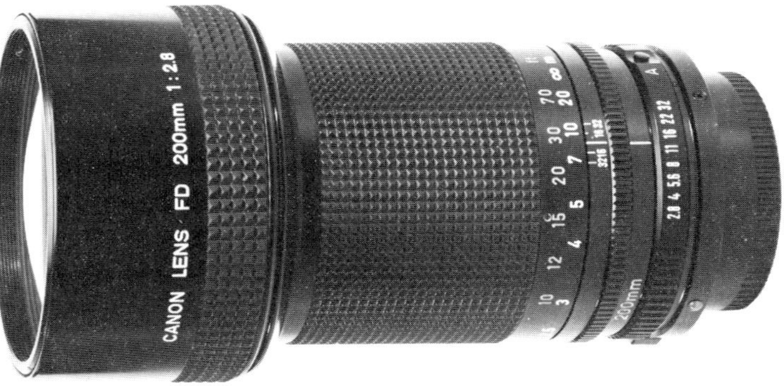

The FD 200mm f/2.8 has now also been fitted with internal focusing. It is thus transformed into an entirely new and effective optical system.

elements in six groups, using a high-refraction glass. The lens speed of f/2.8 is an excellent compromise for the 200mm focal length. It is possible to use this lens in less favourable lighting conditions and the lens diameter at 72mm is not too large. The close-up focusing limit is also 1.5m.

The transition to "telescope" lenses is not clearly defined and I shall take 300mm as the lower limit, because lenses of this range count amongst the specialists.

The 300mm offered in the FD programme is particularly extensive. The FD 300mm f/5.6 is the best-priced one in this range and as such will be of interest to the amateur photographer. Is has internal focusing and can be focused down to 3m. Considering the effective focal length it is very handy at a structural length of 199mm with largest diameter of 65mm.

The FD 300mm f/4 follows, being one stop faster, and thus having a larger diameter. This is the first lens with push-in filters which are inserted in the rear part of the light path. These filters can be changed very quickly and are much more practical and cheaper than screw-in filters, which would have to have a very large diameter for this type of lens.

The FD 300mm f/4 300L is constructed apochromatically of

two types of UD-glass. The result is pin-sharp pictures with excellent contrast.

The fourth in this set is the FD 300mm f/2.8L. This lens is apochromatically corrected by the use of one element of calcium fluoride and another of UD-glass. The lens speed of f/2.8 requires, at this particular focal length, a diameter of 112mm. Weighing a hefty 1900g and reflecting the great technical sophistication in its price, it obviously belongs in the professional class.

In the 400mm range we have first the FD 400mm f/4.5. This was the very first lens with internal focusing and due to the slim construction that is possible with this system can still be used hand-held. The generously sized tripod ring at the centre of gravity serves as a comfortable support for the palm of the hand. The large opening of f/4.5 is the determining factor for the suitability of this lens for hand-held shots, which require a shutter speed of at least $^1/_{500}$ second to ensure sharp pictures.

There is a second lens for this focal length which, due to its almost unbelievable speed of f/2.8, is rather colossal. The ten-element FD 400mm f/2.8L, arranged in eight groups, has two elements of UD glass, which explains the excellent

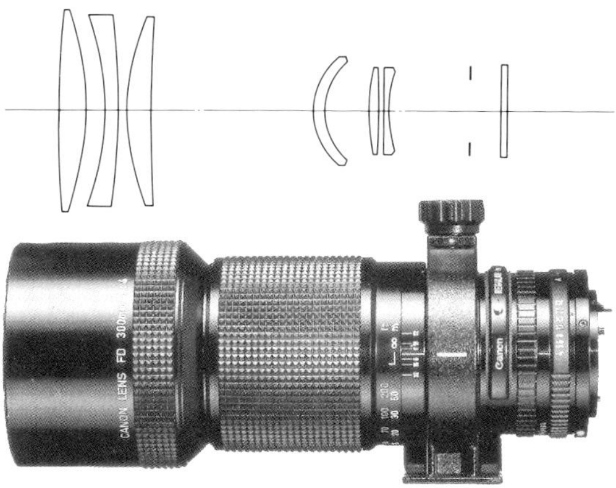

The FD 300mm f/4 is the fast lens for the amateur at this focal length.

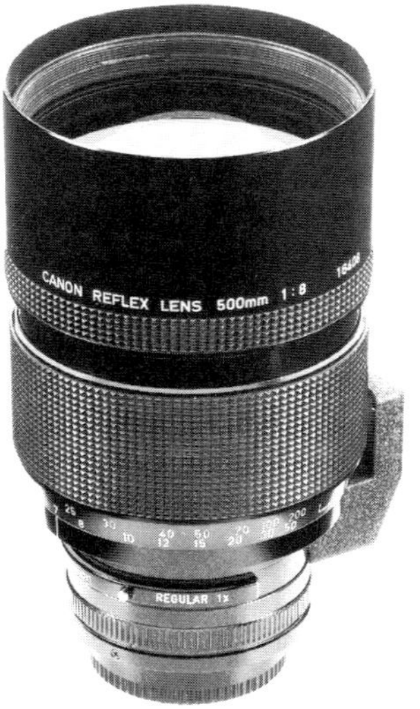

The Canon mirror lens RF 500mm f/8 leaves competitors far behind by its excellent performance.

Comparison between the conventional lens 500mm f/4.5L and the mirror lens 500mm f/8

lens	length	ratio of focal length	weight
FD 1:4,5/500 mm L	395 mm	0,790	2610 g
RF 1:8/500 mm	146 mm	0,292	705 g

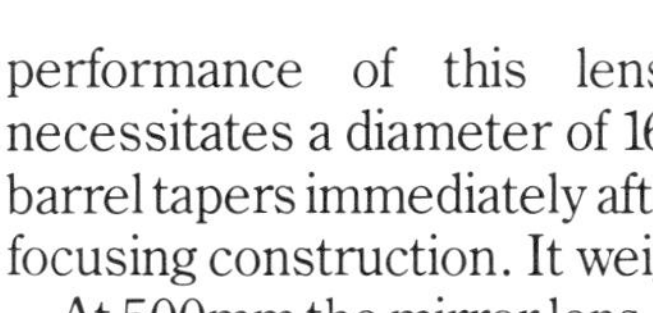

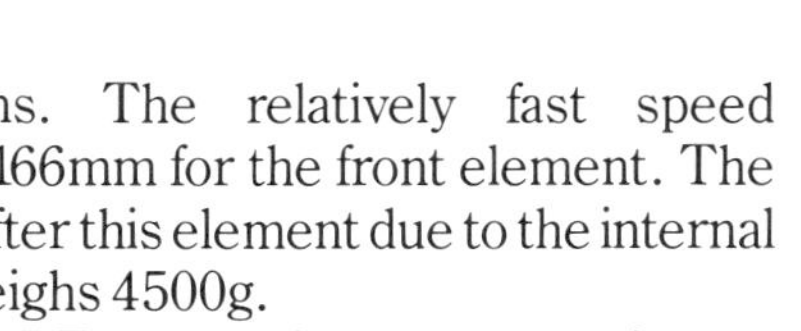

performance of this lens. The relatively fast speed necessitates a diameter of 166mm for the front element. The barrel tapers immediately after this element due to the internal focusing construction. It weighs 4500g.

At 500mm the mirror lens RF 500mm f/8 competes with the conventional FD 500mm f/4.5L. This mirror lens with its excellent performance leaves most other mirror lenses on the market far behind. Together with a fast film it is still suitable for hand-held shots. This lens is probably the absolute limit of sensible equipment for amateur photography. Push-in filters in the rear part of the light path, which can be changed without having to remove the lens from the camera, present a very useful facility. This is the more important if we consider that, for mirror lenses, the use of filters is the only way the incoming light can be controlled. The use of an iris diaphragm is not possible for structural reasons and you are therefore limited to always using aperture f/8, which leaves only the shutter speed as a means for regulating the amount of light. Assuming that the shortest shutter speed at 500mm focal length would be $^1/_{500}$ second, then you are limited to speeds between $^1/_{500}$ to $^1/_{1000}$ second with the T70. In this case you switch the camera to working-aperture mode and are thus being able to utilise all intermediate values within this range. Shutter speed and program modes are of course impossible because of the absence of the iris diaphragm. Generally you will have to use a fast film to be able to stay within the shutter speed limits with this aperture, but if lighting conditions improve, ND filters will be the only way to avoid overexposure.

The 500mm reflex lens has apochromatic correction, obtained by the use of an element of UD-glass and a second of calcium fluoride. Its price and weight definitely put this lens amongst the professionals. The same applies also to the even longer focal lengths which I shall mention only in passing. There is the FD 600mm f/4.5 and the FD 800mm f/5.6L, both high-performance telescope lenses with internal focusing and push-in filters.

Is Zoom Helpful?

The zoom or variable focal length lens has received a lot of attention in recent years. Its advantage, the liberation from fixed focal lengths within certain ranges, is obvious. But there are pitfalls even to progress and technology. Using a zoom lens leads to laziness. Most of us will hardly make the effort to find the best possible angle and viewpoint for a subject, which involves walking, climbing, knee bends and all sorts of contortions if we can just simply bring the subject into the correct framing by a short turn of the wrist. The frame changes smoothly and we press the trigger. Seen in this way we have to consider zoom lenses as a real danger to good photography. It is too easy. This fact should be kept in mind if we smugly twist and turn the focal length adjustment ring.

Zoom lenses have one great advantage. One unit, although usually larger and heavier than individual focal length lenses, can provide us with a kind of mini-equipment in one neat package. If the prime consideration is to move about as unencumbered as possible, then one is probably best served with two zooms lenses. Provided, of course, the moderate speed of these zoom lenses does not present unacceptable limitations under available lighting conditions. You could be fully equipped with one camera and two zoom lenses, which, in theory, replace a set of equipment entirely filling a whole camera bag.

The range of Canon lenses on offer has increased to such an extent that we can talk of two lens series within the programme. Starting with the short focal lengths you may whet your appetite on the following:

A long-standing item in the Canon FD programme is the FD 24-35mm f/3.5L, the first ever aspherical zoom lens for SLR cameras. The considerable technical expenditure was reflected in the very excellent performance which exceeded even that of fixed focal length lenses in that range. This lens covers the entire range of focal lengths that are generally considered as the wide-angle range. In the spring of 1984 it was complemented by a further optical pioneer: the very first super wide-angle zoom, namely the FD 20-35mm f/3.5L. A zoom lens extending down to such a short focal length had been unheard of up to this point. The aspherical surface, the front element, again ensures distortion-free reproduction, which we have come to expect with fixed focal length lenses. In the range of the super wide-angle, distortion presents the problem which is most difficult to correct. This lens will the

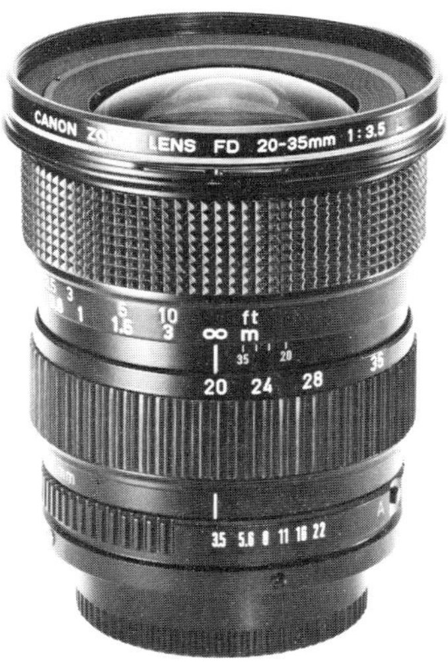

Canon pioneers another advance: the FD 20-35mm f/3.5. The first zoom lens in the world for SLR cameras extending down to the super wide-angle range of 20mm. The front element has an aspherical surface.

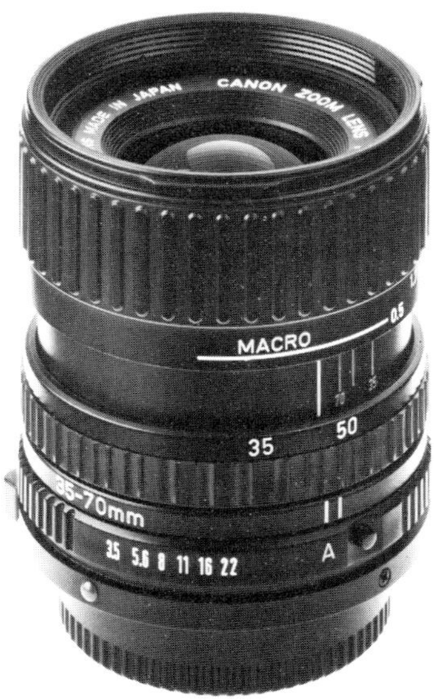

The FD 35-70mm f/3.5-4.5 has continuous focusing down to close-up for the standard focal length, it is possible to move very close to the subject.

delight the wide-angle fan. Despite its greater focal length range, it is even smaller and lighter than its predecessor.

The FD 28-55mm f/3.5-4.5 serves as a standard lens in the FD programme for the T70. By virtue of its light weight of only 220g and structural length of 61mm it may be considered as a minor optical sensation. It will be an obvious choice for those who tend towards the wide-angle ranges and wish to cover the standard focal length and down to the limits of super wide-angles.

Equally sensational is the second of these standard lenses for the T70, the FD 35-70mm f/3.5-4.5. The structural length is again 61mm and it weighs slightly less, only 210g. Similar to the FD 28-55mm it boasts excellent close-up performance and it is possible to achieve considerable reproduction scales with both these lenses. .These two lenses would form an excellent start for a good basic outfit as their performance and prices are altogether most attractive.

Two further variations in the focal length range 35-70mm may be found in Canon literature. There is the old FD 35-70mm f/2.8-3.5, which set beside the new model looks like a giant and has a price to match. Then there is the autofocus model of the former FD 35-70mm f/4. This lens focuses automatically on depressing a button. The compromise for the auto-focusing facility is reflected in the compactness of the lens. Moreover, the value of the auto-focusing facility at this range is also debatable.

The FD 35-105mm f/3.5 could be considered an extended version of the 35-70mm lens. However, weighing as much as 640g and measuring 109mm I doubt whether you would care to have this quite considerable lump attached at all times to your camera, however attractive the availability of a continuous setting from moderate wide-angle to moderate telephoto may be. Even so, compared with the old 35-70mm zoom it is even shorter, but expectations change with improving technology. In line with all the zooms described so far, this lens too possesses separate setting rings for focal length and distance.

The FD 50-135mm f/3.5 is the answer to many a

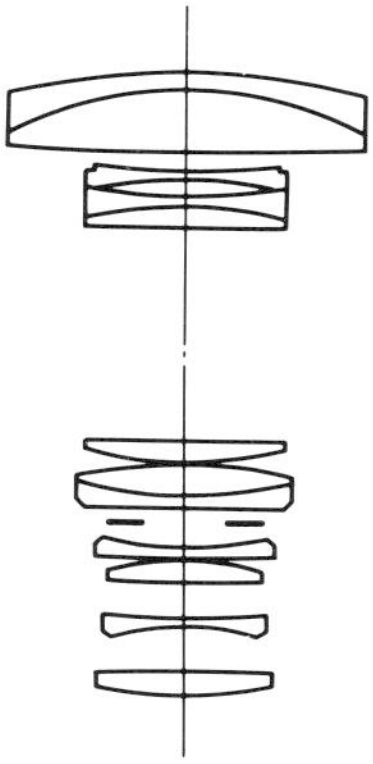

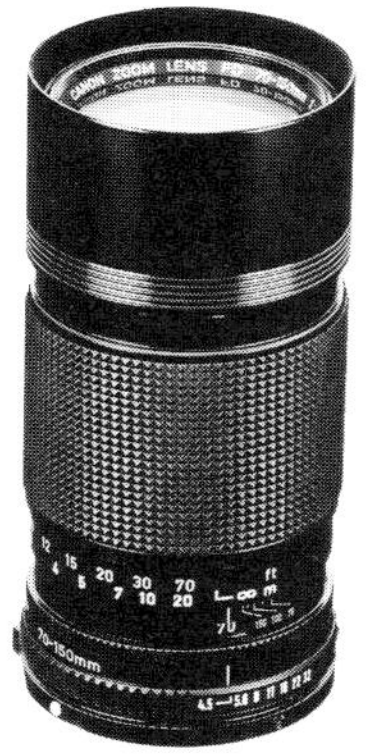

The FD 70-150mm f/4.5 is a very favourably priced universal telephoto lens.

photographer's dream. Starting with the standard focal length it continuously covers the range up to the very popular 135mm telephoto length. The dimensions of this sliding zoom lens are more or less the same as those of the former fast 135mm lenses, which could have been slimmed down recently because of the introduction of the new bayonet fitting. The optical construction of 16 elements in 12 groups demonstrates the high technical expenditure necessary for high performance lenses covering such a range in focal lengths. Therefore you will not be surprised that the price matches the technical effort.

The following zoom lenses are better suited to fit into the budget of most amateur photographers. On the one hand there is the FD 70-150mm f/4.5, which is ideally suited to complement either the FD 35-70mm f/3.5-4.5 or the FD 28-55mm f/3.5-4.5. This lens represents excellent value and you would be able to cover a considerable focal range with two light and compact lenses. By the way, this slide-zoom has a filter diameter of only 52mm, just as the two previously mentioned FD 28-55mm and 35-70mm lenses. However, it is the first in the zoom series that is fitted with an extendable lenshood as standard.

The FD 70-210mm f/4 with its three-fold focal length range,

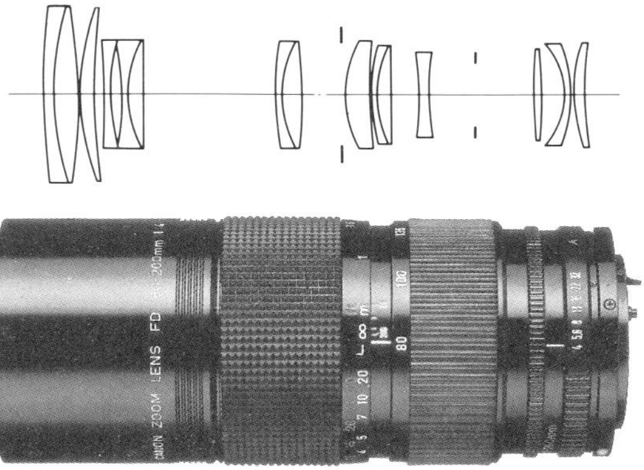

The FD 80-200mm f/4 was highly praised in independent comparative tests. It can be continuously focused down to 1m.

goes even further. This lens is also particularly interesting for its favourable price and is very popular with the amateur photographer. It has a single setting ring for focal length and distance setting. The FD 80-200mm f/4 has a very similar focal length range. It distinguishes itself, however, by its very excellent performance at the limit of its range. This fact has been well documented in the photographic press and in extensive tests. It has separate setting rings for focal length and distance settings and can be focused down to 1m for close-ups. Taking the focal length of 200mm this produces a reproduction scale of 1:3.45 and is therefore ideal for many subjects which would otherwise be inacessible, because the longer focusing distance allows sufficient working distance for shy subjects.

This highly interesting class of zoom lenses welcomed amongst its midst in spring 1984 another little gem in the compact lens series. The FD 75-200mm f/4.5 is a most reasonably priced system, weighing only 510g, filter diameter 52mm and a close focusing limit of 1.8m. The lens designer's endeavours to do away with the former disadvantages of zoom lenses such as weight, bulk and high price, are being increasingly successful, such that the fixed focal length lenses will soon lose their importance in everyday photography. The only factor that is still in the favour of fixed focal length lenses is the lens speed. In this case the speed of f/4.5 is definitely the lowest limit for a zoom lens in this range of focal lengths, as compared with the speeds offered by fixed focal lengths.

The FD 50-300mm f/4.5L is the Canon zoom lens with greatest focal length range, producing excellent performance by use of the UD glass in its construction. Weighing about 2kg and matching in price the considerable technical expense, this will hardly be a lens that many amateur photographers will be choosing.

The FD 100-200mm f/5.6 is a very compact system offered at a reasonable price. This was made possible by a compromise in lens speed. This is also a slide-zoom which is most suitable for any amateur who wishes to cover this most popular range of telephoto focal lengths and is prepared to put up with the slower speed of f/5.6. Just like the FD 80-200mm this lens too is fitted with an extendable lens hood as standard.

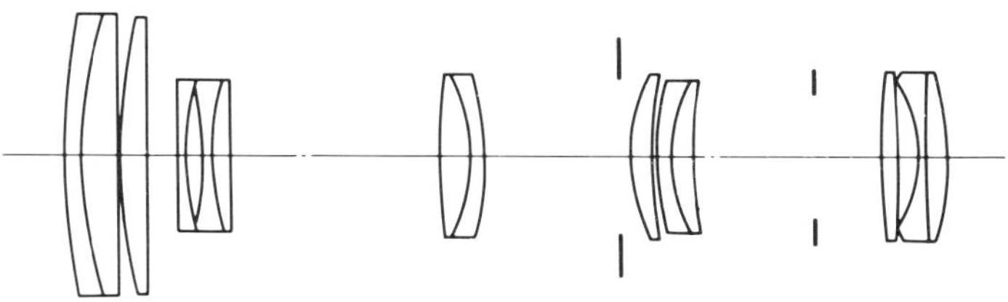

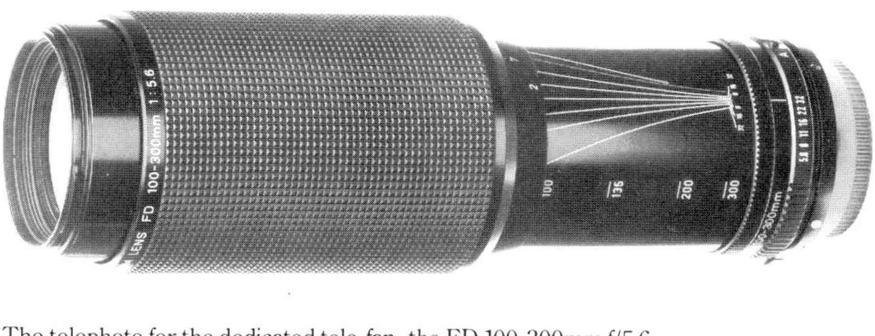

The telephoto for the dedicated tele-fan, the FD 100-300mm f/5.6.

It is the last of the zoom lenses that is still able to offer a 52mm filter diameter.

Here also Canon offers an extended version of the above lens, the FD 100-300mm f/5.6. This too is a particularly slim construction at a reasonable price and should be particularly appealing to telephoto fans amongst amateur photographers. It would also be an excellent companion for, let's say, the FD 35-70mm,

The FD 85-300mm f/4.5 is quite a weighty member in the Canon zoom lens family. Weighing about 1,400g and having a structural length of 250mm, it should really only be used on a tripod and it is equipped with a tripod ring. The high technical expense for this 3.5-fold focal length range is reflected in the price.

Finally there is a specialist lens particularly designed for the professional photographer, the FD 150-600mm f/5.6L. Including UD glass elements and a new type of focusing with 4-fold focal length range, this lens will be needed for sports and animal photography. The photographer will also have to be in good training, carrying a lens weighing 4,350g is no easy task!

Fisheye Lenses

The history of the fisheye lens started with lenses producing a circular image. But most of these were rather misused in the first wave of enthusiasm. Meanwhile most of us have returned to *terra firma* and learnt to employ these lenses rather more sparingly. Now there is another type of fisheye lens available which is the full-format fisheye. Like its predecessor it covers 180° of the entire scene in front of it across the diagonal of the frame, with the difference that the image will cover the entire 35mm format.

The amateur photographer will think twice before investing in one of these rather expensive systems. The application of such a specialist lens is rather limited. Firstly, not every subject lends itself to be shown in this form, and secondly it can be unsatisfactory showing fisheye pictures with our other range of images just because of the unusual perspective. The more extreme an effect, the more rarely should it be used, otherwise it can become quite tiresome for the viewer.

Is a fisheye lens unsuitable for the amateur photographer? Yes and no. The amateur with a minimum of additional lenses would not spend his available cash on one of these lenses. The more committed photographer, who already possesses a good range of lenses, may wish to complement his equipment by the purchase of one to allow him to cover this extreme.

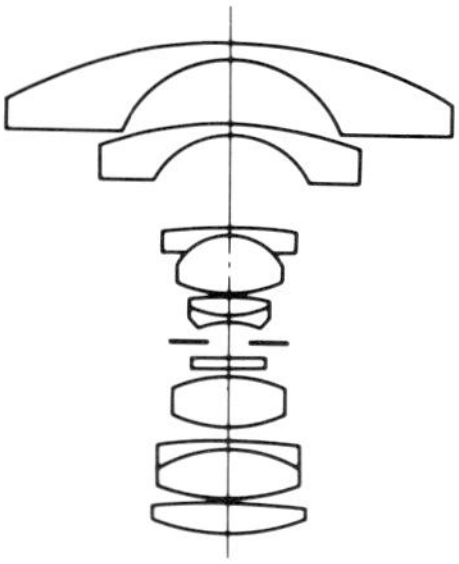

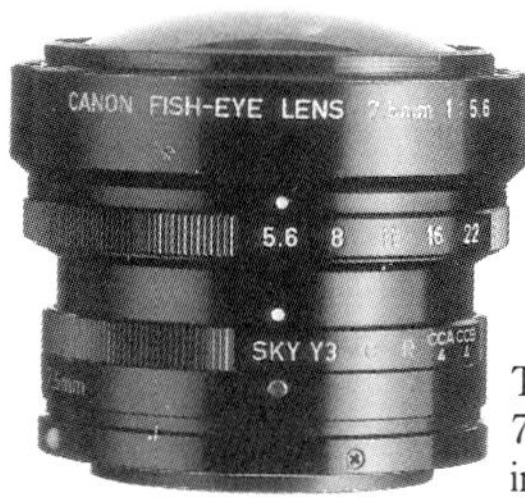

The Canon fisheye 7.5mm f/5.6 with circular image.

Canon offers one lens of each of the above-mentioned types. There is the 7.5mm f/5.6 fisheye which covers a 180° angle and produces a circular image of 23mm diameter within the 35x24mm negative. The extremely large viewing angle does not allow the use of a lenshood. The lens is based on retrofocus construction and the reflex viewfinder is therefore fully operative despite the short effective focal length of 7.5mm. It is not necessary to focus with this lens because, even at f/5.6 the depth of field is so extensive that it covers from the close range to infinity. A skylight filter, an average yellow filter, an orange filter, a red filter and an amber conversion filter CCA 4 and a bluish CCB 4 are all permanently built-in and can be brought into operation by turning the setting ring. The provision of these filters is essential as the insertion of a filter at the front of the lens would reduce the viewing angle. The optical system is adjusted such that it always requires a filter to be in position. Generally this will be the skylight filter for colour shots and in this case it has a slight pink hue as fisheye lenses are well-known for their rather cold rendition. The lens has neither auto diaphragm nor aperture simulator. Using this lens with the T70 presents no problem; you simply switch to working-aperture mode.

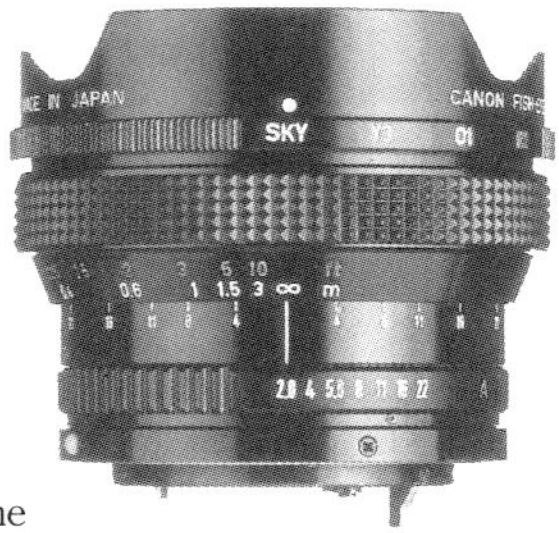

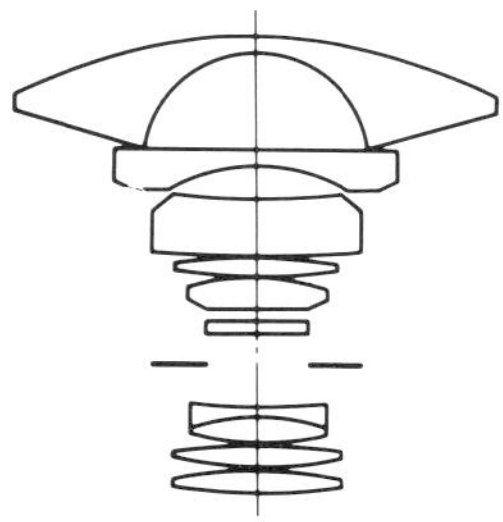

The Canon fisheye FD 15mm f/2.8 with complete coverage of the 35mm format.

The FD 15mm f/2.8 fisheye lens manages to cover the extreme viewing angle of 180° in full 35mm format. Moreover, it has a lens speed of f/2.8. Here too, a set of filters is built-in, namely skylight, average yellow filter, orange filter and red filter. Because of the rectangular format boundaries it is possible to have a mini lenshood which is integrated in the lens fitting and serves primarily to protect the front element. This lens has retrofocus construction and a focusing movement down to 20 cm. It has FD lens fitting and aperture simulator and auto diaphragm so it is possible to shoot in program and shutter-speed priority modes.

The reflex viewfinder of the T70 becomes the most important tool in image creation as shooting with this lens is an entirely new experience. The proper assessment of the final image is only possible through the viewfinder. Even details at close range seem far away and you have to get really close. If you take your eye from the viewfinder to look at the subject you will be surprised to find that you are practically on top of it.

The closer that straight lines are to the edge of the frame, the more curved they will be. This effect can be used to artistic advantage, or it can be counteracted by placing straight lines as close as possible to the centre of the frame; in this position they will be shown more or less realistically. The horizon, running through the centre of the picture, will remain straight. Don't be surprised if you find the sun in almost all your pictures; the chances for it being there are at least 50:50 in view of the viewing angle of 180°. But the sun is often a rather attractive feature in these shots as like a star it emits picturesque rays over the scene. Ghost images are more or less prevented by the multilayer lens coating, but it is impossible to avoid them altogether. This has been accepted as a necessary evil and may be used to good effect. It is often possible to achieve rather effective views by partially hiding the sun behind some details within the view.

There is another important point to look out for; don't stick your tummy out when using this lens, as you may end up with some rather unflattering views of your own anatomy. Every detail that is in front of the lens, elbows, feet, equipment dangling from the shoulder, will be within the view of the fisheye lens. This applies in particular to your own shadow. You will have to watch the edge of the frame very carefully so that you do not include any unwanted items. It is not infrequent that an otherwise perfect composition is completely spoilt by some unwanted details that you had overlooked.

Aspherical Lenses

These are the result of some more pioneering work by Canon in the field of optical engineering. After the introduction of the FD 55mm f/1.2AL early in 1971 Canon have managed to develop production and test procedures which allow acceptable production techniques for the mass production of aspherical lenses. The results of these endeavours are two further giants in lens speed which, without exaggeration, set

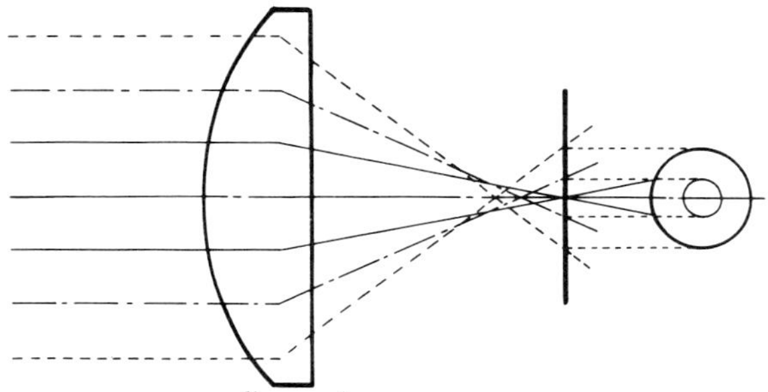

diagram 1

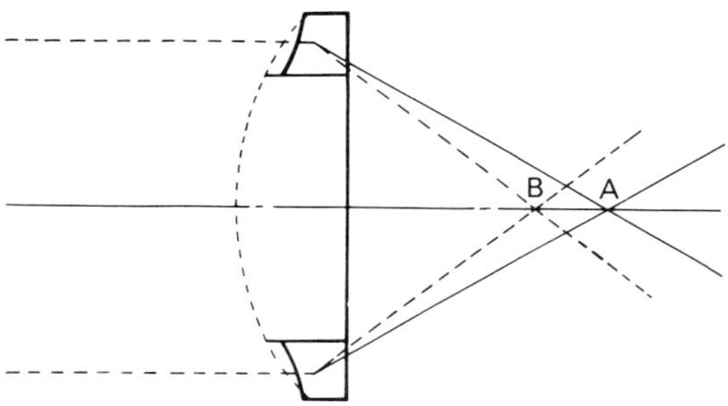

diagram 2

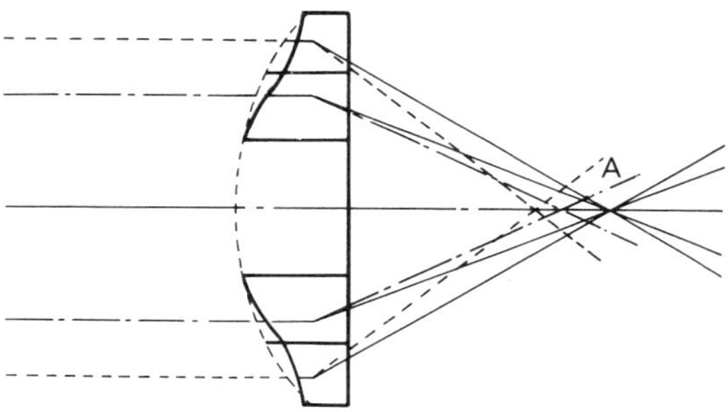

diagram 3

The method for bringing axial and marginal rays to the same focus by an aspherical surface. Refer to text for explanation.

the pace in optical engineering. Let me explain first what is meant by an aspherical lens system and why these aspherical surfaces are such an interesting subject in photography.

Until fairly recently the elements in photographic lenses had spherical surfaces, i.e. they were composed of segments with spherical surfaces with their vertices on the optical axis. Such surfaces have unavoidable limitations for the design of optical systems which make it impossible to correct certain aberrations. Diagram 1 shows that peripheral rays come to a focus much closer behind a spherical area than the rays near the axis. This so-called spherical aberration is responsible for the fact that increasingly large discs superimpose around the sharp nucleus of the main rays, representing the image created by the peripheral rays of the same image point. It is obvious that this phenomenon becomes more pronounced the larger the lens diameter, i.e. the faster the lens. The problem is to focus the peripheral rays at the same point as the rays from near the axis. Diagram 2 demonstrates how a change in radius at the periphery brings ray A to a point of intersection at a greater distance from the lens element, and to the same point as the rays from the vicinity of the axis. The broken line B corresponds to the intersection point for an unchanged lens radius, i.e. to a spherical lens.

Diagram 3 demonstrates the process of how, by deviation from the spherical surface in the peripheral region, the rays refracted at the edge are made to intersect at the same point as rays from the vicinity of the axis. The result is the so-called aspherical surface which deviates from the conventional spherical shape.

The use of aspherical surfaces in optical systems makes it possible to construct very fast lenses with outstanding performance characteristics, even at fully open aperture. This allows photography in areas which so far have appeared impossible for technical reasons. It is obvious that even today such highly sophisticated systems, requiring a high standard of production and test procedures, will cost more than conventional lenses, particularly if we consider that a greater

The new FD 50mm f/1.2L with filter diameter 52mm. This is now a very handy and small version of the previous standard lens.

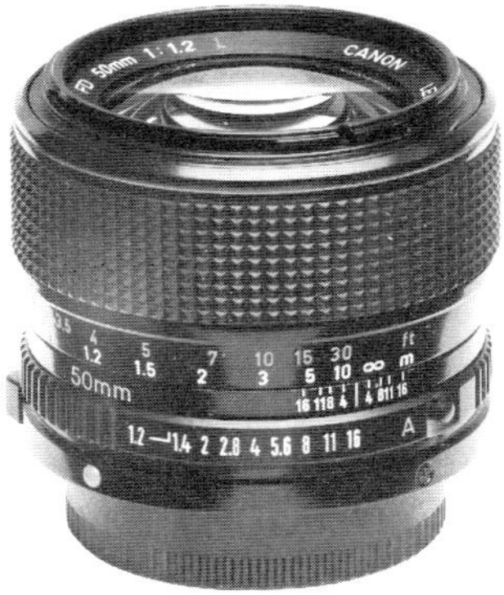

lens speed requires larger lens diameters and therefore a greater construction effort, making even normal lenses more expensive. Seen against this background, and allowing for the excellent performance that these outstanding lenses are able to offer, even their higher price is reasonable.

Before the introduction of the new Canon bayonet these giants of light speed were offered with a focal length of 55mm as the standard lens. The new lenses of this type have the uniform 50mm focal length and a filter diameter of 52mm. The exceedingly fast aspherical standard lens goes under the description FD 50mm f/1.2L. The reduction in weight is also quite remarkable. At only 380g it is slowly shedding its

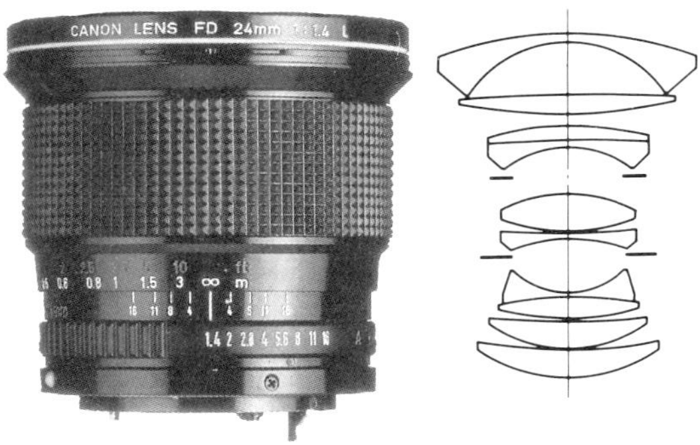

Even this fast wide-angle lens has an aspherical surface for excellent performance at full aperture of f/1.4

reputation as a specialist lens and is now considered the super-standard lens for all those who generally have to work in poor lighting conditions. The close-up limit of 0.5m is also in keeping with that of the normal standard lens.

The fastest 24mm lens for SLR cameras at the moment is the FD 24mm f/1.4L, again with aspherical surfaces and therefore extremely high performance at full aperture. In addition, the very considerable depth of field for the lens speed of f/1.4, at full aperture viewing is sufficiently reduced to allow reasonably comfortable focusing on the screen. On the other hand the depth of field which is quite considerable for the lens speed opens up new photographic possibilities. It also has automatic correction compensation, maintaining the high performance even for the shorter focusing distances.

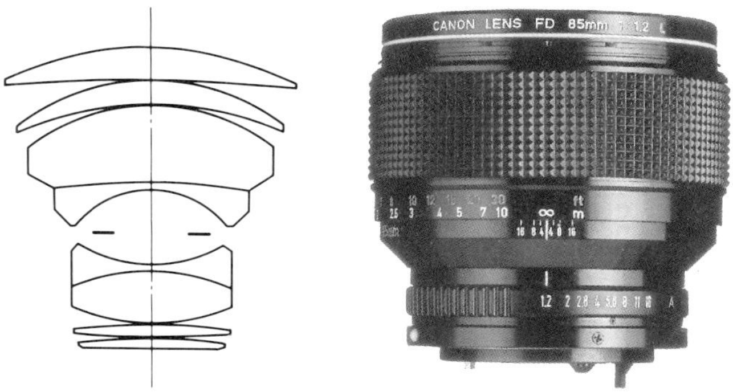

For many years this was the only SLR lens capable of offering a lens speed of f/1.2 at a focal length of 85mm, the FD 85mm f/1.2L.

The third of this type is a particular treasure even amongst these fine lenses. This is the FD 85mm f/1.2L. This is another system, completely unrivalled in the market in its performance and specification. The price that you have to pay for this veritable treasure is not only the financial outlay, but also a levy in size as the inevitable consequence of high lens speed; filter diameter 72mm and the corresponding weight of 680g, the faster the lens, the bigger the "hole" to allow the light in. Even this mild telephoto has been equipped with an automatic correction compensation to retain the excellent performance throughout the entire focusing range.

Focal Length Extenders – or Teleconverters

Teleconverters or extenders are also offered by Canon; in fact there are three. You may already know that a teleconverter is an additional lens inserted between the camera and the lens to increase the focal length of the system. It is important to consider that such an optical accessory should always correspond to the quality of the original equipment, otherwise it would turn a high performance lens into a simple piece of ordinary glass. For this reason Canon offers several of these extenders because the characteristics of the light passing through the lenses are quite different for lenses with different focal lengths.

The teleconverter FD2X-B is meant for lenses up to 300mm. For lenses in excess of 300mm you should use the FD2X-A, which is also suitable for FD zoom lenses including the 300mm focal length. Then there is the FD1.4X-A which is meant exclusively for fixed focal length telephotos in excess of 300mm.

The two converters FD2X double the focal length of the basic lens, the FD1.4X extends it by only 1.4-times, but it

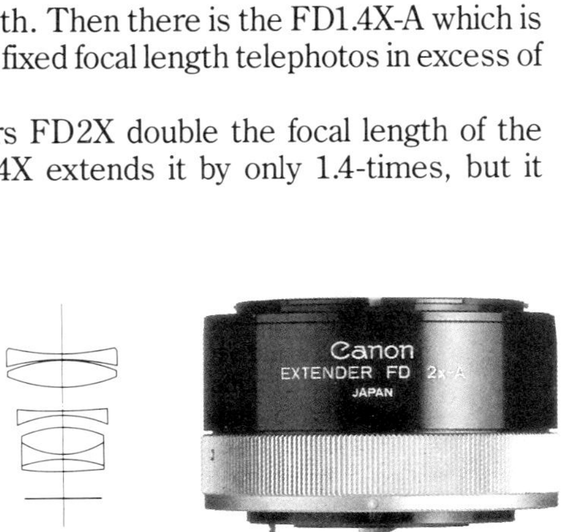

One of the Canon teleconverters, the extender FD2X-A

reduces the lens speed by only one stop, while the other two will cost you a reduction in lens speed of two stops. For the longer fixed focal lengths and converter FD1.4X the 1.4-fold extension in focal length is usually sufficient, whilst the rather slower speeds of the long lenses are not reduced excessively.

For a comparatively small financial outlay a teleconverter multiplies your photographic range as it is possible to use it with more than one lens. You mustn't forget, however, that you will only be able to take very bright subjects, unless you are using a tripod, because the conversion of a basic FD 200mm f/4 by teleconverter to a 400mm f/8 allows very little leeway for hand-held shots.

The serial description of the Canon teleconverters indicates that they are equipped with the necessary FD coupling elements for open aperture metering and are therefore suitable for program and shutter-speed priority modes if used with the T70. The reduction in lens speed causes a few peculiarities which need to be considered when using this accessory. The aperture value displayed in the viewfinder will always be that of the lens system, to which you will have to add the factor of the converter used. If you are using a 2x converter and the viewfinder displays f/5.6, then this corresponds in reality to f/11. Any incorrect exposure warnings, however, correspond to the actual conditions and have to be taken as such.

The distance scale of the basic lens retains its validity with an extender. This could lead to an interesting extension of the setting range, unless the extension of the focal length does not necessitate shutter speeds which are no longer possible by hand. If, for example, you have as basic lens the FD 80-200mm f/4 and the 2X converter you will have as largest aperture, f/8. On the other hand the close-focus limit of 1m and the resulting focal length of 400mm will bring the macro range within your grasp.

Another peculiarity in the use of the Canon 2X converter with the T70 has to be considered. The film speed setting will have to be adjusted. Using the FD2X-A the correction should be a 1/3 stop higher, using the FD2X-B converter a correction will be necessary only for the faster lenses. For lenses with lens speeds between f/1.2 and f/1.8 the film speed setting has to be increased by 2/3 stops, for lenses with lens speed f/2 by 1/3 stop. Apart from this your T70 will always meter correctly as this is always done by measuring the light on the film plane. Any equipment put before the lens will make no difference to this fact. Using converters will take a little thought, though, as it is necessary to reset the film speed again after the converter has been removed. Failing to do this will mean that any subsequent shots taken at the wrong film speed setting will be spoilt.

Corrected Perspective

Finally I shall describe the special lens TS 35mm f/2.8, a special application lens which retains the chromed clamp ring of the former Canon bayonet. This is primarily intended for the professional photographer, although many an amateur will delight in its use. After all, it is the only SLR lens of its type on the market that allows not only a shift parallel to the film plane, but may be tilted as well. In doing so it tries to offer similar facilities to those available on large format stand cameras in the form of tilting lens panels, whose range of facilities can hardly be imagined by the SLR photographer.

These lens movements are required on the one hand in still-life photography and on the other for architectural photographs. Control in perspective is the purpose in still-life photography; the representation of objects such that they are acceptable to our eye as realistic representations and furthermore the sharp rendering over a large range without having to stop down, or perhaps in addition to stopping down. To achieve this we avail ourselves of the "Scheimpflug" rule which says that a subject plane is shown in sharp focus without consideration to the aperture used at the point where the extrapolations of the planes of the subject, of the lens and of the film intersect. In architectural photography the advantage of

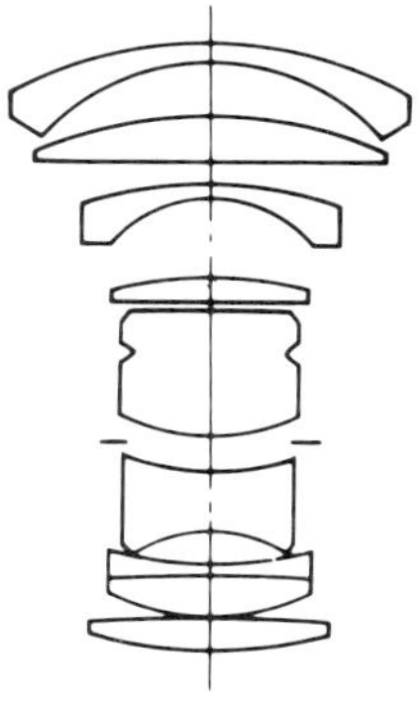

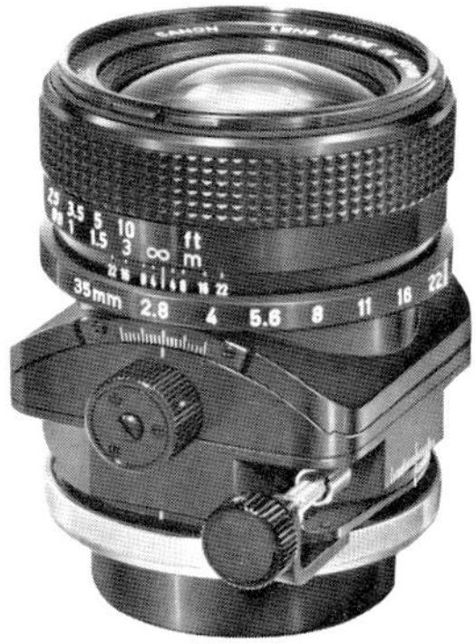

TS 35mm f/2.8, the only SLR lens in the world with both off-centre and tilting movements for perspective correction.

the parallel adjustment of the lens to the optical axis lies in the exclusion of the interfering foreground without converging verticals. The same applies to the representation of extended structures without excessive tapering towards the sides. The amateur photographer may also come to hold this lens in high esteem as a wide-angle lens that is capable, so to speak, of jumping over its own shadow. The possibility, to spirit away unwanted detail in the foreground, to make an optical leap, is welcome in almost every kind of photography. The TS 35mm manages to counteract the greatest disadvantage of a wide-angle lens, namely that the extension of the angle of view restricts you to holding the camera absolutely vertically and in doing so covering details in one half of the frame that are altogether uninteresting or even undesirable. The TS 35mm allows the choice of exactly the right framing whilst at the same time making full use of the wide angle of view.

This lens, with an image diameter of 58.4mm, covers a wide circle, which is necessary to utilize the adjustment and tilting range. It also possesses automatic correction compensation. The inclusion of an auto diaphragm was waived because of the complicated mechanical construction it would have entailed. The aperture is therefore set manually. For metering, the lens is stopped down to working aperture. It would be logical in principle if you thought you could overcome this shortcoming

1. The normal viewing circle (A) is extended by the TS 35mm to 58.4mm (B).

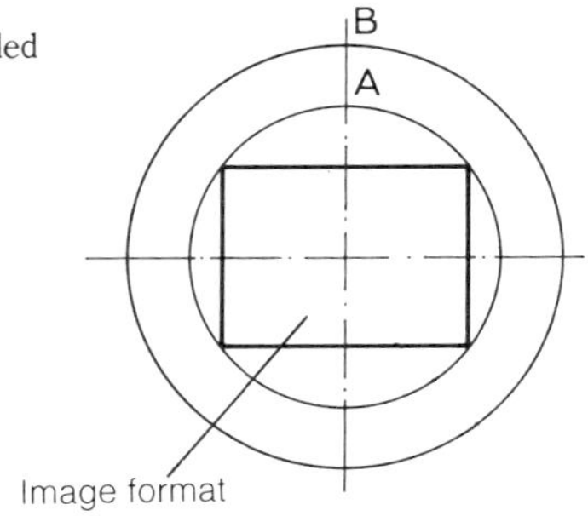

2. Tilting the lens allows a relocation of the depth of field without having to stop down.

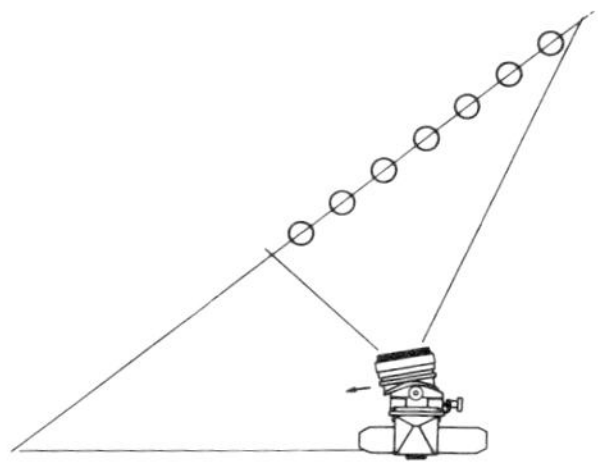

3. The lateral shift of the optical system allows frontal shots despite lateral camera position.

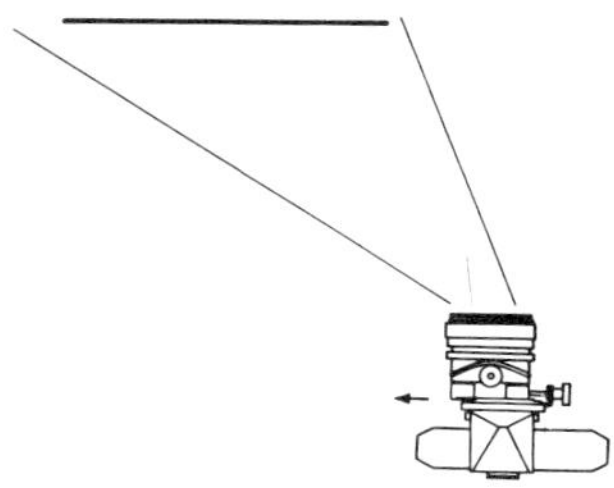

by setting your T70 to working aperture mode. However, in this special case this is not permitted. The working aperture mode is inoperable for optical reasons when utilizing the adjustment facilities of this lens. As long as you use this lens in its basic setting the automatic program will remain operative. I would therefore advise you to perform metering in the basic position and to set the ascertained values manually as soon as the lens has been adjusted. In the extreme positions, where the outermost edge of the viewing circle is utilized, you increase the setting by half a stop to counteract the natural decline in light in the peripheral zones.

Technical data

Technical data of Canon FD Lenses

Description	diagonal angle of view	number of groups/ elements	smallest aperture	close focusing limit(m)	filter diameter(mm)	lenshood	length(mm)	weight(g)
FD 1:5,6/7,5 mm	180°	8/11	22	–	built-in	–	62	365
FD 1:2,8/15 mm	180°	9/10	22	0,2	built-in	built-in	60,5	460
FD 1:2,8/14 mm L	114°	10/14	22	0,25	–	fest	83,5	490
FD 1:4/17 mm	104°	9/11	22	0,25	72	BW-72	56	360
FD 1:2,8/20 mm	94°	9/10	22	0,25	72	BW-72	58	305
FD 1:1,4/24 mm L	84°	8/10	16	0,3	72	BW-72	68	430
FD 1:2/24 mm	84°	9/11	22	0,3	52	BW-52C	50,6	285
FD 1:2,8/24 mm	84°	9/10	22	0,3	52	BW-52C	43	240
FD 1:2/28 mm	75°	9/10	22	0,3	52	BW-52B	47,2	265
FD 1:2,8/28 mm	75°	7/7	22	0,3	52	BW-52B	40	170
FD 1:2/35 mm	63°	8/10	22	0,3	52	BW-52A	46	245
FD 1:2,8/35 mm	63°	5/6	22	0,35	52	BW-52A	40	165
FD 1:1,2/50 mm L	46°	6/8	16	0,5	52	BS-52	50,5	380
FD 1:1,2/50 mm	46°	6/7	16	0,5	52	BS-52	45,6	315
FD 1:1,4/50 mm	46°	6/7	22	0,45	52	BS-52	41	235
FD 1:1,8/50 mm	46°	4/6	22	0,6	52	BS-52	35	170
FD 1:1,2/85 mm L	28°30'	6/8	16	0,9	72	BT-72	71	680
FD 1:1,8/85 mm	28°30'	4/6	22	0,85	52	BT-52	53,5	345
FD 1:2,8/85 mm SF	28°30'	4/6	22	0,8	58	BT-58	69,6	400
FD 1:2/100 mm	24°	4/6	32	1	52	BT-52	70	445
FD 1:2,8/100 mm	24°	5/5	32	1	52	BT-52	53,4	270
FD 1:2/135 mm	18°	5/6	32	1,3	72	built-in	90,4	670
FD 1:2,8/135 mm	18°	5/6	32	1,3	52	built-in	78	395
FD 1:3,5/135 mm	18°	4/4	32	1,3	52	built-in	85	325
FD 1:2,8/200 mm	12°	6/7	32	1,5	72	built-in	134,2	735
FD 1:4/200 mm	12°	6/7	32	1,5	52	built-in	121,5	440
FD 1:2,8/300 mm L	8°15'	7/9	32	3	push-on	built-in	245	2300

Description	of view	groups/ elements	aperture	limit(m)	diameter(mm)	lenshood	length(mm)	weight(g)
FD 1:4/300 mm L	8°15'	7/7	32	3	push-on	built-in	207	1100
FD 1:4/300 mm	8°15'	6/6	32	3	push-on	built-in	204	945
FD 1:5,6/300 mm	8°15'	5/6	32	3	58	built-in	198,5	635
FD 1:2,8/400 mm L	6°10'	8/10	32	4	push-on	built-in	348	4500
FD 1:4,5/400 mm	6°10'	5/6	32	4	push-on	built-in	288	1250
FD 1:4,5/500 mm L	5°	6/7	32	5	push-on	built-in	395	2900
FD 1:8/500 mm	5°	3/6	–	4	push-on	built-in	146	705
FD 1:4,5/600 mm	4°10'	5/6	32	8	push-on	built-in	462	3740
FD 1:5,6/800 mm L	3°06'	6/7	32	14	push-on	built-in	577	4100
FD 1:3,5/20–35 mm L	94°–63°	11/11	22	0,5	72	BW-72	84,2	470
FD 1:3,5/24–35 mm L	84°–63°	9/12	22	0,4	72	BW-72	86,6	495
FD 1:3,5–4,5/28–55 mm	75°–43°	10/10	22	0,4	52	BW-58C	60,9	220
FD 1:2,8–3,5/35–70 mm	63°–34°	10/10	22	1	58	W-69	120	545
FD 1:3,5–4,5/35–70 mm	63°–34°	8/9	22	0,5	52	BW-58C	60,9	200
FD 1:4/35–70 mm AF	63°–34°	8/8	22	1	52	–	84,5	640
FD 1:3,5/35–105 mm	63°–23°20'	13/15	22	1,5	72	BW-72B	108,4	640
FD 1:3,5/50–135 mm	46°–18°	12/16	22	1,5	58	BS-58	125,4	720
FD 1:4,5/50–300 mm L	46–8°15'	13/16	32	2,5	push-on	S-100	250	1945
FD 1:4,5/70–150 mm	34°–16°20'	9/12	32	1,5	52	built-in	132	530
FD 1:4/70–210 mm	34°–11°45'	9/12	32	1,2	58	BT-58	151	705
FD 1:4,5/75–200 mm	32°11'–12°	8/11	32	1,8	52	BT-52B	123	510
FD 1:4/80–200 mm	30°–12°	11/15	32	1	58	built-in	161	765
FD 1:4,5/85–300 mm	28°30'–8°15'	11/15	32	2,5	Serie IX	built-in	246,8	1690
FD 1:5,6/100–200 mm	24°–12°	5/8	32	2,5	52	built-in	167	610
FD 1:5,6/100–300 mm	24°–8°15'	9/14	32	2	58	BT-58	207	835
FD 1:5,6/150–600 mm L	16°20'–4°10'	15/19	32	3	push-on	built-in	468	4350
FD 1:3,5/50 mm Makro	46°	4/6	32	0,23	52	BW-52A	57	235
FD 1:4/100 mm Makro	24°	3/5	32	0,45	52	BT-52	95	455
FD 1:4/200 mm Makro	12°	6/9	32	0,58	58	built-in	182,4	830
TS 1:2,8/35 mm SSC	63°(79°)	8/9	22	0,3	58	BW-58	74,5	550
microscope lens 1:3,5/20 mm	–	3/4	22	–	–	–	20	35
microscope lens 1:2,8/35 mm	–	4/6	22	–	–	–	22,5	60

Index